D0864560

GLADYS TABER'S STILLMEADOW COOK BOOK

By Gladys Taber:

Gladys Taber's
STILLMEADOW
COOK BOOK

DRAWINGS BY ANN GRIFALCONI

PARNASSUS IMPRINTS, INC.
Orleans, Massachusetts 02653

Copyright © 1965, 1958, 1947 by Gladys Taber

Published by arrangement with
Harper & Row, Publishers

All rights reserved

Cover drawing by Ann Grifalconi

Parnassus Imprint edition published May 1983

ISBN 0-940160-18-8

Library of Congress Catalog Card Number 65–20590

Printed in the United States of America

For
The dear friends who have shared their cherished family recipes with me over the picket fence at Stillmeadow or sent them from faraway places.

And for
Barbara Lovely, who not only spent so many long hours helping with this book but inspired me to keep at it until we turned the last page.

Contents

Introduction

I DOUBT IF ANYONE EVER APPROACHED THE FIELD OF COOK-
ing knowing less than I did. Or being, frankly, more scared. My "do-
mestic science" education consisted of one term in sixth grade when we
happened to live temporarily in a town that had that subject. Class
assembled in a rather cobwebby basement room in which there was a
stove, a couple of wooden tables, a Hoosier cabinet and a couple of
wooden chairs. There must have been an icebox but I can't remember
it. All I remember about the teacher is that she taught some other
subjects and never seemed to have her heart in this one. I remember
the chairs because I was usually sitting in one folding a dish towel.

Our repertoire included Shrimp Wiggle and chocolate pudding and
some kind of cake baked in a square tin that was impossible to clean.
And I looked on the whole thing as a hideous waste of time when there
were so many interesting things to do in life.

My other preparation for half a life spent in the kitchen was clearing
the table at home and wiping the dishes. My mother had a reputation as
the best cook in town, although she felt several of her friends were
really more accomplished. She liked Mrs. Ritchie's bread better and
Alma's golden egg noodles, and Mrs. Rector's cloverleaf rolls were, she
said, much lighter than hers. Nevertheless, she managed to feed any
number of Father's college students, plus any of my gang that happened to be around, plus the faculty, plus her town friends, without ever
seeming to feel hurried. She was a round, rosy woman with flyaway
silk-brown hair and smiling eyes, and she never lost her composure
even if Father banged in at five-thirty with three or four men he had
collected on campus. He never, of course, telephoned her ahead of time
because he didn't like telephones.

How often did I most bitterly regret never learning to cook when I
was right at home with a built-in opportunity! I was, alas, upstairs,
reading poetry and trying to make a sonnet come out even.

I was, however, always available for licking the cake batter from the
bowl or consuming the first hot honey-nut bun that came from the pan

9

or eating the round crispy balls that I called the holes in the doughnuts. And it may be that a small bit of mother's skill sank in by osmosis, but not enough to carry me to an easy victory when I began housekeeping as a bride. Far from it. I was a disaster in the kitchen.

I finally learned to stand by the stove and never take my eyes from the carrots or anything else that was boiling. I learned that pies are better if the broiler isn't on as they bake. I learned that getting everything done at the same time requires anguished concern. Too many times, we were eating the potatoes as a separate course, which they aren't. I learned that fried chicken is best when it isn't bloody red at the bone and black outside. And I learned how to make lemon meringue pie, after making it daily for two weeks. I didn't make it for years afterward.

And, in the end, I learned that cooking is not only a basic art but more fun than almost anything. It has a universal appeal because eating is so daily and those few forlorn souls who "only eat to live" are a minority and should go to a doctor. A well-cooked, well-seasoned meal provides something of that gracious living we often think has gone. Few people can sparkle if they are sawing away at an overdone wedge of meat, but a tender, juicy slice comfortably provided with pan gravy inspires good conversation and suggests the world is worth saving. A cheese soufflé, delicate and golden, lifts the spirits. I don't like desserts except for Herman Smith's ginger mold, but I like the sigh of pleasure when I bring in a pineapple upside-down cake. After all, as my daughter says, some people even like cream in their coffee.

When my love affair with cooking got really under way, I began to hunt recipes. I exchanged them with friends the way Jill, who lived with me, was exchanging bulbs and cuttings and special seeds with other gardeners. It is my firm belief that an unshared recipe is a poor thing. Once you invent something delicious, it should be shouted from rooftops, if you can climb to a rooftop. A recipe is like a poem, and a poem is not to be shut away in a drawer but read to anyone who will listen. I know some women who keep their best achievement a dead secret, but they do not need to. Their identity goes along with it, for that particular treasure will always be known as Mrs. Nicholson's oyster scallop or Joan's flounder bake. The creator of a perfect recipe is associated with it always.

Fortunately, the secret-keepers in my life have been few, since most women, and most men too, will copy down their best recipe half an hour after you meet them. Swank restaurants are different. I once ate every day for a week in a special French place trying to figure out a fabulous dish. I approximated it, but it lacked something. What it lacked was ⅓ cup Hollandaise sauce. Eventually I got the recipe and it was Chicken Divan and the Hollandaise was important. I had no luck at all with a request from a friend to tell her how to make a salad dressing she had been served in her home town in Illinois. She said it was out of this world and could I tell her how to make it, as they wouldn't. It was, she said, spicy but not too spicy. It didn't seem feasible to ask her to steal a teaspoonful and mail it to me to taste!

I like the modern kitchens which make cooking easier. I began cooking in a flat (which I suppose would be glorified as a duplex now). The kitchen was sort of a woodshed with an iron sink, wooden drainboard, a gas stove with rusty burners, a wooden table, and a wooden icebox with a hole cut in the floor for the drippings to go through. Later I cooked in one of those big city apartments. The kitchen window gave on a dank well and people in upper apartments often threw milk bottles down to crash below. The kitchen was big enough for two people to stand in, providing one stood sidewise. The gas stove stood on weak legs and it leaked gas. The oven door had to be propped shut when in use because it had a way of flinging itself open just as a soufflé was almost done. The grids (if that is what you call them) were not even, since the stove top slanted to the left. This meant one part of a pan would be high and dry while another was swimming in liquid. I kept most of the canned goods in the hall closet along with the cleaning supplies and the umbrellas and wraps. There were a couple of wooden cupboards but they were too high to get at without a stepladder. We didn't have room enough for a stepladder, and had to borrow one from the janitor six floors down in case I purely needed the turkey platter.

Then, when we moved to the country, I found two kitchens at Stillmeadow. We have always called them the middle kitchen and the back kitchen, and now and then someone asks where is the front kitchen. There isn't any. Two kitchens do give plenty of space, and ours were full of children, cockers, Irish setters, and two cats. The middle kitchen had the refrigerator, stove, sink, and some wide open shelves (it had been the milk room). Jill made a coffin-like wooden box to hold the utensils and we kept it on the radiator. The radiator top was curved, so frequently the whole box crashed to the floor scattering puppies, cats, and eggbeaters and potato mashers all over everything. The back kitchen had an ancient wood range which heated the room in winter and roasted it in summer. I loved it dearly even when we had to get up at midnight on a cold night to put more wood in the firebox.

It is my theory that push-button heat is wonderful, but that you can get more gradations of temperature on the top of an old range by moving the pots and kettles just a quarter of an inch here or there. I also loved the slightly smoky flavor that comes from the oven as the turkey is brought out. I even liked dipping hot water from the reservoir. However, in time we modernized the kitchens, and the old stove retired in favor of counter space and good storage cabinets.

For my kind of cook, counter space is never enough. How I admire the woman who tells you dinner is served, and, as she brings in the golden popovers, I offer to fetch the salad, and I see the kitchen looking as if it were ready to be photographed for a magazine. These divine creatures are able to "wash up as they go along." Whereas Jill used to say anybody would know I had been in the kitchen because I had a gift for leaving everything in a mess. I couldn't, she observed, make an omelet without scattering things all over the place. I have tried to improve but I am a complete failure. I cannot seem to concentrate on the meal itself and keep scouring pans and cleaning egg beaters. After guests have departed, I often take one look at the kitchen and wonder whether it wouldn't be simpler just to move away.

I heartily believe in a place for everything and everything in its place, but never am sure just where I put the double boiler the last time. I was reminded of this last summer when I was on Cape Cod and my daughter kept house at Stillmeadow. She called up long distance one night and said, "Mama, can you tell me where the orange juicer might be? I'm halfway through cranberry mousse and — — "

"Look under the ring molds," I suggested, "and then behind the Swedish casserole in the cupboard by the sink. It's there somewhere. If you can't find it, try using the top of a milk bottle."

I have no trouble locating my herbs, spices, and seasonings because they are ranged on a narrow shelf directly over the cooking counter and I recommend such a shelf for every kitchen. It may be fastened by brackets from a hardware store, and if possible should not be directly over the range because the heat does no good. It is also a great help to hang the most-needed utensils over or near the range.

Today's homemakers have almost everything from self-defrosting refrigerators to automatic coffee makers. Or they can look forward to possessing them as soon as the budget allows. One of my favorites is the electric skillet which cooks fried chicken, beef stew, pancakes, and dozens of other things. Then I love my electric knife sharpener for I never acquired the art of sharpening knives on a whetstone. I usually sharpened my fingers. An electric beater is a miracle. I remember very well beating egg whites with a flat wire thing with the egg whites lying simply on a platter until I nearly gave up. In those days, I only made angel food cakes for birthdays. A pressure cooker is not only a timesaver but makes everything savory as well as tender. It means a working woman can dash in at night and serve the kind of pot roast with vegetables that used to take half a day.

I couldn't catalogue the new products that are now available to make cooking easier and better. The frozen meats, fish, fowl, vegetables, and fruits along with the good packaged mixes and the improved distribution of fresh products mean that nothing is ever out of season any more. You can have oysters in July and strawberries in January. And now there is a new method of processing food which may be even more remarkable – some kind of a flash-dry affair which I cannot understand. The new non-lumpable flour is a mystery to me too, but I enjoy it.

For myself, I have reservations about the frozen dinners. I used them during an emergency time when I was spending all day at a hospital and coming home late. Perhaps if I had taken all the various dibs and dabs out and done things to them, I'd have liked them better. On the other hand, the frozen au gratin potatoes, spinach soufflés, and so on, are fine and very good to keep on hand in the freezer. If you are cooking for a big family, they are expensive and do not serve as many as they claim – at least not for most people.

But servings are impossible to estimate. For instance, when Barbara and I were typing recipes for this book, I read one aloud and said confidently, "Serves 6."

"Slim could eat that all by himself," she said, referring to her tall, lean husband.

So every cook has to consider who is going to eat what, and if it is spaghetti, could they live on it or does it bore them? And have they been out chopping firewood or dashing to catch a commuting train, or have they been lounging by a good fire reading the latest spy story?

Most of us dream of being the perfect hostess. This means being well organized far enough ahead of time to allow for a hot bath, a short rest, and time to put on a pretty frock and spray yourself with White Lilac. This never, never happens to me. Five minutes before I begin to jump into the shower, the plumber comes to fix the washing machine. This involves his going down into the cellar and fussing with the fuse box while I rush around alertly turning on lights as he checks. Or, as I glance out of the window, I see the guests coming down the flagstone walk and I also see a couple of stray cows tramping on the roses. Or the phone rings and someone has arrived unexpectedly at Seymour (the nearest town) and could I pick him up.

I wonder about those women I read of in the magazines who greet their guests feeling relaxed and casual. Even should they have help in the kitchen, does the current never go off as the rolls go in? Does no banished child ever plunge headfirst down the stairs or arrive with a stray kitten that needs attention IMMEDIATELY? And the guests – ah, are they always on time or does their car break down twenty miles away? Is there never a tie-up in city traffic resulting in their turning up an hour and a half late? Do they never take the wrong road or go to 85th instead of 86th Street?

I wonder . . .

At Stillmeadow, there is no predicting. But, in the end, we always manage to sit down to a candle-lit table and the rib roast is not overdone and the Yorkshire pudding is crusty and tender with rich juices bubbling at the edges and the salad is unwilted. I even have remembered to take the cheese from the refrigerator so it has come to room temperature, and I did not park the fruit bowl on the radiator! When everyone takes that first mouthful and breathes a happy sigh, that is the time I relax and become the easy gracious hostess. My hair may not look like a *Vogue* illustration and my face is shiny and I never did find time to slip into that fresh frock, but I am a very happy woman.

One thing I have learned not to do and that is apologize for everything and anything. This is because I have been a guest myself and been pretty bored when the main topic of conversation consisted of the hostess explaining that nothing was really as good as it should be. Then you spend the whole dinner hour reassuring her and as you finally say good night, she says, "I am so sorry the rolls were just not quite right."

"Tasted all right to me," you mumble; "ate three."

But you wish people could take out their insecurities somewhere other than in the kitchen, especially if they cook to perfection.

Another thing I learned after a year or so of struggle in the kitchen. It is better to serve something you know how to make than to try a fancy new dish. I am reminded of my favorite uncle who had a spectacular voice but would never sing anything for company that he had gone over before. He just kept rehearsing strange numbers and stopping in the middle to begin again. I rarely heard him sing a whole aria or ballad. It is better to rehearse ahead of time on the family because they can't do anything about it anyway and have to put up with you. My family ate a number of soufflé soups before I felt secure with a soufflé. And my first popovers were pried from the pan with a carving knife.

I must say a word about cooking times. The reason nobody can accurately estimate how long any given thing should cook is that a stove is a very personal being. Theoretically an oven should be calibrated by an expert frequently, but I have never lived where any expert would come and do that. Top burners get tired and in time do not really go on High when they say they are. But every cook knows the temperament of her or his own range and adjusts to it. My own range would burn everything to a crisp if I put it up to 400°. My best front burner will not, on the other hand, boil potatoes if I put it on second. They sit and simmer endlessly. My small back burner must be treated with caution because a pan of bacon will turn to ash in no time.

But since we are old and devoted friends, we understand each other. I have collected cook books for years, but the cooking time is between me and my range. As far as roasts go, I smell when they are done. For baked things, I see when they draw away from the edges of the pan and look stable in the middle. For top-stove cooking, I use a two-tined fork which is a very old and dear one and never fails. When it slides both tines in with ease, I turn off the heat.

Most things, I have found, continue to cook even with the heat off, and I allow for that while I am getting the muffins out of the muffin tins. A roast or turkey will keep gently cooking while you get the platter warm and find the carving set. No matter how agile you are, some time elapses from stove to table, and in my book this is a continuance of the cooking time. My general tendency is to cut the cooking time of any recipe I find about a quarter. I don't get in a stew about the vitamins because I think in this country we get them, by and large, but I just like vegetables with some personality left and meat that is juicy and tender instead of leathery and dry. I don't like soupy boiled potatoes or asparagus that you could glue stamps on with. But this may be a personal preference.

Most of my cook books get involved with calories. As one who has dieted off and on for years, I take a firm stand on this. When I diet, I do not try to make gourmet dishes without the gourmet ingredients. I broil the chop and dish up the cottage cheese and munch the lettuce. But when I cook a decent meal, I do not substitute non-calory ingredients. I make it the way it was meant to be. If the recipe calls for sour cream, that is what I use. If sugar is called for, I use sugar and not a synthetic flavorer. I think a lot of women fight the battle of the bulge trying to make something taste like something it can never taste like.

The recipes in my personal cook book have met two tests. They call for ingredients usually available and they are economical with time. Occasionally, if there is a free day, I enjoy putting a stack of records on the machine and just giving myself up to hours with the range. But like most women today, I depend on recipes which do not call for long preparation. And I think a simple, well-seasoned dish always gets a warm welcome.

Happy cooking!

Appetizers

APPETIZERS CAN BE A GIRL'S BEST FRIEND. THERE ARE TWO times when I find them invaluable. When I have company for dinner and almost all the guests have arrived, obviously at the point of starvation, but the inevitable late-comers turn up an hour later, appetizers save the day. A tray of things to nibble keeps people happy. The second time is when I foolishly plan a dinner that cannot be cooked ahead of time, or insist on something like popovers or cheese soufflé. I have the appetizers ready and bring them in as I turn on the oven. This means I become a clock watcher so that the appetizer round is over at the right time.

I do not believe in serving a lot of rich snacks if a big roast beef with Yorkshire pudding is to follow. I have occasionally dined out when I ate so many tiny shrimp puffs and cheese balls and so on that I could hardly face dinner itself. Before a hearty dinner, I serve whatever drinks people wish — cocktails, tomato juice, or cranberry juice (my

17

favorite)—and nothing more than a bowl of crisp small crackers. Or a dish of jumbo ripe olives.

One hot appetizer and one or two cold ones make a good balance. For a cocktail party, with no food to follow, it is all right to have a dozen or more kinds of tidbits, but never before dinner. In summer I do like a tray of appetizers (not too many kinds) with iced minted tea instead of cakes.

There are any number of ready-to-serve tidbits available now, and I keep some on the emergency shelf. The packaged dips are excellent, requiring only sour cream or cottage cheese added. Potato chips make good dippers.

QUICK CHEESE PUFFS

1   tube of biscuits
3   tbsp melted butter or margarine
¼   cup (about) grated Parmesan cheese and
¼   cup (about) grated cheddar cheese, mixed

Open tube and separate the biscuits (there are 10 or 12 per package). Cut each biscuit into quarters. Roll each piece in the melted butter or margarine, then in the grated cheese mixture. Place on baking sheet in 450° oven for 10 minutes or until golden brown. Serve hot, with toothpicks.

This is an elegant appetizer.

CHEESE COOKIES FOR COCKTAILS

¼   lb butter   1   tsp salt
1   pkg snappy cheese   ¼   tsp paprika
1   cup flour

Soften butter and cheese for an hour in a warm place. Cream well and add flour, salt, and paprika. Form in round loaf and put in waxed paper overnight in the refrigerator. Slice very thin and bake 12 minutes in a hot oven.

MAKES 15 OR MORE

They're delicious.

BESS CLARENDON'S APPETIZER

3/4 pkg, large size, cream cheese
1 egg yolk
  Grated onion – 1 tsp or more
  Accent

Blend the egg yolk, slightly beaten, with the cream cheese; then add the grated onion and seasoning. Spread on crackers and broil until bubbly and brown.

SERVES 4 – 6

But it is wise to double the recipe!

CHEESE HOOIES

1/4 lb butter
1/4 lb strong American cheese
1 cup sifted flour
1 tsp salt
A good dash of Cayenne

Grate cheese into butter (I hope with a mouli grater). Cream well together, using a wooden spoon or your own clean hands. Add salt and Cayenne, then work in flour until thoroughly blended.

Knead on a board until smooth, roll into a long, thin roll and put in the refrigerator to chill thoroughly. When chilled, slice thinly (use a sharp knife) and bake on a cookie sheet in a moderate oven (350°) until the hooies are beginning to brown (about 8 to 10 minutes).

Dust with powdered sugar, if desired.

Serve with cocktails, highballs, tomato juice, soup or salads.

This was the chief cooking specialty of my Virginia friend, Ida Fitzgerald. When she visited me in summer, we were not above a few cheese hooies with our breakfast coffee. She always doubled the recipe. They keep indefinitely, but are seldom allowed to.

LOBSTER DIP

Cooked or canned lobster
3 or 4 hard-cooked eggs (depending on how much
    lobster you have)
Melted butter
Sour cream (the commercial type)
Seasoned salt and paprika

Chop the lobster fine. Mash egg yolks and add (save the whites for another dish). Add the butter and cream and seasonings and blend well. Serve with crisp crackers or thinly sliced strips of dark bread.

This is good with crab or shrimp or tuna instead of the lobster. The egg whites may be added to the next creamed dish you make. You may add a dash of mustard if you like.

CHEESE CUBES

3 thick slices bread, white (preferably unsliced until
    you slice)
2 tbsp melted butter or margarine
1 egg, beaten
1 cup grated American cheese

Cut the bread into 1-inch cubes. Add egg to butter or margarine and dip the cubes in this mixture, then roll in the cheese. Bake in a moderate oven (350°) until cheese is melted and cubes are golden brown. Serve hot.

AVOCADO DIP

1 cup mashed avocado pulp
½ lb pkg Philadelphia cream cheese
3 tbsp lemon juice
⅓ cup minced onions or shallots
1 tsp salt
   Worcestershire to taste

Blend avocado and cheese well. Add remaining ingredients and mix well. Serve in a bowl with crisp crackers arranged around it.

CHICKEN LIVER PÂTÉ

½ lb chicken livers
1 sliced onion
6 tbsp butter or margarine
   Salt and pepper to taste
   Madeira (if you have it) or mayonnaise

Sauté the onion in the butter or margarine and sauté the chicken livers in another pan about 5 minutes. Add salt and pepper to the chicken livers. Mix onion and livers together and put in a blender or through the finest blade of your food chopper. Let cool and add enough wine or mayonnaise to make spreading consistency. Serve on fingers of toast or plain crackers.

If you have any chicken fat, use that instead of the butter.

LOUELLA'S CUCUMBER DIP

1 pint commercial sour cream
1 tbsp plus 1 tsp prepared horse-
     radish
1 tbsp paprika
1 tbsp minced chives
1 tsp salt
1 tsp dill (fresh if you can get it)
¼ tsp garlic salt and monosodium
     glutamate
1 clove garlic, crushed
   Freshly ground pepper
   Basil vinegar to taste

Blend all ingredients together and chill at least an hour. The amount of basil vinegar depends on the sour cream, which varies in sharpness.
   Serve in a bowl set in a larger bowl of crushed ice.
   For the cucumber sticks, peel 4 large fresh cucumbers. Cut in thin strips and slice off the seedy part. Crisp them in ice water. Drain thoroughly.

Leftover dip, if there is any, makes a fine addition to your salad dressing.

MUSHROOMS IN WINE

Fresh button mushrooms, 4 or 5 for each
   person to be served
Dry white wine
Olive oil
1 tbsp finely chopped onion
1 tbsp chopped chives
1 tbsp chopped parsley
1 bay leaf
3 whole cloves
   Pepper, tabasco sauce (dash of this), salt
1 clove garlic

Cover the mushrooms with the wine and let stand in the refrigerator for an hour. Then drain and cover the mushrooms with olive oil and put them in a jar. The seasonings above will serve for a pound of mushrooms. Add them to the jar and cover. Let stand 2 days in the refrigerator.

Serve with toothpicks for spearing.

HOT CLAM CHEESE DIP

1 10½-oz can minced clams
¼ lb process cheese, cut in
   small pieces
1 small onion, finely chopped
3 tbsp butter or margarine
½ green sweet pepper, diced
4 tbsp catsup
1 tbsp Worcestershire
1 tbsp sherry (or milk)
¼ tsp Cayenne

Sauté onion and pepper in the butter or margarine 3 minutes. Add the rest of the ingredients and cook until the cheese melts, stirring constantly. Keep hot while you serve it, either in a chafing dish or in an earthenware casserole over a warmer. It must stay hot.

Serve with Melba toast, crisp crackers, or pumpernickel.

I have known a man who does not like clams to have seven dunks of this. Better serve small plates when you have the clam dip as it may drip off the crackers on your newly cleaned best rug. Worth it anyway.

CRAB CURRY CANAPÉ

1 medium or large can of crab meat
⅔ can cream of mushroom soup
2 tbsp pimiento, minced
¼ tsp curry powder (I use a little more)
¼ tsp salt.

Heat in a double boiler or chafing dish. If it seems to be too thick, thin with a little cream. Serve in a bowl with crackers or crisp potato chips for dunking.

If you use frozen crab meat, follow directions on the package for thawing and cooking (if uncooked). One package will equal a large-size can of crab meat.

BARBARA'S HOT CANAPÉS

Cut slices of bread with a doughnut or cooky cutter into rounds. Use firm bread, day old, that will not crumble.

Mix deviled ham (a small or large can according to how many people you are serving) with horseradish to taste. (Use freshly ground horseradish if you have a garden.)

Taste as you mix.

Butter the bread rounds lightly and spread with the mix. Sprinkle a few capers on top of each canapé. Bake in a hot oven (400°) until bubbly.

Serve hot.

Save the crusts to toast and crumble for toppings on casseroles or creamed dishes. No waste. We find men like these canapés especially, so make enough if you have men to feed — and what is more fun than feeding men?

RIPE OLIVES CURRIED

Heat the olives in their own liquor with curry powder added to taste. Serve hot or cold.

BARBECUED BEEF BOWL

1½ lbs hamburger (or 4 cups diced cooked beef)			Salt, pepper, Cayenne to taste
1½ cups water		3	thin lemon slices
¼ cup vinegar		2	medium onions, diced
¼ cup sugar		½	cup butter or margarine
5 tsp prepared mustard		1	cup catsup
		4	tbsp Worcestershire

Sauté the onions in the butter or margarine until golden in a deep heavy pan. Add water, vinegar, sugar, mustard, seasonings, and lemons and simmer 20 minutes. Meanwhile brown the hamburger. Add hamburger, catsup and Worcestershire and simmer about 30 minutes. Serve with toast rounds for dunking, and be sure the guests have plates.

If you use leftover already cooked meat, do not sauté it. This is good for a party that will run latish, because the barbecue is hearty fare.

SARDINE CANAPÉS

1 can sardines packed in oil	Lemon juice
2 tbsp mayonnaise	Toast strips
1 tbsp pickle relish	

Mix mayonnaise and pickle relish and spread on the toast. Lay a drained sardine on top of each strip and drizzle with lemon juice. Put in a hot oven (450°) for 5 minutes. Serve with extra lemon wedges dusted with paprika.

The main trick is to drain the sardines well. One reason some people do not like sardines is because they find them too rich.

ANNE'S ANTIPASTO

1 can chick peas	Salt
Italian salad dressing	Mayonnaise
Chopped scallions	

Heat the chick peas, then drain and immediately pour Italian salad dressing over them. Mix in the scallions and add salt to taste. Let stand in refrigerator overnight. Just before serving add enough mayonnaise to moisten.

SERVES 3–4

You may use your own oil, vinegar and garlic dressing. If you have no scallions, use minced red onion. Use plenty of salt. This goes well with almost anything you have—slivers of ham, smoked fish, sliced toma-toes, salami, cheeses.

HOT ONION CANAPÉS

Cut rounds of bread in bite-sized circles, using a small cooky cutter. Then cut very thin slices of onion to fit the rounds, and place a slice of onion on each.

Mix grated Parmesan cheese with mayonnaise (about 3 tablespoons of cheese to a cup of mayonnaise). Top the onion slices with this mix-ture. Broil in a hot oven (400°) until the canapés are puffed up and beginning to brown.

Serve hot.

RED CAVIAR ISLAND

Red Caviar
Cottage cheese, fine grain

Make a mound of the cottage cheese and frost it with the red caviar, leaving some of the cheese showing around the bottom edges.

Serve with Melba toast or crackers for dipping.

For the amount, suit yourself. But this is very popular and is so easy. The red caviar is milder than the black, and also less expensive. You may, if you are in the mood for it, squeeze a little lemon juice on the caviar. Or a bit of grated onion does no harm.

BLENDER PARTY DIP

1 No. 2½ can pork and beans or chili (without meat)
½ cup shredded Cheddar cheese
½ clove garlic, minced
½ tsp salt
1 tsp chili powder (omit this if you use canned chili)
    Dash Tabasco
2 tsp vinegar
2 tsp Worcestershire
4 slices bacon, broiled and broken in bits

Combine all ingredients, except the bacon, in the blender, and blend on medium speed. Turn into a chafing dish and heat in the *blazer*. When simmering, keep hot by putting the blazer over the under pan in which you have enough hot water to make a little steam.

Sprinkle the bacon over the top, and serve with potato chips, Melba toast, crisp crackers or small toast triangles as a dunk.

MUSHROOM CANAPÉS

16 large mushrooms
1   lb seasoned country sausage

Wipe mushrooms with a damp cloth. (I take a dim view of peeling them and taking away most of the flavor.) Remove the stems and save them for soup or gravy. Stuff the caps with sausage and broil under low heat for 20 minutes. Lower the broiler rack if the fire is too hot.

Serve on rounds of buttered thin toast.

Thin toast should be thin. If you have regular sliced bread and do not own one of those tiger-toothed bread slicers, lay your bread flat on the counter, and put a piece of aluminum foil over the top. Then slide your sharpest knife through the center of the slice while keeping it in place with the foil, and there you are, I hope.

VERA'S PICKLED MUSHROOMS

1 large clove garlic, crushed
¾ cup salad oil
¼ cup olive oil
½ cup lemon juice
1 medium onion chopped (or 5 green onions,
      chopped)
1 tsp salt
¼ tsp pepper
½ tsp dry mustard
2 or 3 bay leaves
1 sprig fresh rosemary (½ teaspoon if dried)
½ tsp oregano
2 4-oz cans big button mushrooms

Mix sauce, and taste for seasoning. Add dash of wine vinegar if desired. Pour into a jar with a top, add drained mushrooms, and cover. Store in the refrigerator at least 24 hours. Remove bay leaves after a few hours. Drain on paper towels and stick a cocktail pick in each mushroom. Serve with cocktails or on the hors d'oeuvre tray.

CHICKEN LIVER NIBLETS

1 pkg frozen chicken livers
   Flour to dredge
   Garlic salt
   Butter or margarine

Thaw the livers enough to separate them easily, then dredge with flour, sprinkle thoroughly with garlic salt. Sauté over medium heat in butter or margarine in a heavy saucepan until tender and brown.
   Serve with cocktail picks.

SERVES 4–6

This is easy and always a favorite. The garlic does something to the livers.

Soups

I IMAGINE THE INVENTION OF SOUP WAS PRIMITIVE MAN'S
first step toward civilization. I wish I could have known that first man
who got tired of gnawing raw meat and threw the bones in a clay pot
and added some water. If, later, he threw in some weeds, he was all set.
When mankind lived by the sea, it was easy to toss in fish, and perhaps
the clamshells provided spoons. Inland, I suppose they just slurped
from the pot.

In any case, soup has progressed along with man. It may be as sophis-
ticated as jellied cucumber soup or as simple as pot au feu, but soup it
is, and when the tureen comes to the table, nobody waits to be called.
But the basis of soup is still using what you have around, backed up
with soup bones or fish or chicken. Soup should be simmered slowly a
long, long time with the quick-cooking ingredients added toward serving time. Unless you are making consommé, soup should never be thin.
When you lift a spoonful of the stock, it should be rich and sturdy. If you
have used chicken or turkey bones, the soup will almost stand by itself

29

when cool. For a beef soup, if you are short of marrow bones (ask your dog to please let you have one or two) you may add a can of beef bouillon and a can of one of the cream soups (which gives it body).

Soup must be served so hot that guests can sit and breathe the elegant richness before they dip in. Of, if you are having a cold soup, it should be like the first snowfall in December. There is no halfway, none at all.

Canned and dehydrated soups have many uses. I like to experiment, combining two or three kinds. The liquid from canned vegetables may be used instead of water. On cream soups, I often float a thin slice of lemon on each bowl, or a slice of hard-cooked egg, or a spoonful of sour cream.

If soup is the main dish for the meal, I have plenty of hot bread, chunks of French or Italian bread or popovers or corn sticks, or toasted English muffins sprinkled with herbs or grated Parmesan cheese.

HOLIDAY SOUP

Leftover turkey or chicken or duckling
Onion, diced
Celery tops, chopped
Parsley
Seasoned salt and pepper
Dressing
Cooked peas, carrots, green beans, etc.
Gravy

Use the bones, skin and leftover meat from the turkey or chicken or duckling and simmer for about 2 hours with water to cover. At the end of an hour add the vegetables, dressing, and any leftover gravy. If you are short of bones and meat, add 1 chicken bouillon cube or 1 teaspoon meat extract for each 2 cans soup. A spoonful of chicken concentrate, if you can get it, adds flavor.

For the duck soup, allow plenty of time for it to cool and then skim off excess fat. Reheat for serving. Remove skin and bones and cut up any meat before serving.

This is a substantial soup and needs only a green salad to make a meal. If there is no leftover dressing, add rice a half hour before serving time, or very fine egg noodles.

MINESTRONE

1½ qts beef stock
½ lb salt pork, diced
1 pkg frozen peas
½ lb frozen lima beans
½ head medium-sized cabbage, shredded
½ lb fresh spinach, cut fine
3 medium-sized carrots, diced
2 stalks celery, cut fine
1 medium onion, diced
2 cloves garlic, chopped
2 tomatoes, cut in small pieces
¼ cup raw brown or long-grain white rice
1 tbsp chopped parsley
Salt and pepper and paprika to taste

Bring the stock to a boil. Meanwhile lightly fry the salt pork until it just turns color but is not brown. Add the salt pork and the remaining ingredients to the stock, reduce the heat and simmer gently until the vegetables are tender.

SERVES 4-6

Serve with a bowl of grated Parmesan cheese or stir the cheese right into the soup (about ½ cup). Serve in soup plates. This soup is too thick for dunking, but stick with the Italian bread (wrapped in aluminum foil and heated to piping).

I have eaten minestrone in any number of Italian restaurants and have yet to find it twice the same. The only thing I find is that it is always better than the last. I think you may add almost any vegetables, from chick peas to fresh green beans. Kidney beans are fine too. I use the canned and add juice and all, but this is no doubt unethical. If you are short on rice, elbow macaroni does no harm.

I do not know the origin of minestrone but I always suspect an Italian housewife had a good soup bone simmering half the day, and just tossed in whatever she had because there was not money enough to buy veal for Parmigiana for a large and very hungry family.

If you have a country garden, it is quite possible to find a few pods of okra, a Brussels sprout or so, and even a few slivers of turnip in that soup.

STILLMEADOW SOUP

2 or 3 lbs soup meat with bones
2 veal bones
1 can beef bouillon
1 pkg dehydrated soup, beef, onion, vegetable, etc.
   Chopped celery with leaves
   Diced carrots
   Chopped cabbage
   Onion, cut rather fine
   Noodles, spaghetti, macaroni, or almost any
      pasta or rice
   Seasonings

Simmer meat slowly in water to cover. Add the bouillon when more liquid is needed. Continue to cook until the meat is almost tender. Add the dehydrated soup with a cup or two of water. Add the vegetables and noodles, putting the cabbage in last. Taste for seasoning.

SERVES 6

Proportions are impossible to set. If the bones are large, you will need more liquid in the pot. I usually buy the meat in a chunk, not cut up, and any inexpensive cut will do. I add whatever vegetables I have on hand, left-over corn or peas or canned tomatoes. A can of tomato paste will make a thicker soup. It is never the same twice running, but the secret is the canned bouillon and dehydrated soup which flavor and reinforce the stock. One or two parsnips go well, but parsnips are sweet and must be used very sparingly. I do not use asparagus because it gets mushy and gives a bitter taste. This soup is even better the next day, so it pays to make a lot of it.

HERMAN SMITH'S BOUILLABAISSE

3 lbs fresh-water fish, in serving pieces (keep heads)
1 can (8-oz) shrimp
1 can (medium or large) lobster
4 cups water
2 onions, sliced
3 leeks, sliced
1 large clove garlic, mashed
½ cup oil
2 tomatoes, peeled, chopped
  Pinch saffron
1 strip orange rind
1 bay leaf
4 whole cloves
6 peppercorns
1 cup dry white table wine
6 slices toast
1 clove garlic, cut in half
3 tbsp soft butter or margarine
3 tbsp chopped chives
2 tbsp butter or margarine, melted
1 tbsp parsley, minced

Cook fish heads and liquid from shrimp and lobster for 10 minutes. Drain, reserve stock. Cook onions, leek and garlic in hot oil until soft. Add 4 cups reserved stock, tomatoes, saffron, orange rind.

Tie bay leaf, cloves, peppercorns in cheesecloth bag and add to mixture. Simmer about 30 minutes. Then remove the bag, and add fish and shrimp and cook about 10 minutes more. Then add the wine. Rub the toast with the cut garlic, spread with soft butter and sprinkle with chives. Heat the lobster in butter or margarine and place a spoonful on each slice of toast in deep soup plates. Pour in the stew, sprinkle with parsley and serve at once.

SERVES 6

Or you may put the stew in the soup plates and lay the lobster toast on top. This is a complete dinner, but have extra toast ready for dunking. A tossed salad goes well.

SMILEY'S SHORT-CUT BOUILLABAISSE

2 1-lb pkgs frozen halibut, sole, or any filleted fish
   (boneless)
1 can clams in the shell
1 can shelled clams
2 cans Manhattan-type clam chowder (or red-hot
   clam chowder if you can get it)
1 medium cooked lobster with shell
1 lb shrimp, canned or frozen or fresh (cooked)
⅛ tsp monosodium glutamate
⅛ tsp saffron
1 tbsp salt

Pressure cook 1 pound of the halibut in 2 cups water at 15 pounds for 15 minutes: pulverize in a blender and remove to another container. Put the 2 cans of clam chowder in the blender and beat 3 minutes, then add to halibut with salt, monosodium glutamate, saffron, both cans of clams, and more water, if needed. Next, pressure cook the remaining 1 pound of halibut 5 minutes at 15 pounds pressure, break into chunks and add this to the mixture with the shrimp. Break up the lobster in the shell and add to the mixture, then simmer all this for 20 to 30 minutes over a slow heat.

SERVES 6–8

Smiley travels in his trailer when on location for Western shows, personal tours, or public performances. The kitchen in this particular trailer is his pride, and he is always cooking up something for anyone around, from acrobats to cowboys.

"No use," he says, "not eating well even if you are on the go all the time!"

I once visited him when he was forced to stay in a hotel in a big city, and he had talked the management into letting him bring his portable cooking equipment into his suite. He served four of us a fine dinner, of what he called decent home cooking.

GLADYS TABER'S FISH SOUP

1 medium onion, sliced
1 tbsp olive oil
½ cup potatoes, sliced
2 medium carrots, cut in slivers
1 green pepper, medium or small, diced
1 quart scalded milk
1 tbsp butter
2 small cans fish flakes
½ cup parsley, chopped
   Seasoned salt and seasoned pepper to taste

Brown onion in the oil (adding a little more oil if needed). Add potatoes, carrots and pepper and simmer until tender. If they begin to stick, add 3 tablespoons water. Add milk, butter, fish flakes, seasonings, and heat slowly but do not let boil. Serve in warm soup plates with the parsley sprinkled on each.

SERVES 4

The charm of this is not only how easy it is but that the vegetables do not get mushy.

CRAB BISQUE

4 cups cooked or canned crab meat
4 tbsp butter or margarine
3 tbsp flour
2 cups top milk
½ cup cream
   Worcestershire (2 or 3 tbsp)
1 tsp mustard
   Chopped chives
   Sherry to taste

Melt the butter and blend in flour, then add milk and cream and seasonings. Cook, stirring constantly, until creamy, then add crab. Do not boil after crab is added. Before serving, stir in about 3 tablespoon sherry.

SERVES 4–6

You may thin this with top milk as needed. Place a thin slice of lemon in the soup plates before serving. Actually a bisque is a cream soup, but this isn't a stew, either, and bisque sounds prettier.

NEW ENGLAND CLAM CHOWDER

2 dozen hardshell clams in the shell (or 3 dozen if
      small)
¼ lb salt pork
1 minced onion
2 cups raw sliced or diced potatoes
3 tbsp flour
3 tbsp butter or margarine
4 cups milk
    Parsley, salt, paprika, pinch of dry thyme

Scrub the clams well in several waters with a firm brush. Put them in a deep kettle and pour over 1 cup water. Steam, tightly covered, until the shells open.

Remove the clams and chop the hard portions with a sharp knife (or use a food chopper).

Strain the juice through cheesecloth and add 2 cups of water.

Meanwhile dice the salt pork and heat over a low flame until it is crisp and golden brown. Add the onion and cook until the onion is transparent. Add the hard part of the clams.

Cook slowly for five minutes.

Sprinkle the flour over and add clam juice and water. Next add the potatoes, cover, and simmer until the potatoes are done. Add the soft part of the clams and the butter, and when the chowder comes to a boil add the milk (heated but not boiling).

Add seasonings.

Let the chowder ripen at least half an hour. Serve hot with toasted chowder crackers.

SERVES 6

You may use 2 cans minced clams. You may also use part light cream for a richer chowder. You will, if you are sensible, float an extra dollop of butter on top and more paprika.

NEW YEAR'S EVE OYSTER STEW

3 dozen oysters, shucked and with liquid
5 tbsp butter
2 tbsp Worcestershire
1 tsp seasoned salt
½ tsp seasoned pepper
Paprika to taste
6 cups top milk, or half milk and half cream
½ bunch parsley, minced

Heat the butter in a deep heavy kettle. When bubbling, add oysters and seasonings. Cook gently until the edges of the oysters begin to curl (about a minute). Meanwhile, in a separate kettle heat the milk. When the milk is hot but not boiling, combine with the oysters and simmer briefly but do not boil. Let stand to blend the flavors. When ready to serve, heat until hot but not boiling. Pour into a warm tureen and top with parsley, paprika, and bits of butter.

SERVES 8

This was the way my mother made it for me when I brought my friends in after sleighing or skating on New Year's Day. In that innocent and happy time, there was no problem of teen-age drunken driving or wild parties. We hitched Grace, the livery stable horse (who also drew the hearse for funerals), to an old-fashioned sleigh and went up and down the Wisconsin hills singing "Sweet Adeline." Then we came home to my house, and the oyster stew was ready with plenty of oyster crackers. It was flavored with youth and happiness and there was never any left over.

The main trick is not to overcook the oysters, or they get rubbery. Never boil the milk or cream.

SHIRLEY BOOTH'S PURÉE MONGOLE

1 can cream of tomato soup, condensed
1 can cream of green pea soup, condensed
2 cans top milk or thin cream
1 tbsp sherry

Heat the two soups with the milk or cream until just simmering, but not boiling. Add the sherry. Serve in heated soup bowls or mugs.

SERVES 4–5

The reason we now call this Shirley's soup is that when we were discussing recipes, she said she made this soup one time, and it was good. She couldn't think how she had dreamed it up, and then it burst over her that she read it in my Diary! I think the soup people originally thought of it, but from now on, it is Shirley's soup to us.

We like it with croutons (add garlic salt to the butter or margarine you fry them in) and a gelatin fruit salad with sour cream and mayonnaise dressing. No dessert, unless the green and white grapes just happen to be ready to pick.

QUICK BORSCH

1	No. 2 can beets (shredded)	Salt and pepper to taste
1	tsp minced onion	1 tbsp lemon juice, fresh,
1½	cups beef stock or bouillon	canned or frozen
1	cup water	Sour cream

Drain the beets, reserving the juice. Combine the juice, onion, bouillon, water; add the beets and cook for about 5 minutes, or until simmering. Add seasonings and lemon juice. Pour into hot soup bowls and top each bowl with a spoonful of sour cream.

SERVES 4–6

If you use whole beets, shred them on your biggest grater (as for cole slaw).

This is an excellent first course for dinner, especially a mixed-grill platter of lamb chops, tiny broiled sausages, grilled pineapple slices, and sliced cooked sweet potatoes brushed with butter or margarine and broiled just as the chops are about done.

MURRAY EDWARDS' VICHYSSOISE

2 cups diced raw potatoes
2 cups diced raw leeks or onions (leeks are better)
1 cup chicken broth
1 cup sour cream
1 tsp Worcestershire
  Salt to taste
  Chopped chives

Cook potatoes and leeks in a very little water until soft. Press through a food mill, or use your blender. Add the broth. Let cool. Then add the sour cream and beat well. Add seasonings and chill.

Serve in individual cups, topped with the chives.

SERVES 4-5

I have tried many variations of Vichyssoise, and this is my true love as far as this soup goes. I first had it at dinner in Murray's house on the Virginia Military Institute grounds. I knew at the first spoonful that a colonel can cook for me any day. Afterward we sat on the back veranda and watched the sun go down over the blue Virginia mountains while we sipped the colonel's own specially ground coffee.

CHEDDAR SOUP

¾ cup Cheddar cheese, grated
1 tbsp onion, chopped
1 tbsp butter or margarine
1 tbsp flour
1 cup chicken stock or consommé
2 cups milk

Melt butter or margarine, add the onion and cook until golden. Blend in the flour, then add the chicken stock and milk, stirring. Bring to boiling, add cheese, and stir until cheese is melted.

Garnish with chopped parsley or chives or croutons.

SERVES 6

SPAGHETTI SOUP

1 large soup bone, veal, beef or lamb,
    prèferably with some meat on it.
8 bay leaves
2 or 3 whole cloves
1 cup sliced onions
2 tsp salt; freshly ground pepper to taste
1 No. 2 can tomatoes
1 lb spaghetti

Cover the soup bone with cold water. Add the first 4 ingredients, and when the soup comes to a boil, add the tomatoes. Turn the heat low, and simmer 2 or 3 hours. Taste for seasoning, and if the stock is not rich enough add 1 dessert spoonful of beef concentrate or 2 bouillon cubes.

When it is time to eat, cook the spaghetti in rapidly boiling water, salted, until tender but not mushy.

Heap the spaghetti, at serving time, in big warm soup plates, and pour the soup over. You may remove the bay leaves and cloves by straining the soup.

Serve with a big bowl of grated Parmesan cheese.

SERVES 8

If you use a pressure cooker for 3-pound bone, 2 quarts water, cook at 10 pounds' pressure for 40 minutes.

You may add garlic salt, a dash of chili powder, ½ can tomato paste, a dash or so of Worcestershire, or what you will. But serve only a green salad and a lot of crusty French bread for sopping.

CREAMY ONION SOUP

4 medium onions, sliced
2 tbsp olive oil
2 tbsp butter or margarine
2 cups chicken broth
1 cup cream
Salt, pepper, to taste
Parsley, chopped
Parmesan cheese, grated

Cook the onions in the olive oil and butter or margarine until golden but not brown. Add the broth and cream. Bring just to boiling point, but do not boil. Top with the parsley and serve with grated Parmesan cheese.

SERVES 4

Serve hot buttered crackers dusted with paprika with this, and any kind of salad at all, except onion and orange!

We like this as a change from the customary French onion soup, and it is substantial enough for a one-dish supper.

ONION SOUP

1 cup chopped onions	1 tsp salt
2 cups water	Butter (any quantity desired)
½ cup cornmeal	1 quart sweet milk

Cook 1 cup of chopped onions until tender (about 10 minutes) in 2 cups water. Stir in ½ cup sifted cornmeal to thicken, cook again until meal is done (about 10 minutes). Add salt, 1 quart sweet milk and butter. Heat to boiling point and serve.

SERVES 4–6

This comes from my friend Mrs. Tate in South Carolina, and I agree with her that it is a really special kind of onion soup.

CREAM OF CHICKEN AND CUCUMBER SOUP

2 tbsp butter or margarine
2 tbsp grated onion
¼ tsp curry powder
1 cup peeled and diced cucumber
1 can cream of mushroom soup, diluted
    with ½ can water
1 can cream of chicken soup, diluted
    with ½ can water
½ cup top milk or light cream
    Salt, pepper, paprika to taste

Melt butter or margarine in a deep kettle, add curry, onion and cucumber. Simmer, covered, until the cucumber is tender (5 minutes or less). Add the soups and the cream and heat to simmering, but do not boil. Season to taste and serve at once in warm soup bowls.

SERVES 4–6

You may like more curry, but taste after adding. On a broiling August day, try this served frosty cold with a sprig of watercress in each bowl. To complete the meal, if the soup is hot, serve grapefruit and orange salad, adding a bit of mayonnaise to a French dressing to pour over. Tiny hot biscuits (use the smallest cutter or the center of a doughnut cutter) and currant jelly go well, winter or summer. Make the coffee hot or the tea iced according to the time. In summer, our choice is a chef's salad with fresh crisp mixed greens, slivers of tongue, chicken, ham, Swiss cheese, minced scallions.

RITA'S ITALIAN RAG SOUP

4 cups chicken broth
2 heaping tbsp seasoned bread crumbs
2 eggs
2 heaping tbsp grated Parmesan cheese
½ tsp nutmeg
   Salt and pepper to taste

Bring the broth to a boil. Mix the remaining ingredients together, adding a little water if the mixture is too thick. Add to the boiling broth, stir and simmer 5 minutes.

SERVES 4–6

Don't be misled by the name! This is probably a cousin of beef soup with marrow balls, but in this version the crumb mix does not stay in balls but floats through the soup (hence rag?). The seasoned or flavored bread crumbs may be found at most groceries.

LOBSTER CHOWDER

1 medium-sized lobster, boiled
3 tbsp butter or margarine
¼ cup cracker crumbs
4 cups top milk (or 3 cups milk and 1 cup
   thin cream)
1 medium onion, diced
1 cup chicken or clam broth
   Seasonings

Cut the meat from the lobster in small pieces. Cream the butter or margarine with the green liver of the lobster and the crumbs. Meanwhile scald the milk with the onion, and strain into the first mixture.

Cook the shell of the lobster in the broth for about ten minutes and strain into the milk. Add lobster meat and reheat, but do not boil. Season with seasoned salt, paprika, and a spoonful of sherry, if desired.

SERVES 4–6

You may use frozen lobster or a large can of lobster.

POOR MAN'S STEW

4   slices salt pork, diced
4   medium onions, chopped or cut fine
3   medium potatoes, peeled and diced
1½ qts water
Pepper to taste

Fry the salt pork in a heavy deep kettle until crisp and brown. When the pork is nearly done, add the onions. When the onions are golden, add the water and potatoes. Simmer, covered, until the potatoes are tender. Add pepper. Then drop in dumplings, cover and cook 15 minutes.

DUMPLINGS

2   cups biscuit mix
2   tbsp parsley flakes

Mix as directed on the package.

SERVES 4–5

You may use part chicken broth or beef stock in place of the water, but this is delicious as is.

We first had it during a February blizzard, when "the electric" was off. We did not dare open the deep-freeze with the current off, and the shelves were pretty bare after a three-day storm. A guest from Vermont asked if we had any salt pork. . . . We hung the iron soup kettle over the fire in the fireplace, and shortly the wonderful smell of salt pork and onions filled the house. That was a memorable dinner, that one. We served cole slaw (plenty of cabbage stored in the cellar), coffee (boiled, with an egg shell dropped in it), and for dessert rosy Delicious apples and Port Salut cheese.

CREAM OF CLAM SOUP

1 cup canned minced clams
2 cups top milk
1/2 cup whipped cream with 1/4 tsp salt
   Paprika
   Parsley

Heat the clams. Scald the milk in the top of a double boiler. Combine clams and milk and season to taste. Keep under boiling point.

   Serve in heated soup cups topped with whipped cream and sprinkled with chopped parsley and paprika.

SERVES 3

This is a quick and satisfying soup.

CORN CHOWDER

2 slices salt pork, diced
1 can (medium size) cream-style corn
1 small onion, diced
2 medium potatoes, peeled and diced
2 cups water
2 cups light cream or top milk

In a heavy kettle fry the salt pork to a light brown (add no fat) and then the onion. Cook gently until the onion is golden, then add the potatoes and season with freshly ground pepper and salt, and add the water. Cook until the potatoes are tender but not mushy. Meanwhile heat the cream or milk but do not boil. Add with the corn to the first mixture, and reheat to simmering (no boiling).

SERVES 4–6

This is a robust supper soup. Serve in a warm tureen with a good dusting of paprika and a little chopped parsley on top. With it serve crisp cucumber slices and chilled tomato slices dressed with a light French dressing. Add crusty French bread cut in chunks and spread with garlic butter.

BEET CONSOMMÉ

1   can whole or sliced beets
(These have more flavor than the shoestring kind.)
2   cans condensed consommé
1   can water (1½ cups)
2   medium onions, chopped, not too fine
6   whole cloves
1½ tbsp vinegar
¼   tsp salt
A dash of pepper

Drain juice from beets and put it in a deep saucepan. Add consommé and water. Chop the drained beets and add beets and onions to the juice. Add cloves, vinegar, salt and pepper. Bring to a boil and simmer 20 minutes. Strain. Serve consommé hot or cold with spoonfuls of thick sour cream and a sprinkling of chopped chives.

SERVES 4–6

This soup tastes like a clear borsch. It is equally good hot or cold.

JELLIED CUCUMBER SOUP

4   cups chicken broth (no fat, please)
2   envelopes unflavored gelatin
¼   cup cold water
¼   cup lemon juice, fresh, canned or frozen
A few drops green vegetable coloring
Salt, pepper, paprika to taste
1½ cups peeled, seeded, diced cucumber

Heat the broth to boiling. Soften the gelatin in the cold water and add to the broth, then add lemon juice and coloring. Season well. Cool until it begins to thicken, then add the cucumber and chill again until set. At serving time, break it up with a fork and serve in chilled cups or bowls. Garnish with lemon slices dusted with paprika. (Use the Hungarian sweet paprika if you can get it.)

SERVES 4–6

This is a cool, light luncheon soup and low in calories too. Makes a fine prelude to a cold buffet. Or serve sliced cold chicken, tongue, turkey, or cold cuts and ripe tomatoes stuffed with cottage cheese. Fill the bread basket with rye or pumpernickel. Add tall glasses of strong iced tea.

LEEK AND POTATO SOUP

¼ cup butter (½ stick)
6–8　leeks, finely chopped
¼ cup chopped celery
1　qt chicken broth
⅛ tsp pepper
4　medium potatoes, sliced thin
1　tsp salt
2　cup light cream
1　tbsp chopped chives

In 3-quart pan heat butter, add leeks (white part only), celery, and cook over low heat for 5 minutes. Add the potatoes with broth (or consommé, or 4 chicken bouillon cubes in 4 cups hot water), salt, pepper. Cover and simmer for 20 to 30 minutes until potatoes are tender.

Put mixture through fine sieve and blend in light cream. Pour soup into tureen and sprinkle with chopped chives over top.

Can also be chilled and served cold.

SERVES 4 for main dish; or 6 for first course

ANNE'S SUPPER SOUP

1 large can minestrone (Progresso if possible)
1 cup red or white clam sauce (Buitoni)
Grated Parmesan cheese

Combine the minestrone and clam sauce and heat. Serve the cheese in a separate bowl.

SERVES 3–4

This is a rib-sticking soup and we like it for supper with a green salad and bread sticks and hot coffee.

WATERCRESS SOUP

2   cups chopped fresh watercress
½   pkg Old English style Process cheese
      sliced thin
2   tbsp butter or margarine
2   tbsp flour
4   cups top milk
      Salt and pepper to taste

Melt the butter or margarine, blend in the flour, add the milk gradually, stirring constantly over a medium heat. When it begins to thicken, add the cheese, and stir until the cheese is melted and the soup is smooth.

   Add seasonings and the watercress and cook 2 or 3 minutes longer. Serve at once.

SERVES 4

Try this as the one hot dish needed with a cold supper, particularly good with cold thinly-sliced ham and a fresh vegetable salad, and wedges of French or Italian bread (heat the bread in the oven first).

GAZPACHO

2 tbsp olive oil
1 clove garlic mashed with ½ tsp salt
5 or 6 ripe tomatoes, cut in pieces
1 medium onion, chopped
1½ cups cold water or consommé
1½ tbsp vinegar
   Freshly ground pepper
   Paprika
¼ cup dry bread crumbs
   Croutons
   Cucumber, diced

Add garlic to the olive oil, then the rest of the ingredients. Let stand about an hour then put through a grinder or coarse strainer. Correct seasoning. Stir in bread crumbs. Serve in chilled bowls, adding an ice cube to each. Add croutons and cucumber at the last minute.

SERVES 4–6

This is a traditional Spanish soup except for the ice cubes! Fine for a luncheon dish on a hot summer day. Add crusty French bread and coffee.

Eggs, Cheese, and Pasta

ON THE SUBJECT OF EGGS AND CHEESE, I AM A FANATIC. BOTH are basic, and both vary a good deal. An egg that has been around too long looks tired and smells stale. The yolk should be firm and the white clear and not watery. A blood spot has nothing to do with it, it merely means it is a fertile egg. I am a brown egg addict. When I lived in the city, I walked endlessly hunting for brown eggs. City people, I was told, wanted white ones. Now I am a country dweller I have a hard time at Easter finding white eggs, which do take dye better.

I do not know how many kinds of cheese there are, but each has its

51

own province from the lusty Vermont Cheddar to the gentle Port Salut
from the Swiss Colony in Wisconsin. Except for a few recipes, I never
use what I call patchwork cheese, which is a cheese base with added
milk solids. I do not want pasteurized cheese or milk solids. I want real
cheese. Fortunately most stores carry some true cheese along with the
dozens of synthetics. And there are many cheesemakers who will ship
sound cheeses. I will admit weakly that I seldom take time to grate my
Parmesan — I buy it grated in a can. I once grated several jars, wearing
my fingers out, and covered them tightly and the cheese molded. If you
buy a wheel of cheese, keep it in the refrigerator until you use it and if
it molds, cut off the molded edges and sprinkle a few drops of white
vinegar on the wrapping. Use it in cooking, but for table cheese, have it
new and fresh.

Pasta covers almost as many categories as the dictionary does words.
I keep several kinds — the wide egg noodles, the thin noodles (for soups),
macaroni, spaghetti, lasagne noodles, the pasta shaped like bowknots,
and so on. I have not succumbed as yet to the squared-edged type, but I
daresay I shall. The main trick in cooking the various pastas is not to
overcook so they get mushy. They should be what the Italians call *al
dente,* which means your teeth know they are there. And do not break
spaghetti in pieces, cook it whole and then work at winding it on your
spoon when you eat it. I always add a tablespoon of butter to the salted
boiling water, but don't ask me why. I just do.

DAISY EGGS

1 egg to a person

Separate yolks from whites, keeping yolks unbroken and each yolk in a
separate dish.

Beat whites well, and add seasoned salt, plenty of paprika, a dash of
Worcestershire or A-1 sauce.

Put the whites in greased individual flat ramekins, or pile them in
individual mounds on a baking sheet.

Slip the yolks carefully into the center of the beaten whites. Season
with paprika and seasoned salt. Bake in a moderate oven (325°) until
the yolks are firmly set.

DEVILED EGGS CASSEROLE

6 hard-cooked eggs, deviled (*see* Curried Eggs,
    p. 54)
16 shrimp, cooked
¾ cup sliced mushrooms
3 tbsp butter or margarine
2 cups cheese sauce

Place the deviled eggs in a shallow greased baking pan. Break the shrimp in pieces and lay around the top of the eggs. Sauté the mushrooms in the butter or margarine, and, when brown, put on top of the shrimp. Pour the cheese sauce over, and bake in a moderate oven (350°) about 15 minutes or until it bubbles.

SERVES 4–6

CHEESE SAUCE

2 tbsp butter or margarine
2 tbsp flour
½ tsp salt
2 cups milk
½ cup grated sharp cheese

Melt butter or margarine in a saucepan, stir in flour and salt, cook until smooth and free from lumps, stirring constantly, then gradually add milk and cheese and continue stirring until cheese is thoroughly blended and sauce bubbles.

EGGS CARACAS

2 tbsp butter   ½ cup grated American cheese
4 ozs shredded dried beef   2 cups stewed tomatoes
1 tsp chili powder   6 beaten eggs

Melt the butter in a heavy skillet. Add dried beef, chili powder, cheese and tomatoes. Cook over low heat until the mixture bubbles. Add the beaten eggs and stir constantly until it thickens. Serve on crisp toast.

SERVES 6

Perfect for a chafing dish supper.

EGGS MORNAY

2 tbsp butter or margarine
2 tbsp flour
2 cups milk
   Salt, pepper, paprika to taste
   Dash tabasco or Worcestershire
1 tsp mild prepared mustard
⅓ cup Cheddar cheese, diced or grated
6 eggs

Melt the butter or margarine, blend in the flour and seasonings, and gradually add the milk, stirring constantly. When the sauce is smooth, add the cheese and stir until melted. Now put a layer of the cheese sauce in 3 greased individual baking dishes (or use a flat glass baking dish big enough to accommodate the 6 eggs). Slide 2 eggs into each ramekin on top of the sauce, cover partially with the remaining sauce, dust with paprika. Bake in a moderate oven (350°) 20 minutes or until the yolks are set, the sauce bubbly.

If you leave a little of each egg yolk showing, the eye appeal is greater. Tastes the same!

CURRIED EGGS

Hard-cooked eggs
Mayonnaise
Curry powder
Paprika
Finely cut sweet gherkins

Cut the eggs lengthwise after shelling and remove yolks. Mash yolks with a fork and add enough mayonnaise mixed with curry powder to make the mixture smooth. Pile in the whites and tuck a bit of pickle in the center of each. Dust with paprika.

This has been a Stillmeadow favorite for years. I make the yolk mixture very creamy. My quarrel with regular deviled eggs is that they taste good, but can be rather dry.

CREOLE EGGS

Butter or margarine
1 tbsp onion, diced
1 cup tomatoes, peeled and chopped
3 or 4 mushrooms, sliced
6 eggs, slightly beaten
1 dessert spoon of capers, if desired

Sauté the onion and mushrooms in the butter or margarine until tender but not brown. Add the tomatoes and cook about 8 minutes. In a double boiler or chafing dish, pour the onion mixture, then add the eggs, capers and seasonings (use seasoned salt if you have it), paprika, a dash of Cayenne. Cook gently until the eggs are creamy, stirring (a wooden spoon is fine for this).

Serve crisp crackers or buttered toast triangles.

SERVES 4–5

This is an easy, quick supper dish, and perfect for a chafing dish.

BAKED EGGS SPECIAL

1 can (large size) cream-style corn
4 green-pepper rings
4 eggs
Salt, pepper, paprika
1 tbsp crumbs
2 tbsp grated Parmesan cheese
Butter or margarine

Season the corn with salt and pepper, and place in greased individual baking dishes or ramekins. Parboil the pepper rings 5 minutes and place a ring in each baking dish.

Break eggs into the rings, sprinkle with seasonings, crumbs and cheese. Dust with paprika. Bake 15 minutes in a moderate oven (350°).

SERVES 4

EGGS AND MUSHROOMS IN CHEESE SAUCE

¼ cup butter melted in a pan

Mix in:

¼ cup flour
1 tsp paprika
1 tsp salt
¼ tsp pepper
¼ tsp mustard

Stir in:

3 cups milk

And cook slowly till thickened.

Add:

1 cup grated American cheese

And stir till melted.

Then fold in:

6 hard-cooked eggs
1 – 1½ cups cooked mushrooms

Serve piping hot on toast or in a wild rice ring.

SERVES 4 – 5

HOPPEL POPPEL

(also called Bauern Breakfast, a hearty sportsman's brunch)

4 potatoes
8 eggs
8 slices bacon
2 onions
2 tbsp butter

Boil potatoes and slice. Sauté onions, chopped, in butter, add bacon cut in small pieces. Scramble the eggs into this mixture, adding potatoes.

SERVES 4

TABASCO EGGS

1   cup thick cream
1   cup whole milk
1   tsp salt
    Dash Cayenne and tabasco to season
6   eggs
½   cup fine buttered bread crumbs
½   cup grated cheese, Parmesan or Cheddar

Heat the cream and milk in a chafing dish or ironware skillet. Add salt, Cayenne, tabasco.

When mixture is scalding, slip the eggs in one at a time, carefully. Keep the heat low if you are doing this on a range. As the eggs begin to set, sprinkle the crumbs and cheese over them. Keep dipping the sauce over the eggs until they are firmly set.

Serve on hot buttered toast.

ALLOW 2 eggs per person if this is the main dish

This is a recipe I started housekeeping with, and it saved the day for me many a time.

WELSH RABBIT

2   tbsp butter
3   cups Cheddar cheese, grated
½   tsp dry mustard
½   tsp salt
1   tsp Worcestershire

Pinch of Cayenne
2   egg yolks, lightly beaten
½   cup ale or beer
    Crisp buttered toast

In a double boiler or chafing dish, melt the butter, add the cheese and stir with a wooden spoon in one direction only. When the cheese melts, add the seasonings. Combine the egg yolks with the ale, and add gradually, stirring constantly. Do not let it boil. When piping hot, pour on the toast and serve immediately.

SERVES 2–4

MEXICAN RABBIT

3   tbsp butter or margarine
1   onion, chopped
½   green pepper, chopped
2   tbsp flour
1   cup milk
2   cups grated Cheddar cheese
1½   cups stewed tomatoes (or 1 medium can)
     Salt, Cayenne
2   egg yolks, beaten

Sauté the onion and pepper in the butter or margarine in the top pan of a chafing dish. Put the pan over hot water, add the flour and stir until blended. Then add the milk and stir until smooth. Add the cheese, and when it has melted, add tomatoes and seasonings. Cook for 10 minutes, stirring occasionally; then add the egg yolks and stir for 2 minutes.

Serve on hot toast points.

SERVES 4

EXTRA SPECIAL SCRAMBLED EGGS

2 eggs per person and an extra egg for the pan
Salt, pepper, paprika, pinch of chili powder
Cottage cheese, preferably the big curd

Beat the eggs in a bowl with a fork. Meanwhile melt butter or margarine in a heavy pan or chafing dish. When the butter is hot but not brown, turn the eggs in, and add the cottage cheese. You may use 2 tablespoons for 4 or 5 eggs, but the amount of cheese depends on how moist it is. A firm, creamed cottage cheese you use sparingly. A loose curd cheese you may be reckless with. Stir gently until the cheese is mixed through the eggs as they set. Turn the heat off before they are really done, for eggs keep on cooking.

The secret is to cook slowly over a low heat. After a time or two, you will know how much cheese your family likes in this creamy, delicate dish.

CHEESE SOUFFLÉ

    2 tbsp butter or margarine
    2 tbsp flour
    ¾ cup milk
       A dash of Worcestershire
       Salt (taste for this as some cheese is strong),
          pepper, paprika
    4 egg yolks
    5 egg whites, beaten until stiff
    1 cup crumbled or grated cheese (Cheddar,
          American, or Swiss)

Melt the butter or margarine over medium heat, blend in the flour. Add milk gradually, and stir until smooth, adding the seasonings as you stir. Remove the pan from the fire and beat the egg yolks in, one at a time, alternately adding the cheese. Put back on the range over low heat and stir until the cheese melts. Remove from stove and let cool a few minutes. Then fold in the egg whites (with a wooden spoon if you have one).

Bake in an ungreased quart casserole in a moderate oven (350°) for about 45 minutes, or until the soufflé begins to draw away from the sides of the casserole and the top is delicately browned.

SERVES 3–4

Serve with crisp buttered toast points, asparagus, a mixed green salad with a light French dressing, coffee. Add catsup, chili sauce or Sauce Diable for those who wish a dribble on the soufflé.

QUICHE LORRAINE

Pastry to line a 10-inch pie tin (see pastry recipe or use a pastry mix as directed). Line the pan with pastry. Prick with a fork on the bottom. Chill until you make the filling.

> Soft butter to cover pastry
> 1 cup grated Swiss cheese (use a mouli rotary
>   grater if you have one)
> 4 eggs, slightly beaten
> 2 cups thin or thick cream
> 1 pinch Cayenne
> 1 pinch sugar
> 1 tsp salt, and pepper to taste
> Bacon or cooked ham
> 1 white onion

Spread the surface of the pastry with soft butter. Beat eggs and cream together until blended. Add the seasonings, and stir lightly. Meanwhile grill a dozen slices of bacon, break in bits and sprinkle on the crust. Sauté a small diced onion in butter or margarine until transparent. Sprinkle on the crust. Then sprinkle the cheese on. Pour the egg mixture over. Bake in a hot oven (450°) for 12 minutes, reduce to 325° and bake until a knife inserted in the middle comes out clean. For most ovens 25 minutes is enough.

SERVES 4, but 3 will finish it. For 6–8 persons, I make two pies.

You may omit the bacon and onion, or you may substitute chopped cooked ham for them. I happen to like the bacon and onion best.

Serve with a green vegetable such as fresh peas cooked with mint leaf, broccoli (no Hollandaise this time) or spinach. Add a fruit salad and coffee and skip dessert as this is a rich dinner.

Quiche Lorraine freezes beautifully. Freeze after baking. I first had Quiche Lorraine at Rose Feld's, when we both were celebrating successful new books. Most of the time as we ate the whole Lorraine, we talked about food, not books. I copied down the recipe as we sat by the fire drinking hot black coffee and watching the moonlight silvering the wide floor boards.

PIZZA

CRUST

1 envelope active dry yeast	½ tsp salt
1 cup lukewarm water	3½ cups all-purpose flour

Soften yeast in water. Add salt and stir in 2 cups of the flour. Turn onto a floured pastry board and knead in the rest of the flour. Knead until smooth and shiny. Cover and let rise in a warm place until double in bulk. Punch dough down, place on the board and pound lightly with rolling pin to flatten dough. Cover and let rise again. Then roll and pull and stretch dough to make a 12-inch round, not more than ¼ inch thick. Ease dough onto greased pizza pan and let rise 30 minutes at room temperature. Then fill with sauce.

PIZZA SAUCE

2 cups Italian tomatoes	Freshly ground pepper
2 tbsp tomato paste	½ pound mozzarella cheese,
½ tsp salt	sliced thin
½ tsp garlic powder	¼ cup grated Parmesan cheese
¼ tsp onion powder	3 tbsp olive oil
½ tsp sugar	

Mash tomatoes and blend with next 6 ingredients. Spread over dough. Place mozzarella in layers over tomatoes. Sprinkle Parmesan over and drizzle olive oil on. Bake in hot oven (400°) about 30 minutes or until crust is brown.

This is plain pizza. You may vary it by using anchovies, sausage, mushrooms Italian ham. Or whatever you feel like! The added ingredients go over the mozzarella.

If you can get whole oregano leaves, add a teaspoon to the tomato sauce. As to how many this serves — in my family one to a person and it is the whole meal. You may cut it in fours and serve four and they may accept it. For two, it is quite adequate. For six it is just enough to cut in slim wedges and have as an appetizer.

ESTHER KONOTOPHA'S VERNICKE

1 pkg noodles	A pinch of salt
1 qt cottage cheese	1 tbsp sugar
5 eggs	1 cup thick sour cream

Cook package of noodles or use a pint of cooked ones. Add one egg to cottage cheese, pinch of salt and 1 tablespoon sugar. Mix these together; then add them to the noodles and pour into a buttered baking dish (2 inches deep).

Mix sour cream and 4 eggs (do not beat the eggs). Fork this lightly through the first mixture, leaving a rough surface of cheese on the top and allowing the cream and egg mixture to seep through around the sides.

Bake 1 hour in a slow oven (325°) or until the center is quite firm and the top slightly brown.

The last helping can be dessert if you top it with a sauce made of thick sour cream, a touch of salt, and jam, jelly, preserves, or fresh sugared fruit.

SERVES 4–6

This is an Old World recipe and one of our favorites. It is worth every calorie. The cottage cheese should be fresh and preferably large curd.

HOMEMADE NOODLES

1   egg
½ tsp salt
2   cups flour (or a little more)

Beat the egg and salt and mix in the flour so that you have a very stiff dough. Knead on a floured board or pastry cloth until it forms a firm ball; then roll out as thin as possible. Cover with a towel and let rest 20 minutes. Then cut in strips and spread out on a board to dry. Store in a tightly covered jar.

A German friend of ours used to make these and give us a jar for Christmas. I like them cooked in boiling salted water until just tender and served in a warm bowl with butter and cottage cheese stirred in.

FETTUCINE LENTEN SPECIAL

1 lb fettucine noodles
   Boiling salted water
1 stick butter or margarine (½ cup)
1 cup thick cream
¼ lb grated Parmesan cheese
   Seasoned pepper or freshly grated pepper

Cook noodles in boiling water about 10 minutes. Do not let them become mushy. Drain and put them in a chafing dish or electric skillet or in a heavy pot over low heat on the stove. Add butter gradually and stir so it will coat the noodles; then add the cream and pepper. Stir gently until cream begins to thicken. Add cheese and stir again.

SERVES 6

Serve with salad and plenty of hot coffee. If you want dessert, have a bowl of fresh fruit.

OPEN CHEESE AND BACON SANDWICH

¾ lb store cheese (Cheddar cut from a wheel is best)
3 eggs
1 tsp dry mustard
1 tsp Worcestershire
   A dash of Cayenne
   Salt to taste
1 or 2 slices bacon to each serving
1 slice tomato to each serving (if desired)

Grate the cheese and add the eggs one at a time beating in well. Add remaining ingredients and stir until blended. Store in a covered jar in the refrigerator. It will keep 3 weeks.

This was invented by my Cape Cod friend Peg. She says pile it on thickly over bread which has been toasted on one side and broil it until it begins to brown, then add a slice of bacon and the tomato slice if you wish. It puffs up almost like a small soufflé and makes a fine luncheon dish with a green salad and coffee. As to how many it serves, this depends on how you pile it! It should make 6 or more open sandwiches.

GNOCCHI

1   cup cornmeal (preferably white, but
       yellow will do)
3/4 cup grated Parmesan cheese
3   cups cold water
2   tsp dry mustard
1   egg, beaten
    Salt
    Freshly ground pepper
1/3 cup melted butter or margarine
1/3 cup grated Parmesan cheese
4   medium tomatoes
2   pkgs brown-and-serve sausages

Put the water and salt in a deep sauce pan and bring to boil. Stir in the cornmeal slowly, stirring constantly. Continue to stir and cook until the cornmeal is thickened and creamy. It will begin to draw from the sides of the pan when it is done. Then cover, reduce heat to low, and cook 10 minutes.

Remove from heat, stir in cheese, mustard, egg, salt, pepper. Turn into a greased 10″ × 6″ × 2″ baking dish, smoothing evenly with a spatula. Set in the refrigerator until 15–20 minutes before dinner. Then cut the gnocchi into squares and arrange in the center of a large flat baking dish (or metal skillet). Top with the 1/3 cup of grated cheese and the melted butter or margarine.

Start the broiler in the range. While it heats, cut the tomatoes in wedges and arrange at one end of the dish. Sprinkle with seasonings and remaining cheese. Broil 5 minutes, then add the sausages at the opposite end of the dish and continue broiling until sausages are brown, cheese bubbly.

SERVES 6

Tomatoes and sausages may be omitted.

ANNE'S LASAGNE

1   lb lasagne noodles
1½ lbs Italian sausage (optional)
1   lb ricotta cheese
1   lb mozzarella cheese, sliced
     Grated Parmesan or Romano cheese
¼   cup chopped parsley

SAUCE

Either 2 large cans spaghetti sauce simmered 10–15 minutes with 1 lb ground beef browned in 3 tbsp olive oil. *Or* sauce made with:

4   tbsp olive oil
1   lb ground beef
1   carrot, grated
¼   tsp thyme
1   tsp oregano
½   tsp sweet basil
     Large can solid pack tomatoes
     Salt and pepper
     Small can tomato paste
1   paste can of water (use the can you have
       removed the tomato paste from)

Sauté sausage until browned. Drain and slice thin. Cook the lasagne, following directions on package until tender but not mushy. Drain. Butter a large baking dish (9″ × 14″ is good) and line bottom with lasagne, overlapped slightly. Add a layer of sauce, sprinkle with sausage slices, ricotta, mozzarella slices, parsley, and a good handful of grated cheese. Add another layer of lasagne, and continue alternating layers, ending with a layer of lasagne. Pour over any remaining sauce, sprinkle with grated cheese, and bake in a 350° oven for 25 to 30 minutes or until bubbling and lightly browned. Can be assembled several hours ahead of baking; also excellent reheated. If dry, pass additional sauce.

SERVES 4–6

If Italian sausage is not available, use any good sausage you can get. You may, if necessary, omit the sausage and still have a good dish.

TOMATO CHEDDAR FONDUE

1   10½-oz can condensed tomato soup
2   cups Cheddar cheese, grated
2   egg yolks
½   cup milk
1½   tsp Worcestershire
2   egg whites
     Pinch of salt

Combine tomato soup and cheese and heat in a chafing dish until cheese melts. Beat egg yolks and milk together and add seasonings. Add to soup mixture. Beat egg whites, with salt, until stiff. Fold into the mixture.

SERVES 6

Serve with chunks of hot French bread or toast triangles for a Sunday brunch. Add a green salad and a fruit compote and hot coffee for a quick supper when guests happen in.

BAKED MACARONI AND CHEESE

1 cup elbow macaroni	¼ tsp pepper
1 cup soft bread crumbs	½ tsp Worcestershire
1½ cup milk	½ cup mushrooms cooked
1 egg, beaten slightly	in butter 2 minutes
1½ cup grated cheese	1 pimiento, diced
½ tsp salt	2 tbsp melted butter

Cook macaroni in boiling salted water. Drain. Place in well-greased casserole. Add bread crumbs to milk. Let stand 5 minutes. Add remaining ingredients. Pour over macaroni. Bake in moderate oven (350°) 45 to 50 minutes.

SERVES 4–6

SPAGHETTI WITH ANCHOVIES

2	lbs spaghetti		Bunch of parsley
2	tbsp salt	¼	lb butter
4	small onions, diced or chopped	2	cans anchovies
		12	black olives

Have water boiling in a large kettle, add salt and spaghetti and stir until done "al dente," or about ten minutes. Meanwhile sauté onions in butter with chopped parsley, the anchovies, sliced, and the pitted olives.

Drain spaghetti, place in serving dish and pour sauce over. This is to be served *without* Parmesan. Garlic bread is nice with it.

SERVES 4–6

TAMALE SCRAMBLE

1	15½-oz can tamales
8	eggs
1	cup milk
	Salt
3	tbsp butter or margarine
1½	cups grated cheese (Cheddar or American)

Take the husks from the tamales and cut each tamale in bite-size pieces. Place tamales in a baking dish and add the sauce from the can. Beat the eggs lightly and add milk and seasoning. Melt the butter or margarine in a skillet and add the egg mixture. Cook gently until the eggs begin to set. Pour the eggs over the tamales, top with the cheese and place the dish under the broiler (about 3 or 4 inches from the heat.) When the cheese is melted, turn off the broiler and leave the dish in for two or three more minutes. Garnish with fresh sprigs of watercress.

SERVES 4–5

If you heat the tamales first, you can shorten the oven time.

STILLMEADOW CHEESE BAKE

6   slices white bread, with crusts removed
2½ cups grated Cheddar or Swiss cheese
3   eggs, beaten slightly
2½ cups milk
1   tsp salt
     Pepper to taste
     Dry mustard (½ to 1 tsp)

Lay the bread in a greased baking pan, spreading each slice with butter or margarine and fitting one layer in the pan. Sprinkle the cheese over the bottom layer, add the mustard, lay another layer of bread over this, and then pour over the eggs mixed with the milk and seasonings.

Let stand an hour. Bake in a slow oven (325°) 30 to 40 minutes, or until it puffs up and begins to brown. If a straw inserted in the center comes out clean, it is done.

SERVES 3–4

You may increase the bread slices and cheese and add 1 extra egg with ½ cup more milk to serve 6.

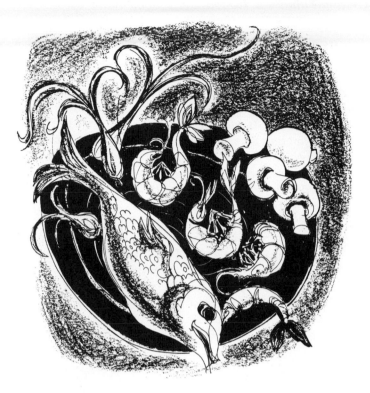

Fish and Shellfish

THE BEST FISH IS, OF COURSE, THE ONE YOU JUST CAUGHT.
Brook trout is tops, flounder is elegant, perch and small-mouthed bass
delicious. The first thing you need is someone to clean it, and I have always arranged to fish with such a one. I build the fire and get the spider
hot (it is not a skillet to me) and have the coffee ready. For frying fish, I
use half margarine or oil and half butter. I do not use bacon fat because
I think the flavor is too strong. Since margarine or oil burns less quickly
than butter, the fish will fry to a golden brown and not get too black. The
butter gives the flavor.

My cousin dips fish in cornmeal, I use seasoned flour. Some people lay
the fish in the pan as is. A good many people, alas, cook fish too long. I
stick a two-tined fork in mine after 5 minutes or so, and if the fork slides
in, I call it done. Of course, if you are cooking a large fish, you will have

69

to cook it longer. Sea bass has a firm texture and is a slow cooker; so is swordfish steak.

The only shellfish I have ever garnered is clams. A cherrystone opened on the beach and eaten without seasoning is an experience. Oysters, shrimp, lobsters, scallops, steamers, are now available almost everywhere, frozen or canned. If you live by the sea, you go to the fish pier and buy them fresh. You may also get so-called fresh shellfish in fish markets in the inland cities. If you shop for lobsters, be sure they are a good blackish-green color and are lively. If a lobster seems limp and lifeless, it probably is. And you may regret buying it. I don't advise buying clams, quahogs, or other seafood from roadside stands. They often sit in the sun all day. Seafood needs to be bedded in ice until cooked.

If you have a freezer, you may have fish shipped to you. I once ordered a shipment from Wisconsin because I was hungry for fresh lake fish. Part of the ice had melted and I still remember the frantic time Jill, my housemate, and I had wrapping and freezing pounds and pounds and pounds of fish. We had fish sliding all over the kitchen!

SEAFOOD BORLANDIA

Fillets, frozen or fresh, flounder or whitefish, 2 to a person
Oysters, fresh or frozen, 4 to a person. (A container of frozen
  oysters serves 4.)
Shrimp, 1 6-oz can to 4 persons
Cheese sauce

Place drained fillets in a greased casserole or baking dish, add the raw oysters, then the shrimp. For the sauce, make a cream sauce (see SAUCES) and add ¼ cup grated Cheddar cheese. Pour over the fish, and bake in a moderate (350°) oven for 30–40 minutes, depending on whether fillets are frozen or fresh. Test with a fork. When the fillets are flaky, and the sauce bubbly, dinner is ready.

Serve with garlic buttered French or Italian bread and a green salad.
Pass a bowl of frosty white grapes for dessert, or ripe peaches.

JANET'S FILLET OF SOLE

1 pkg frozen fillets of sole or flounder
1 lb fresh or 1 pkg frozen spinach
  Parmesan cheese, grated
  Sauce
  Croutons

Cover the bottom of a casserole with the spinach, cooked and seasoned.
  Lay seasoned fillets over the spinach and sprinkle well with the cheese.
Pour the sauce over, sprinkle again with cheese and add croutons. Bake
in a moderate (375°) oven for 25 minutes or until golden brown.

SAUCE

Melt 2 tablespoons butter or margarine, blend in 2 tablespoons flour, add
1 cup canned consommé and cook until thickened. Season to taste and
add ½ cup cream (evaporated milk if the cream is gone). Stir well, remove from fire. (Or use Béchamel Sauce recipe in SAUCE section.)

SERVES 2-4

DEVILED SALMON

1   large can salmon, flaked and with skin removed
1   cup canned tomato soup, undiluted
¼ onion
¼ green pepper, diced
3 tbsp butter
1 tsp salt
1 tsp prepared mustard
1 slice lemon with peel

Put in a blender and blend well. (Or mince onion, pepper, lemon very
fine.)
  Pour the tomato mix over the salmon and stir. Pile in greased ramekins. Top each ramekin with buttered crumbs and a thin slice of lemon.
Dust with paprika. Bake in a hot oven until bubbly (about 25 minutes).

SERVES 4

BAKED SEA BASS

1 3- to 4-lb sea bass
Thin slices of salt pork

Wipe fish with a damp paper towel, then rub salt outside and in. Stuff with the following:

2 cups fine bread crumbs	1 tbsp lemon juice
1½ tsp grated onion	½ tsp salt
½ cup chopped celery (with some leaves)	3 tbsp melted butter
	2 tbsp white wine or water

Mix all ingredients well, then spoon the stuffing into the fish. Skewer opening. Place fish in baking tin or flat casserole. Lay salt pork strips over. Bake in a very hot oven (500°) 10 minutes, then reduce heat to hot (425°) and bake about 45 minutes longer. Slide gently onto a hot platter, garnish with lemon slices dusted with paprika and parsley flakes.

If you wish a sauce, heat a can of frozen shrimp soup with ⅓ can of top milk and pour over.

SERVES 4–6

If your fish is 5 pounds, add a little more celery and ⅓ cup crumbs to the stuffing.

CREAMED FLOUNDER

8 flounder fillets	Salt
Cooked shrimp or oysters, or both	Paprika
Cream	Thyme
Parmesan cheese	Butter

Butter a large flat casserole (large enough to hold the fillets without overlapping). Lay fish on the bottom, distribute the chopped shrimp or oysters on top. Barely cover with cream. Sprinkle with salt and cheese, paprika and thyme. Dot with butter. Bake in a 350° oven for about a half hour, or until fish is done and cream begins to thicken.

SERVES 4–8, depending on size of fillets

FISH PUDDING

1 lb flounder fillets	2 tbsp potato starch
1¼ cups milk	¼ cup dry vermouth
2 eggs	1 cup heavy cream

Cut flounder into pieces and put in blender with 1 cup milk, eggs, starch. Cover container and put on high speed for 2 minutes. Take cover off. Add ¼ cup milk and vermouth. (It should be ¾ full. Add water if necessary.) Add cream to the rest and turn off blender.

Pour in greased round 1 quart mold, set in pan of warm water and bake at 325°, or moderate, until set in center – about an hour. Turn out on warm platter and garnish with cooked shrimp or lobster. Serve with sour cream sauce.

SOUR CREAM SAUCE

1 cup sour cream
1 bunch chopped fresh dill

Put in blender and run at high speed for 20 seconds. Then heat in double boiler over hot water. Do not boil.

SERVES 4

If fresh dill is not available, sprinkle dill seed in the cream.

PICKLED FLOUNDER

¾ cup vinegar	¾ tsp salt
2½ cups water	½ tsp black pepper
2 sections garlic, minced	1½ to 2 lbs flounder
½ tsp cumin seed	

Combine vinegar with water, garlic, cumin seed, salt and pepper. Cut flounder into pieces suitable for frying, and let stand in solution in icebox for 12 hours. Drain and dry. Roll in cornmeal and fry.

SERVES 4–6

SMILEY'S CORN AND SALMON LOAF

1   can (7¼ oz) salmon
2   cups cream-style corn
1   tbsp melted butter
1   cup bread crumbs
1   cup milk (or half milk, half cream)
2   eggs, beaten
1   tsp lemon juice
½   tsp salt
⅛   tsp pepper

Remove skin and small bones from salmon and mix salmon with corn. Sprinkle melted butter over bread crumbs and toast lightly in oven. After reserving some of crumbs for topping, mix remainder with salmon and corn and add remaining ingredients. Place in a buttered casserole dish, top with reserved crumbs, and bake at 325° for 45 to 50 minutes, or until loaf is firm in center.

SERVES 4–6

SALMON CASSEROLE

1   No. 2 can salmon   ½ can whole potatoes
½ onion, diced   ⅓ cup sour cream
½ green pepper, diced   Paprika

Drain salmon, saving the liquid. Place salmon in center of greased casserole. Sprinkle with black pepper. Top with the onion and green pepper and add ⅓ cup of the salmon liquor. Slice the potatoes and arrange around the fish. Dot with butter and season. Pour the sour cream over the salmon. Sprinkle the paprika over. Bake in a hot (425°) oven about 20 minutes.

SERVES 2–3

This is a quick and easy dish and fine for a winter night.

BAKED FILLETS WITH LOBSTER SAUCE

1 pkg frozen flounder or sole fillets
1 can frozen lobster soup (or shrimp soup)
  Butter or margarine
  Freshly ground pepper
  Chopped parsley

Separate the fillets and lay them in a greased flat baking dish. Thaw the soup by immersing it in hot water until it sloshes in the can when you shake it. (Or you can thaw it on a sunny window sill in 2 hours, if you happen to think of it.)

Pour the soup over the fillets, add pepper and parsley. Bake in a medium oven (350°) until the fish is tender when you pierce it with a fork and the soup is reduced to a creamy sauce.

SERVES 2–4

Serve garnished with fresh watercress. Add a tossed salad made with plain French dressing (the fish will be rich) and pass wedges of hot crusty French bread for sopping up that sauce. If you must have a vegetable, use tiny canned peas with half a can of mushrooms added. And to top off a meal that almost does itself, serve canned grapefruit sections with a dash of crème de menthe and a sprig of fresh mint dipped in powdered sugar. Keep the coffee hot.

SOLE BAKED IN WINE SAUCE

2   lbs sole or flounder fillets
2   tbsp lemon juice
2   tbsp dry white wine
    Salt and pepper
4   tbsp butter or margarine
4   tbsp flour (¼ cup)
2   cups milk
¼   tsp freshly ground pepper
½   tsp dry mustard
1   tsp Worcestershire
½   tsp tarragon, crumbled
2   tbsp each, chopped green pepper, parsley, chives
2   tbsp grated Parmesan cheese
4   tbsp dry sherry

Sprinkle fillets with lemon juice, wine, salt and pepper. Chill several hours.

Melt butter in a saucepan, blend in flour. When smooth add milk slowly, and stir over low heat until thick. Add the pepper, mustard, Worcestershire, tarragon, green pepper, chives, parsley, cheese and sherry.

Arrange fillets in a flat casserole or baking pan (greased) and pour the sauce over. Bake in a moderate oven (350°) for 30 minutes, or until fish flakes with a fork.

SERVES 6

BOILED SALMON AND SHRIMP SAUCE

2-lb salmon
2 qts court bouillon
1 tbsp butter or margarine
1 tbsp flour
½ lb cooked shrimps (fresh, frozen or canned)
   Seasoned salt and pepper
1 egg yolk
1 cup light cream
2 tbsp Madeira (if desired)

Wrap the salmon in a piece of clean cheesecloth and place it gently in the court bouillon. Cover and simmer about 20 minutes.

COURT BOUILLON WITH WINE

4 cups dry white wine
2 cups water
1 diced carrot
1 diced onion

1 stalk celery with leaves
Bouquet garni (parsley, bay leaf, peppercorns, 3 cloves)

Simmer for 35 minutes. Strain, bring just to the boiling point.

SAUCE

For the sauce, melt 1 tablespoon butter or margarine and stir in 1 tablespoon flour. Add shrimps (cut in pieces) and ½ cup of the court bouillon. Season with salt and freshly ground pepper and cook until smooth. Then pour the cream (scalded) over the beaten egg yolk, and add slowly to the shrimps. Lay salmon on a warm platter. Add Madeira to sauce and pour over. Garnish with watercress.

SERVES 6

Boiled salmon belongs to the Fourth of July according to my family tradition. However, there was no wine used in Father's house with the exception of a kind of imitation cooking sherry which was quite frightful. Mama used a little vinegar in the court bouillon. Tasted just fine to us. The salmon was served cold for supper with mayonnaise and lemon wedges. We ate on the lawn at sunset and set off our modest fireworks as soon as it was dark. Neither Mama nor I could stand noise, but Father always had a few bangs available.

SHAD ROE WITH TOAST TRIANGLES

2 lbs fresh shad roe (or 3 cans roe)
½ cup butter or margarine
   Salt, pepper, monosodium glutamate, paprika
3 or 4 slices bread

In a chafing dish or skillet, heat the butter, but do not let it brown. Lay the fresh roe in, cover, and cook over low heat about twelve minutes or until tender. Turn once. Add butter or margarine if it gets dry. Heat canned roe in butter.

Arrange toast triangles on a heated platter and lay roe on top. Season to taste and arrange lemon wedges sprinkled with paprika around the platter.

SERVES 6

When the shad roe man comes down our road, we buy six or twelve. Roe freezes very well. But when the shad are not in season, the canned roe is excellent. It makes a special Sunday breakfast as well as a fine supper dish.

CREAMED FINNAN HADDIE

2 lbs finnan haddie
2 tbsp minced onion
1½ tbsp minced green pepper
4 tbsp butter or margarine
4 tbsp flour

1 cup milk
1 cup cream or top milk
   Seasoned salt and pepper
   Chopped parsley

Soak the finnan haddie in lukewarm water for about half an hour, then drain. Cover with fresh water and poach the fish (simmer, do not boil). Drain and flake fish and keep warm. Cook the onion and green pepper in the butter about 5 minutes. Blend in flour and seasonings and stir constantly, adding the milk and cream. When the sauce is thick and smooth, pour it over the finnan haddie.

SERVES 4–5

This is a favorite for Sunday breakfast. It is also fine for supper with baked potatoes and sliced tomato and cucumber salad.

LOIS KLAKRING'S BAKED TUNA CASSEROLE

¼ cup shortening—butter, margarine, vegetable
1   tsp minced onion
1   tbsp minced green pepper
4   tbsp flour
1   tsp salt
½ tsp paprika
2   cups milk
2   tsp chopped pimiento
2   7-oz cans tuna
    Buttered bread crumbs

Sauté onion and pepper in fat about 2 minutes. Add flour, salt, paprika, and blend. Add milk gradually and cook until thickened, stirring constantly. Add pimiento. Separate tuna into flakes. Mix bread crumbs in melted butter or margarine. Arrange alternate layers of sauce, tuna and crumbs in a greased casserole. Top with crumbs and bake, covered, at 375° or moderately hot oven for about 30 minutes. It will bubble when it is done, and the top will be brown.

SERVES 4–6, but 3 can do a good job of it, and never mind

Serve with a grapefruit and avocado salad and lemon juice in the French dressing. Hot buttermilk biscuits do no harm, and you can buy these ready to bake. Don't bother with dessert, unless you have some of the Wisconsin Port Salut to serve with toasted crackers. But double the coffee.

TUNA AVOCADO PIE

Pastry for a 9-in. pie plate
¼ cup grated Parmesan cheese
2 cans tuna
1 avocado, peeled, pitted and
    cut into 1-in. cubes
1 chicken bouillon cube
½ cup boiling water
¼ cup butter or margarine

2 tbsp finely chopped onion
¼ cup flour
¾ cup heavy cream
1 tbsp lemon juice
¼ cup chili sauce
  Salt; chopped parsley to
    taste
½ cup shredded Swiss cheese

Make your usual recipe for pastry, but add the Parmesan cheese to the flour first. Line the 9-inch pan with the pastry. Drain the tuna and break into bite-sized pieces. Dissolve the bouillon cube in boiling water. Meanwhile, melt butter or margarine in a skillet, sauté the onion in it, then blend in the flour. Add bouillon and cream, stirring constantly until thickened, then the lemon juice, chili sauce, seasonings, tuna and avocado.

Mix all together well and pour into the pie shell. Sprinkle with the Swiss cheese and bake in a hot oven (400°) for 25 to 30 minutes or until filling is bubbly and crust is brown.

SERVES 6

FILLET BORLANDIA

Fillets of flounder, whitefish or haddock, fresh or frozen,
  2 to each person
Creole sauce, canned (1 can for 4–5 fillets)
Salt, pepper, oregano to taste

Dry fillets thoroughly on paper towels. Lay them in a greased baking dish, cover with the sauce. Sprinkle the seasonings lightly over. Bake in a hot (400°) oven until the fillets are tender when tested with a fork. The time will vary from 25 to 40 minutes depending on whether you use frozen or fresh fillets.

Spaghetti sauce may be substituted, or canned mushroom sauce. Or if you have time you may make your own Creole sauce.
  Serve with baked potatoes or fluffy rice and a tossed salad and coffee. Keep dessert light; a fruit compote is best.

CRAB AND TUNA CASSEROLE

1   can crab meat, shredded
1   7-oz can tuna (drained)
4   hard-cooked eggs, sliced
½   pkg frozen peas, thawed
1   can mushroom soup, undiluted
1   cup milk
1   tbsp grated onion
2   tbsp chopped green pepper
1   cup bread crumbs (or crushed potato chips)

Combine crab, tuna, 3 eggs and peas. Heat soup, milk and seasonings. Arrange ingredients in layers, sprinkling bread crumbs on each layer and adding liquid last. Place slices of 1 egg on top. Cover and bake at 350° for a half hour. Remove cover for last 5 minutes.

SERVES 4–6

SEAFOOD CASSEROLE

1   can (½ pound) lobster, shrimp, or salmon
1   box frozen peas, thawed
1   can condensed celery soup
1¼ cups milk
    Salt, pepper, paprika
1   tbsp lemon juice, fresh or canned
1⅓ cups cooked rice
    Parmesan cheese, grated

Cook soup, milk, seasonings, stirring until well blended. In a greased 1½-quart casserole, pour half of the soup. Then add alternate layers of seafood, rice, peas. Add the remaining soup. Sprinkle the cheese over the top. Bake, covered, in a moderate oven (350°) until bubbly (20 minutes).

SERVES 4

This may be varied endlessly. You may use a mixture of tuna, salmon, crab, lobster. You may add diced onion and green pepper, sautéed in butter or margarine. You may like to add a dash of sherry. You may garnish with freshly chopped parsley and slivers of pimiento. You may use cream of mushroom soup if you prefer.

HOT CRAB-MEAT SANDWICH

1 6½-oz. can crab meat
   Mayonnaise
4 slices white bread, toasted on one side
4 slices Swiss or American cheese
4 slices tomatoes
4 strips bacon, cut in half
   Dry mustard

Remove any shells from crab meat, and add enough mayonnaise to make the mixture spread easily. Spread crab mixture on 4 slices bread, on untoasted side. Cover each slice with cheese, top with tomato, sprinkle lightly with dry mustard, arrange bacon on top.
   Broil until bacon is crisp and cheese melts.

SERVES 4

MARYLAND CRAB SHELLS

½ lb crab meat (fresh or canned)
1 tsp onion, finely chopped
1 tsp green pepper, chopped
2 tbsp butter or margarine
   Salt
   Cayenne

1 cup thick cream sauce:
   3 tbsp butter or margarine
   3 tbsp flour
   ½ tsp dry mustard
   1 cup milk
      Salt and pepper

½ tsp minced chives
1 tsp chopped parsley
⅛ tsp Worcestershire
   Prepared mustard
   Buttered bread crumbs
1 egg yolk, unbeaten
2 tbsp cream

Remove any bits of bone from crab meat. Sauté with onion and pepper in 2 tablespoons butter. Season to taste with salt and Cayenne pepper. Add thick cream sauce, chives, parsley and Worcestershire. Heat just to boiling. Blend unbeaten egg with cream — add hot mixture to this gradually. Heap into crab or scallop shells or into 2 individual casseroles. Spread mustard thinly over the top; then sprinkle with buttered crumbs. Put under broiler or in 450° oven just long enough to get bubbly and brown.

SERVES 2

GRILLED MARINATED SHRIMP

2 lbs shrimp	1 tsp dry mustard
3 cloves garlic	1 tsp salt
⅔ cup minced onion	½ cup olive oil
¼ cup chopped parsley	2 tbsp lemon juice
1 tsp dried basil	

Split the shrimps down the back of the shells. Remove the vein, leave shells on but cut into the flesh about halfway. Place in a bowl and cover with the marinade. (Mix all ingredients together for the marinade and stir until blended). Marinate 2 hours, then pour all into a pan for broiling. Broil about 3 inches from heat, turning frequently until the shrimp are pink, the shells browned slightly and curl back.

SERVES 4–6

There is a deveining gadget on the market which helps most people, but not me. I use a sharp pointed knife. Serve the shrimp with buttered rice and a green salad. You may like a dessert like cream puffs as the shrimp is not a heavy dish.

GOLDEN SHRIMP CASSEROLE

8   slices bread, slightly dry, trimmed, buttered and
    cubed (amounts to about 5 cups)
2   cups cooked fresh shrimp (or 2 7-oz pkgs, frozen,
    shelled, deveined cooked shrimp)
1   3-oz can mushrooms (drained)
½   lb sharp American cheese, grated
3   eggs, beaten
½   tsp salt
½   tsp dry mustard
    Paprika and pepper (a dash of each)
2   cups milk

Place half the bread in a baking dish about 11″ × 7″ × 1½″. Add shrimp, mushrooms and half the grated cheese. The remaining bread and grated cheese go on top of the casserole. Then beat eggs, salt, dry mustard, paprika and pepper together; add milk and pour over the casserole. Bake for about 45 minutes in a 325° oven, until mixture is set.

SERVES 6 to 8

With a green salad, iced strong coffee, and fruit, this makes a perfect meal. My friend Marie Hinz serves this often when guests drop in for supper.

LOBSTER STEW – THE NEW ENGLAND WAY

2   lobsters (at least 1 pound each)
1/2   cup butter or margarine
1 1/2 qts light cream (top milk will do, if necessary)
2   tbsp or more sherry
     Seasoning to taste

Boil the lobsters for 15 minutes (in sea water if you can get it). Remove to a dripping pan and, when cool enough, split open and remove the meat. Do not skip the coral and tomalley (red roe and green liver). Press the juice from the feelers. Put the lobster meat, tomalley, roe, and juice from the dripping pan into a pan with the melted butter or margarine, and stir constantly until the butter or margarine covers everything except your apron. Cover and let stand several hours. Then heat the cream in a double boiler until it is hot but not boiling, add lobster meat and juice and seasonings. Watch the salt if you have used sea water.

Let cool. Then put in the refrigerator for 24 hours.

Reheat, check the seasoning, and add the sherry.

SERVES 6

Lobster stew, like clam chowder, needs to mellow. Or, as we say in my part of the country, it has to ripen.

Serve this in a big tureen, preferably ironstone, for the creamy color is just right with the pink-rose of the stew. Add crusty French or Italian bread, a green salad, and plenty of hot coffee. Nobody will want dessert. You may offer them fresh fruit, crisp crackers and Camembert cheese, if you must. But don't use a strong cheese, this is no time for the robust Cheddar after the rich savory lobster!

CREOLE SHRIMP

¼   cup butter or margarine
1   large onion, minced
1   cup green pepper, chopped
1   clove garlic
2   tsp flour
2   cups canned tomatoes
1½ tsp salt
     Dash of rosemary
     Paprika and pepper to taste
1   lb fresh or frozen shrimp, cooked

Melt butter or margarine and sauté onion, pepper, garlic for 10 minutes. Then stir in flour, and when blended add tomatoes and seasonings and bring to boiling point. Cover, reduce the heat, and simmer for about 15 minutes. Then add the shrimp and reheat, but do not boil.
    Serve on fluffy rice.

SERVES 4–5

SHRIMP AMANDINE

2 lbs shrimp, fresh or frozen, cooked
¾ cup raw rice
2 tbsp butter or margarine
¼ cup chopped green pepper
½ cup chopped onion

Salt and pepper to taste
1 can condensed tomato soup
1 cup cream
½ cup sherry, dry
½ cup sliced blanched almonds

Cook the rice as the package directs, drain, and let cool. Meanwhile, sauté the onion and green pepper in butter or margarine about 5 or 6 minutes. Then add seasonings, the soup, cream, sherry and almonds. Reserve a few whole shrimps for garnish and mix the rest with the rice and sauce. Turn into a 2-quart casserole, greased, and bake about 30 minutes in a moderate oven (350°). Add the whole shrimps, chopped parsley, paprika, and a few more almonds, and bake about 10 minutes longer.
    A sprinkle of Parmesan does no harm.
    Garnish with celery tips, watercress or more parsley.

SERVES 6 very well, more if you have enough side dishes

LOBSTER NEWBURG

    2 cups boiled diced lobster meat, or 2 6½-oz cans
    1 cup light cream
    2 egg yolks, beaten
    1 tbsp flour
    ¼ tsp salt
    4 tbsp melted butter
    1 tsp lemon juice
       Paprika to taste

Heat lobster in 3 tablespoons of melted butter. Do not let butter brown. In another saucepan stir flour into 1 tablespoon of melted butter, add cream and heat, stirring until smooth. Remove from fire as it begins to boil, add beaten egg yolks and stir until mixture thickens.

Add lobster and seasonings.

Serve at once on thin dry toast or crisp crackers.

SERVES 4

This is a variation of the usual sherry in Newburg, and is more delicate. The lemon juice does not mask the taste of the lobster.

LOUELLA'S CLAM PIE

       Pastry to line a 9-in. pie tin
    2 7½-oz cans minced clams, drained (save liquor)
    6 slices cooked bacon, crumbled
    3 tbsp minced onion cooked until golden in 2 tbsp of
          the bacon drippings
    4 eggs, slightly beaten
    1 cup milk
    1 cup clam liquor
       Pepper and salt to taste

Combine eggs, milk, clam liquor, seasonings. Sprinkle bacon over pastry shell. Add diced clams. Pour the egg mixture over. Bake in a moderate hot oven (375°) for 40 minutes, or until a knife inserted in the center comes out clean.

SERVES 4–6

CAPE COD CLAM PIE

1 pint raw clams, including liquor, or an equal
    amount of frozen clams, thawed
2 tbsp butter or margarine
1 tbsp flour
1 egg yolk, beaten
1 tsp minced parsley
⅔ cup evaporated milk or thin cream
    Pastry

Chop the hard part of the clams, or grind them. Make a roux of butter, flour, and liquor. (This merely means melt butter, blend in flour, over a medium heat, stir constantly, add liquor and keep stirring until smooth. Easy.) Add clams, milk or cream, egg and freshly ground pepper.

Line a deep pie dish with pastry. Pour in the clams. Cover with an upper crust and bake until the pastry is brown, about 40 minutes.

SERVES 4–5

You may use canned minced clams, but shorten the baking time as these are already cooked.

PISELLI À LA ZINGARELLA

2 tbsp olive oil
2 onions, chopped
1 can tomato paste
1 tbsp butter
1 lb frozen shrimp

1 can of whole mushrooms
2 cans of peas
Garlic salt to taste
Basil to taste

Sauté onions in oil slowly, add tomato paste after 5 minutes, add butter. Then add shrimp and cook for 10 minutes. Add peas and mushrooms last, stirring constantly.

Ham and chicken livers may be used instead of shrimp: 1 pound of chicken livers and 1 thick ham slice, diced; Canadian bacon can be substituted for the ham.

SERVES 4

CHINA SCALLOP À LA SHIRLEY

1½	lbs scallops, fresh or frozen	¼	tsp salt
1	medium cucumber	1½	cups milk
¼	cup butter	1½	tbsp cornstarch
1	4-oz can pimiento (diced)	2	tbsp dry sherry
¼	tsp catsup		Toast points or noodles

If you use sea scallops, slice them crosswise in ¼-in. slices. Peel and remove seeds from cucumber and cut lengthwise into 16 strips, then crosswise in small pieces. Cook scallops in the butter about 3 minutes, or until light brown. Add cucumber, pimiento and salt. Cover and simmer 3 minutes, then stir in catsup and 1 cup of the milk. Blend cornstarch in remaining milk, add and stir over medium heat until the mix thickens and comes to a boil. Stir in sherry.

SERVES 6

Shirley serves this as an entree in individual casseroles with toast points. You may serve it in a large dish surrounded by noodles if you prefer. Four can eat it with no problem, it is really tops.

SCALLOP BAKE

2	lbs scallops	½	cup bread crumbs
¼	lb mushrooms	⅛	tsp pepper
4	sprigs parsley	¼	cup margarine
1	tsp salt	1	tbsp lemon juice

Wash scallops. Chop mushrooms coarsely and mix with chopped parsley, crumbs, salt, pepper. Melt margarine. Spread scallops in baking dish. Sprinkle mixture over them. Pour margarine and lemon juice over all. Bake 15 minutes.

SERVES 6

It is gilding the lily to add anything to scallops, but during scallop season one may like a change from plain broiled.

COOKY SHEET SCALLOPS

Scallops (allow 10 per person)
Finely rolled cornflakes crumbs

Wash scallops and dry on a towel (NOT a paper towel). Roll in crumbs. Grease cooky sheet with barely enough butter to call it greased, just as little as possible. Arrange scallops on the sheet, not touching each other. Put in 350°–400° oven or under broiler. In about 5 minutes shake the cooky sheet to loosen scallops. Another 5 minutes and they are done. They look nice, they stay separated, and they are not greasy.

OYSTER PIE I

1 qt oysters
2 cups sliced mushrooms
2/3 cup butter
2/3 cup flour
1 tsp celery salt
1 qt milk
1 tsp salt
1 cup oyster liquor
1/4 tsp pepper
Pastry

Shuck oysters and drain liquor, saving it. Slice mushrooms and cook in butter until browned, about 3 minutes. Stir flour in and, when blended, add milk and oyster liquor slowly. When the mixture comes to a boil and is smooth, add oysters and seasonings. Pour into a 2-quart casserole. Cover with pastry and crimp the edges with a fork. Cut a gash in top to allow steam to escape. Bake in a hot oven (450°) until pastry is brown.

SERVES 4

This is the version of oyster pie I like best and it came to me from the Poconos. Dorothy Lambert and Linda Pipher are responsible. I think the mushrooms make the difference.

OYSTER PIE II

1 qt oysters, shucked	1 qt fresh milk
¼ lb butter	Pepper and salt to taste
Cracker crumbs	

Line bottom of a shallow baking pan with the crumbs (roll crackers fine). Put over this a layer of the oysters, then the butter and seasonings. Add another layer of oysters and crumbs until pan is filled, having crumbs for the top layer. Pour the milk in and bake about 20 minutes or until bubbly.

SERVES 2–4

This is Mary Margaret MacBride's recipe, and she says doubtfully that maybe it isn't a pie, but that is what they called it in Missouri when she was growing up. It was a rare treat in Missouri as it was in Wisconsin!

CRAB CASSEROLE I

1 pkg chopped frozen spinach	1 6-oz can tomato paste
1 cup grated Cheddar cheese	½ pint sour cream
1 can (large size) crab meat	Salt, pepper, paprika
1 tbsp lemon juice	1 tbsp dry sherry
1 small onion, minced	

Cook the spinach as directed. Fork it lightly into a greased casserole (1-quart size). Sprinkle with half the cheese, then place the crab meat in, and add lemon juice. Mix remaining ingredients and pour over the casserole. Add remaining cheese.

Bake in a moderate oven (350°) for 35 minutes.

SERVES 4

This is almost a version of Chicken Divan. We like to use half sharp cheese and half Parmesan, grated.

CRAB CASSEROLE II

½ cup butter
½ cup flour
2 cup milk
3 6½-oz cans king crab (remove cartilage and flake)
½ cup chopped green pepper
2 pimientos, chopped
4 hard-cooked eggs, chopped
1 tsp salt
   Pepper
½ cup to 1 cup grated sharp Cheddar cheese
   Buttered bread crumbs

Melt butter in large saucepan. Add flour and mix well. Remove from heat, and slowly add milk. Return to heat and cook, stirring constantly till white sauce thickens. Add crab meat, pimiento, peppers, eggs, salt and pepper. Pour into 2-quart casserole and top with grated cheese and buttered crumbs. Bake at 350° for 1 hour.

SERVES 4–6

Good with a green salad and hot rolls or garlic French bread.

BROILED SEA SCALLOPS

1   lb sea scallops
   Melted butter
   Lemon juice
   Salt and freshly ground pepper

Spread the scallops on a shallow pan and pour the butter over them. Sprinkle with the seasonings. Preheat broiler and broil the scallops 3 inches from the heat for 2 minutes; then turn and broil 2 or 3 more minutes, or until tender. Sprinkle with lemon juice after turning. Serve with lemon wedges or herb butter.

For herb butter, combine softened butter with equal parts minced chives, parsley, tarragon.

SERVES 4

LOBSTER MOUSSE

1   lb lobster meat, cut finely
   Salt and pepper to taste
¾   cup heavy cream
2   egg whites, stiffly beaten

Put lobster in a bowl, season it, and slowly beat in the cream. Then fold in the egg whites and turn into a mold, preferably a fish mold. Set in a pan of hot water and bake in a moderate (350°) oven for 20 minutes, or until firm. Unmold on a warm platter, garnish with watercress or parsley and lemon wedges.

SERVES 3–4

This is rich, but you can diet later. Have a tossed salad with French dressing and nothing heavier than a fresh fruit compote for dessert.

LEAH'S SCALLOPED OYSTERS I

1 pint oysters
1 pint milk
4 eggs, well beaten
¼ lb melted butter
20 to 25 saltines, coarsely crushed
   Salt and pepper to taste

Mix oysters, liquid, and milk in well-buttered casserole. Add beaten eggs and melted butter. Add crushed saltines and let sit until moisture is absorbed. Add more saltines if necessary to take up excess liquid, but mixture should be *sloppy*, not dry! Salt and pepper to taste, dot with butter and bake in 400° oven until well puffed up and delicately browned, about 1 hour. Serve immediately.

This may also be made with bay scallops, or minced clams, or a combination of all three.

SERVES 4–6

This is a glorified scallop and may be one reason oysters were invented. It is a tradition in the family of Barbara Lovely, who lives on one of those Cape Cod roads that bend to the sea. The spicy smell of.pine and salt fill the outside air, and inside, in the big living-kitchen, the smell of the oyster scallop is purely heaven.

SCALLOPED OYSTERS II

1 pint oysters, drained   2 tbsp oyster liquor
1 cup cracker crumbs   1 tbsp cream
½ cup bread crumbs   Salt and pepper
½ cup melted butter

Drain the oysters, saving the liquor. In a shallow greased baking pan, put a layer of the crumbs mixed with the melted butter. Lay the oysters over this and cover with crumbs. Pour over the oyster liquor and cream and season. Bake about 25 minutes in a hot oven (450°).

SERVES 4

This is the New England version of scalloped oysters. Especially nice for Sunday night supper, with a fresh garden salad.

SCALLOPED OYSTERS III

1   qt oysters
½ cup butter or margarine
½ cup flour
1½ tsp paprika
½ tsp salt
¼ tsp black pepper
    Dash Cayenne
1   onion, finely minced
½ green pepper, chopped or minced
½ bud garlic, crushed
1   tsp lemon juice
1   tbsp Worcestershire
¼ cup cracker crumbs

Melt butter or margarine, add flour, and cook until light brown—about 5 minutes. Stir constantly. Add paprika, salt, pepper, cayenne and cook 3 minutes more. Add onion, green pepper, garlic and simmer 5 minutes. Remove from fire and add lemon juice, Worcestershire.

Meanwhile heat oysters in their own liquor until edges curl. Add oysters to the first mixture and pour into a baking dish. Sprinkle crumbs over top and bake in a hot oven (400°) for about 30 minutes.

SERVES 4–6

I first ate this dish in Williamsburg and begged the recipe from Travis House as it was the best I ever tasted.

CRAB MOUSSE

1 tbsp gelatin
1 tbsp cold water
2 tbsp hot water
1 cup cream, whipped until fluffy but not stiff
   Salt to taste
1 small jar pimiento strips
½ green pepper, cut in strips
1 large can crab meat
⅔ cup mayonnaise
   Salt to taste
   Cayenne to taste

Soften gelatin in cold water; add hot water and stir until dissolved. Fold into whipped cream; add salt to taste and stir until the cream thickens. Lightly butter a mold and decorate with pimiento and pepper strips. With a spatula or knife, spread a thin layer of cream over the bottom and sides of the mold. Fill with crab flakes blended with mayonnaise, salt and Cayenne to taste. Cover with cream, chill several hours. Unmold, garnish with cress or shredded lettuce.

SERVES 8

BALTIMORE CRAB CAKES

1 lb cooked crab meat	1 tsp Worcestershire
1 egg	1 tbsp mayonnaise
2 tsp minced onion	2 tbsp chopped parsley
1 tsp dry mustard	Salt and pepper

Mix together and chill for an hour or two. Form into 4 cakes, pressing firmly. Dip in seasoned flour, then beaten egg, then bread crumbs. Sauté in hot fat, turning once.

SERVES 3–4

This is something you can make in the morning and sauté at the last minute. Or make them the night before and have them for a Harvest breakfast.

SMILEY'S OYSTERS À LA ROCKEFELLER

5   tbsp butter
5   tsp finely minced spinach
2   tbsp finely minced onion
1½ tbsp minced cooked lettuce
2   tsp minced celery
3   tbsp fine dry bread crumbs
¼   tsp herb blend for fish
¼   tsp anchovy paste
     Few grains of papper
¼   tsp salt
24   oysters on half shells

Heat butter, add spinach, onion, lettuce, celery, dry crumbs, anchovy paste, pepper and salt. Mix well. Remove oysters from shell, scrub oyster shells, boil to be sure all sand is washed away. Set 6 shells on each of 4 pie plates holding rock salt. Place oyster in each shell, broil slowly for 5 minutes, place 1 spoon of the spinach mixture on each oyster, broil until thoroughly heated, serve immediately.

SERVES 4

You don't think of a cowboy movie and television actor in connection with oysters Rockefeller but here it is. I like to watch him cook while he sings "Ridin' Down the Cayon" or "This Is My Lazy Day."

STUFFED ACORN SQUASH WITH CRAB MEAT

4 acorn squash, small size	1 cup crab meat
½ cup butter or margarine	1 egg beaten
3 tbsp minced onion	1 tbsp lemon juice
3 cups soft bread cubes	

Melt half the butter in a small baking pan. Cut the squash in half lengthwise and scrape out the seeds and membrane. Lay the halves in the pan skin side up and bake in a moderate oven (350°) for 30 minutes. Meanwhile sauté the onion in the rest of the butter and add bread cubes, crab meat, lemon juice and egg. Season to taste. Remove squash from oven and turn. Fill with the crab mixture and return to the oven. Bake until browned, 20 to 30 minutes.

SERVES 4 as a main dish or 8 as a side dish

This recipe has infinite variations. Creamed chicken may be used or sausage or ham. If you use sausage, partially cook it to remove some of the fat before you fill the shells.

STUFFED CLAMS

24 littleneck clams	Salt and pepper
4 fresh chopped mushrooms	Bread crumbs
1 tsp chopped parsley	Butter

Scrub clams well and lay in a flat pan on a bed of rock salt. Put in a hot oven (400°) until clam shells open. Then remove clams from shells, saving the liquor. Chop clams, add liquor and remaining ingredients. Use only enough crumbs to have the mixture keep its shape. Pack lightly into the shells and place ½ tsp butter on each. Bake in a moderate oven (350°) until browned, about 12 minutes.

SERVES 4

The secret of successful stuffed clams is to not make the mixture too dry and stiff. It should not fall from the fork when you eat it, but it should not be stiff, either.

BAKED STUFFED CLAMS

1 7½-oz can minced clams	½ tsp lemon juice
½ cup clam juice	Salt to taste
2 tbsp melted butter	Few drops Worcestershire
¼ cup seasoned bread crumbs	Grated cheese, Parmesan
¼ tsp each: basil, marjoram, thyme	Paprika

Drain clams, reserving the juice. Mix butter, crumbs, the seasonings, and add ⅓ cup of the clam juice. Add this to the clams. Spread mixture in clean clam shells, dot with butter, sprinkle grated cheese over and paprika.

Heat in moderate oven (350°) for 10 to 20 minutes. Let cool slightly before serving.

THIS MAKES 6 CLAMS, better double the recipe

You make these up ahead of time and freeze. It is an easy and delicious first course, but is even better as an accompaniment to cocktails or tomato juice. I first had this on Cape Cod, and not one of the ardent clammers knew the clams came from a can! We ate on a porch overlooking the ocean on one hand and the prettiest Cape Cod garden I know. A bevy of quail and four mourning doves attended outside the screens.

DEVILED CLAMS

1 dozen large hard-shelled clams or quahogs
6 tbsp prepared seasoned stuffing
2 tbsp light cream
3 tbsp chopped parsley
1 tbsp chopped green pepper
1 tsp Worcestershire
1½ tsp lemon juice
1 tbsp butter or margarine
1 drop tabasco
Freshly ground pepper to taste

Scrub clams and put in a flat baking pan in a hot oven (450°) until the shells open. Save the clam juice. Finely mince the clams, then add 2 tablespoons of the juice, half the stuffing and the rest of the ingredients.

When the juice is absorbed, spoon mixture into the clam shells, top with the rest of the stuffing and dot with butter. Lay the stuffed clams on a baking sheet and bake in a moderate oven (350°) until browned. This takes 15 to 10 minutes. Do not overcook or the clams will be tough.

SERVES 6 as a first course or luncheon dish

MRS. BARABEE'S MUSHROOM SUPPER DISH

1 lb button mushrooms
1 lb fresh or frozen peas *or* 2 cups canned peas
1 medium-sized can of shrimp *or* 1 lb of boiled, shelled shrimp
6 hard-cooked eggs, diced
3 cups hot medium cream sauce

Put mushrooms, peas, and shrimp in a double boiler. Add diced eggs. Stir gently into 3 cups of hot medium cream sauce to which a dash of sherry has been added.

Serve on toast or fluffy boiled rice.

THIS SHOULD SERVE 8, but I have seen 5 demolish it

Meats

I HAVE READ SOMEWHERE, BUT DON'T ASK ME WHERE, THAT Americans consume more meat than any nation in the world. And we are steak eaters. My father believed that any illness could be cured by a nice thick piece of steak.

"You'll get your strength back," he would say.

And even now, if I feel under par, I find myself broiling a steak, to strengthen me!

Meat is expensive nowadays (steak used to be 25 cents a pound), but the cheaper cuts are better than they used to be and, properly cooked, often have more flavor than the tenderloins and *filet mignon*. A chuck or rump steak or a thick round steak or a flank steak can be gourmet eating. A pot roast may make a company dinner as well as a rolled rib roast. Shoulder cuts are savory.

One of the best of the modern inventions is the meat tenderizer which can make even a tough piece of meat fork-tender. You sprinkle it on according to the directions on the bottle. It comes either seasoned or unseasoned and regular or instant. I keep some of each on my spice shelf. I use the unseasoned if I am having a spicy sauce on the meat, and the seasoned for chops or steak. I use the instant if I am in a hurry; otherwise I use the regular. In the meat recipes that follow, use the tenderizer for the thrifty cuts of meat.

Also there is something called monosodium glutamate, usually known as Accent, which I speak of from time to time. It brings out the flavor in meat. I go in heavily for seasoned salt and seasoned pepper and for garlic salt as well as mixed herbs, chopped celery leaves, and so on.

If you are cooking from old cook books, remember to cut the timing. Modern ranges are more efficient, and modern meat is better in quality. I tend to cut cooking time a third.

A meat thermometer is a great help, but I admit I don't trust mine all the way. I take the roast out before that red line has gone up to the proper point. I open the oven door and sniff, and my nose tells me when the roast is done.

A word about lamb. One reason, I think, some people have not liked lamb is that it has been consistently overcooked. If pinkish in the center, it will be juicy and tender and make better eating.

Pork does have to be well cooked, although I think Government-tested pork is highly unlikely to give you that trichinosis. In the old days, pork was not properly cured and cared for and it is subject, under adverse conditions, to this bug or whatever it is. Nowadays, if you buy your meat at a reputable market, pork is perfectly safe. However, I am sure we shall all go on overcooking it, just in case.

Finally, remember that a roast continues cooking for about 15 minutes after it is removed from the oven, so count that in as you time it.

BEEF BURGUNDY

2 lbs beef stew meat, cubed	1 cup diced carrots
Flour	1 can condensed consommé
3 tbsp bacon fat or shortening	1 cup water
½ cup diced onion	½ cup burgundy wine
1 cup diced celery	Salt and pepper to taste

Dredge meat with flour, brown slowly in the fat. Add remaining ingredients, cover and simmer gently until meat is tender, about 1½ hours. Stir often, adding a little water if needed.

SERVES 5–6

GLAMOR VERSION BEEF BURGUNDY

Use top round or round steak for the beef. Use leeks, carrots, onions, chopped parsley, chives, 1 crushed clove garlic, and brown separately.

Brown cubed and floured beef in a braising kettle. Light 2 tablespoons brandy in a ladle and pour over the beef, burning. Add vegetable mixture, and a *bouquet garni* of 2 whole cloves, 8 crushed peppercorns, pinch marjoram, salt. Pour over burgundy to cover, cover tightly, bake in a moderate oven (350°) for 3 hours.

Discard bouquet, transfer meat to hot platter, heat sauce to boiling point and pour over the meat.

ROLLED RIB ROAST WITH YORKSHIRE PUDDING

THE ROAST

Wipe the meat with a damp cloth but do not wash it. Season well with salt and pepper, and mixed herbs if you desire. Place in roasting pan and roast uncovered in a slow oven, 300° to 350°, allowing 25 or 30 minutes per pound. Half an hour before it is done make the Yorkshire Pudding.

YORKSHIRE PUDDING

1 cup flour   3 eggs, well beaten
1 tsp salt   1 pint milk

Sift flour and salt, mix beaten eggs and milk and add to flour, stirring until smooth. A rotary beater is best for this. Now pour off drippings from the roasting pan except ¼ cup, push roast to the side and pour in the batter. Increase oven to 400° and bake for 30 minutes.

Or you can bake the pudding in a separate 8-in.-square pan with the drippings in it. The pudding should be crusty and brown and rich with the drippings.

EVA'S FOIL-BAKED BEEF

4 minute steaks, frozen, per person
2 slices sweet onion per person
½ peeled sliced potato per person
   Salt, pepper, butter or margarine

Cut 2 pieces of aluminum foil per serving (½ again as large as the steaks). Lay the first 2 steaks on the bottom piece of aluminum foil, then the onion, seasonings, then the potato slices. Season, add the butter or margarine. Top with the remaining steaks. Now lay the second piece of foil on top, bring the edges of the bottom piece up and fold over snugly, sealing by pressing well with your fingers. Bake in a moderate over (350°) for 50 minutes.

You may vary this by adding a slice of fresh tomato or some chopped green pepper on top of the upper steaks.

This may be cooked on a picnic grill. Turn once, and allow an hour. Add crusty French bread and a tossed salad. For a picnic, just remove the top foil, unfold the edges of the bottom piece and slide a paper plate under for support.

HUNGARIAN STEAK

1½ lbs round steak, cubed
¼ cup chopped green pepper
½ cup chopped onion
1 No. 2 can tomatoes
   Salt and pepper

Dredge steak in flour and brown in butter or margarine or fat. Arrange in layers in a frying pan, with the tomatoes, pepper and onion between the layers and on top. Cover and simmer slowly for 1½ hours.

Add salt and pepper the last twenty minutes.

SERVES 4–6

Serve with fluffy baked potatoes and a green salad.

STILLMEADOW HAMBURGER BAKE

Amounts vary according to how many hungry people have descended on you.

> Hamburger
> Prepared mustard, salt, pepper
> Onion, sliced thin
> Tomatoes, sliced
> Green peppers, sliced

Pat hamburger (ground round steak if possible) into a round cake tin. Spread with prepared mustard, sprinkle with salt and pepper. Lay thin slices of onion over it, covering the meat well.

Then lay slices of tomatoes over the onion, and do not spare the horses on the tomatoes. Lay sliced green pepper over the tomatoes.

Put another layer of the beef on top for a lid, and top that with several slices of tomato.

Bake in a moderate oven (350°) until the hamburger is done. It takes about half an hour, depending, of course, on how thick your layers are. The onion and tomato will cook into the meat and the juices will blend.

If you use regular hamburger, which has fat added, be sure your pan is deep.

Serve with fluffy baked potatoes or, if you haven't time for them, noodles or instant rice. Potatoes, by the way, bake in half the time if you slice them lengthwise, serrate them with a sharp knife—which means make cuts crosswise and lengthwise, but not very deep—and spread shortening on the cut surface.

BEEFSTEAK AND KIDNEY PIE I

1	lb lamb or veal kidneys		Seasoned salt and pepper
2	lbs round steak	1	cup beef bouillon
1	medium onion	1	cup dry red wine
3	tbsp butter or margarine	1	cup sliced mushrooms
1½	tbsp Worcestershire		Pastry or mashed potatoes
1	clove garlic	2	tbsp vinegar

Soak kidneys in cold salted water with 2 tablespoons vinegar for half an hour, then drain, remove gristle and skin and slice thin. Cut the meat into 1-in. cubes.

In a heavy kettle sauté the garlic in 1 tablespoon butter. Remove garlic and add the beef (dredged with flour). Brown the meat; then add the onion, chopped fine, the Worcestershire, and salt and pepper. Pour over the bouillon and wine. Cover and simmer for 1½ hours. Add more bouillon and wine if needed.

Now, in a saucepan cook the kidneys 5 minutes in butter, then add them to the meat (which should be tender by this time). Sauté the mushrooms about 8 minutes in the rest of the butter (or get out another spoonful if you are short).

Add the mushrooms to the meat. You will want to thicken the juices. Shake 2 tablespoons flour in a little cold water and add to the stew, or make a roux in the saucepan with 2 tablespoons butter and 2 of flour and add it when it is thick.

Pour into a buttered casserole and top with pastry or mashed potatoes. Bake at 400°, a hot oven, until brown.

SERVES 6–8

BEEFSTEAK AND KIDNEY PIE II

        Beef suet, size of an egg
1   large or two medium onions, chopped
2   lbs beef chuck cut in 1-in. cubes
1   lb lamb kidneys cut in quarters
1   cup beef stock or bouillon
1½ tsp Worcestershire
        Salt, pepper, Cayenne to taste
        Flour (if needed)
        Pastry

In a heavy kettle try out the suet and then remove cracklings and add onion. When the onion is transparent, add beef and kidneys and brown, stirring constantly. Pour stock or bouillon over, add seasoning and Worcestershire and cover the kettle. Simmer for an hour and a half or until beef is tender. Add more liquid if needed. Thicken the sauce with a little flour mixed until smooth with water. Put the mixture in a casserole or baking dish and let cool. Then cover with pie crust and bake for 10 minutes in a hot oven (450°). Lower heat and bake 15 minutes more until crust is delicately browned.

SERVES 4-6

This makes me think of green lanes in English villages and old inns and strawberries with Devonshire cream and the pie, delicately brown and savory.

TERIYAKI

Sirloin steak, cut in 2-in. cubes
¾ cup soy sauce
⅓ cup dry sherry
1 clove garlic, crushed

Marinate the steak cubes in the soy sauce, sherry and garlic for at least an hour. Thread the cubes on skewers and broil, preferably on a charcoal grill in the back yard.

Count on 4 to 5 cubes per person, or at least 3 for delicate guests. If the budget is bent, try round steak, and tenderize it with a meat tenderizer, according to directions on the bottle.

While the steak is marinating, cook individual packages of sliced potatotes, sliced onion, seasoned with butter or margarine, salt, freshly ground pepper, on the grill. Use aluminum foil, and be sure you double-wrap those edges. Cut two squares of foil for each serving, put the vegetables in the center of one, fold the bottom layer over the top and turn the edges tightly together. Allow about 40 minutes on the grill.

Make the coffee in the house; there isn't room for it.

FLANK STEAK

1 flank steak, *unscored*
Garlic
Butter

Crush the garlic well and rub into steak after first trimming off fat and hard edges. Sprinkle with tenderizing salt. Roll up and wrap in foil. Put in refrigerator for at least 2 hours. Broil for about 7 minutes on one side, 5 minutes on the other. Slice at an angle, as flat as possible, and *very* thin.

SERVES 4 – 6

LONDON BROIL (FLANK STEAK)

1 flank steak (1 lb or more)
  Meat tenderizer
1 clove garlic
  Salad oil
  Butter, salt, pepper.

Sprinkle the steak with meat tenderizer and let stand (follow directions on the bottle). Rub the cut garlic over both sides, sprinkle the salad oil over and place in a preheated broiler about 1½ inches from the heat. Broil 5 minutes; then turn and broil 5 minutes or less on the other side. Dot with butter and season with salt and pepper. Using a very sharp knife, cut the steak in thin slanting slices *against* the grain.

SERVES 4

If the steak is too thick and obviously tough, pound it with the back of a cleaver or the back of your heaviest knife. This is one of the best flavored in the steak family, but needs the right handling. My friend Vicky dropped in one night to say she had just thrown away a flank steak. "I cooked it and cooked it and cooked it," she said dismally, "and we couldn't cut it at all."

BEEF RICE GOULASH

1 lb ground meat
2 small onions
1 can chicken noodle soup
1 can mushroom soup
1 can water
½ cup uncooked rice (raw)

Brown meat and onions, add soup, water and rice. Mix well. Place in buttered casserole. Bake about 1½ hours or longer at 350°.

SERVES 4 –6

BURTON'S SAVORY MEAT LOAF

2 lbs beef chuck or round steak with a good chunk
       of suet (approximately ½ cup), cut fine
2 cups bread crumbs or prepared dressing
2 eggs, beaten

Into the beaten eggs mix:

2 tbsp prepared mustard
3 tbsp horseradish
2 tsp salt
   Pepper to taste
½ cup catsup
1 large onion, minced
1 crushed clove garlic

Mix suet with meat and crumbs and knead well. Add eggs—mix and add other ingredients. Turn into a greased loaf pan and bake in a moderate oven (325°) about an hour or until well browned on top.

Pour off surplus fat and save it for soups or gravies.

SERVES 4–6

Wonderful sliced cold, as it keeps its shape better than most loaves.

POT ROAST SPECIAL

1 pot roast (or 3–4 lbs short ribs)
2 tbsp hot prepared mustard
½ tsp salt
½ tsp black pepper
½ tsp chili powder
1 crushed clove garlic
5 tbsp olive oil
½ cup burgundy

Marinate the pot roast or ribs in the rest of the ingredients (blend them together first) for 6–12 hours.

Heat 2 tablespoons olive oil in heavy kettle. Brown meat. Add the marinade and ½ cup water. Cover closely and simmer until tender.

SERVES 6–8

BOEUF À LA MODE

5 or 6 lb top round of beef	4½ cups red wine
¼ lb salt pork	½ cup cognac, if desired
1 cup carrots, sliced	½ cup oil (olive or salad)
1 cup onions, sliced	1 tbsp salt
Herb bouquet of thyme,	4 cloves garlic cut in half
bay leaves, 4 allspice,	2 or 3 veal bones
6 peppercorns, parsley	

Wipe meat with a damp cloth. If you have a larding needle, lard the beef with thin slices of the pork. If not, try to tuck slivers of pork in any open spaces in meat. Now tie the meat lengthwise and crosswise firmly with clean twine. This is to keep it in shape for slicing. Marinate it for 6 hours—or a day or two—in the wine and cognac, oil, salt, garlic, carrots, onions, and herbs. Tie herbs in cheesecloth so they can be removed easily.

Drain and wipe dry. The meat will not brown properly unless it is dry. (I use paper towels.) Brown meat over moderate heat 10 minutes, turning to brown evenly. Boil down the marinade after removing herbs until it is reduced about half. Remove fat. Now add beef and 2 or 3 veal bones. (If you want to be fancy, simmer the rind of the salt pork 10 minutes and add it too.)

Bring to a boil, cover and cook slowly in a slow oven (300° to 325°) for 3 or 4 hours, or until meat is tender. Remove beef and put in a warm deep platter. Discard bones and salt pork rind. Tilt pan and remove all you can of the fat with a big spoon.

Strain the sauce and boil down to concentrate the juices. The time for this depends on how juicy the meat is, watch and stir until it is reduced. Blend 1 tablespoon cornstarch with 1½ cups liquid (stock, wine, or water) and add to sauce. Simmer until thickened. Remove strings from the beef and pour the sauce over.

Arrange braised onions and carrots on the platter and garnish with watercress.

SERVES 8

FLANK STEAK BRAISED WITH VEGETABLES

1½ lbs flank steak
2   tbsp flour and 1 tsp salt for dredging
     Butter or margarine
1½ cups raw sliced potatoes
½   cup sliced onions
1   green pepper, sliced
1   cup canned tomatoes (or an equal amount of
        fresh stewed tomatoes)

Have your butcher, if he is your friend, make shallow cuts on the flank steak. If he does not like you, do it yourself, cutting across the grain with a sharp knife.

Dredge on both sides with the flour and salt, dot with butter or margarine and place in a rectangular baking pan. Cover with the potatoes, then with onions, and tomatoes.

Cover tightly and cook in a slow oven for 2 hours or until tender. Add tomato juice if it seems dry.

Lift onto a hot platter carefully, to preserve the layers of vegetables, and serve at once.

SERVES 4 – 6

You can add mushrooms, fresh or canned, if company comes. The tomato tenderizes the meat and the flavor of a properly done flank steak is second to none, not even porterhouse. You may add MSG and garlic salt and a whiff of parsley flakes. But, as they say, good wine needs no bush, and this needs no extras to taste good!

BEEF STROGANOFF

2 lbs beef tenderloin cut in strips (2½ by 1 inch)
1 medium onion, minced
1 cup fresh mushrooms
½ pint sour cream
4 tbsp butter or margarine.
   Seasoned salt and pepper

Season the beef strips with salt and pepper. Melt 2 tablespoons of butter in a heavy pan and sauté the onion in it until golden. Add beef and cook over a hot fire about 5 minutes (do not overcook). Slice the mushrooms in and cook about 5 minutes more with the remaining 2 tablespoons butter. Add the sour cream and correct the seasoning.

SERVES 6

The beef strips should be rare and the outside browned. Do not let the sour cream cook or it may curdle. Serve with rice or fine egg noodles.

LAWRENCE'S BEEF STROGANOFF

1½ lbs top round steak cut in 1-in. strips
   Flour for dredging
2 or 3 tbsp fat
½ cup water
½ can tomato sauce (the small size can).
¼ cup Marsala wine
1 pint sour cream
   Oregano, salt and pepper to taste

Dredge the meat strips with flour and sauté in the fat in a heavy skillet. Add tomato sauce and seasonings and enough water to thin the sauce. Simmer until tender, adding the Marsala when the meat is almost done. This will take about 20 minutes. Test the meat with a fork for tenderness. Don't overcook or the beef will be tough. When ready to serve, add the sour cream.

SERVES 4–6

If you have leftover roast beef, you may cut it in thin strips and just heat with the sauce and it will still taste good.

CRANBERRY ISLAND STEW

2 lbs stewing beef (marrow bone included)
Few sprigs summer savory
1 onion, sliced
Salt and pepper
3 or 4 small beets, raw, peeled and quartered
1 small turnip, sliced
3 or 4 sliced carrots
4 small potatoes, peeled and halved.

Cook stewing beef with marrow bone slowly till almost tender. Add savory, onion, salt and pepper. One hour before serving add beets; after 15 minutes add turnip. When these are done, add carrots and potatoes. Cook slowly till done and serve in soup plates.

SERVES 4–6

I don't know how old this recipe is, but it goes far back and I think originated in Maine. It is best if you dig your own beets and make it while they are crisp and juicy and, oh, so delicate in flavor.

MEXICAN SPECIAL

2 cups cornmeal	2 cups canned tomatoes
2 tsp salt	1 tbsp chili powder
1 onion, thinly sliced	1 green pepper, sliced
3 tbsp margarine or fat	Grated cheese
1 lb hamburger	

Stir cornmeal into 1 cup cold water to make a smooth paste. Add salt and stir into 3 pints of boiling water. Cook over low heat in a heavy pot, stirring constantly until quite thick. Place in double boiler and continue cooking another 45 minutes. Brown onion in margarine or fat. Add hamburger and stir until browned. Add tomatoes and chili powder. Finally add green pepper, cover, and simmer for 25 minutes.

Pour half the sauce into a buttered casserole; then pour in the hot cornmeal mush. Cover this with the rest of the sauce. Top with a layer of grated cheese. Bake in a hot oven (450°) about 20 minutes.

SERVES 4–6

BEEF ENCHILADAS

ENCHILADAS

10 tortillas, canned or frozen
1 cup grated cheese, American, Cheddar or
   Monterey Jack

MEAT FILLING

1 lb hamburger
1 clove garlic, finely chopped
2 tsp salt
1 tbsp vinegar

1 tbsp water
1 tbsp chili powder
1 can (1 lb) kidney beans,
   drained

In medium skillet over low heat, sauté hamburger with garlic, salt, vinegar, water and chili powder until hamburger is browned. Then stir in kidney beans. Set aside.

TOMATO SAUCE

3 tbsp salad oil
1 clove garlic, very finely
   chopped
¼ cup chopped onion
2 tbsp flour
2 cans (10 ½ oz) tomato soup
1 tbsp vinegar

1 beef bouillon cube
1 cup boiling water
2 tbsp finely chopped canned
   green chilies
½ tsp salt
   Dash each of pepper and
   cumin

In hot oil in skillet, sauté garlic and onion until golden. Remove from heat. Stir in flour until smooth; then stir in tomato soup, vinegar and bouillon cube (dissolved in boiling water). Bring mixture to boiling point, stirring over medium heat. Add chilies, cumin, salt and pepper; simmer uncovered and stirring occasionally, about 5 minutes. Set aside.

To assemble:

Preheat oven to 350°. Place about ⅓ cup meat filling in center of each tortilla; roll up; arrange, seam side down, in a 13″ × 9″ × 2″ baking dish. Pour tomato sauce over all; sprinkle with cheese; bake 25 minutes.

SERVES 4

Meat filling and tomato sauce may be made ahead of time and refrigerated. Reheat slightly when ready to use.

CHILI CON CARNE

STOCK FOR THE CHILI

1 gal. cold water
1 large can tomato juice
2 medium potatoes, sliced thin
3 large white onions, chopped fine

Put the water in a large pot or heavy kettle. Add remaining ingredients and cook slowly about 3 hours, stirring now and then and keeping the fire low so as not to burn. When the stock has become slightly thickened (mushy is the word), strain it and return strained liquid to the pot.

CHILI

3   lbs beef round coarsely ground
½   lb kidney suet, coarsely ground or chopped
3   tbsp chili blend or powder
     Salt to taste
3   large cans kidney beans
     Salt, pepper, more chili if needed

Cook beef and suet in a heavy iron skillet until browned well. You will need 3 skilletfuls unless you have a very large skillet. Add salt and chili (1 tablespoon to each skilletful). Put the cooked meat into the stock and stir but do not cook. Add beans and more seasoning as desired. Cool and put in the refrigerator until the next day. Reheat carefully so as not to burn.

SERVES 6–10

This is from a Texas friend who says they cook their own beans, either pinto or frijole, using 2½ cups for the recipe above. But she says the canned beans are much less trouble!

As to how many this serves, she tells me it sounds as if it would feed a regiment, but it disappears so fast you'll be amazed. Also it gets better if put back in the refrigerator and reheated another day. It makes a satisfying party dish and all you need is that green salad and crusty French bread and something like honeydew melon with lime wedges — or watermelon, cut in cubes and served in a glass bowl with blueberries.

QUICK CHILI CON CARNE

3	small onions, chopped		Salt, pepper
2	tbsp oil	1	clove garlic
1½	lbs ground chuck or round steak		Chili powder to taste
		1	cup water
¼	cup kidney suet, cut fine	2	No. 2 cans kidney beans

Sauté the onions in the oil until transparent, then add the beef, suet and seasonings and cook until the meat is brown. Add water and simmer 15 minutes. Stir in the kidney beans and turn into a greased casserole. Heat in a hot oven (400°), covered, for about 20 minutes.

SERVES 4–6

Sometimes short cuts are a great help and make very good eating. When the family has been out skating on a January day, this means supper on before everyone starves. A bowl of fruit and a pot of hot coffee go with this meal.

CHILI CON CARNE AND TAMALES

2 cans chili con carne
1 can tamales

Turn chili into a greased casserole and arrange the tamales (with their sauce) on top. Heat in a moderate oven (350°) for 20 minutes.

SERVES 3–4

Fortunate are those Western friends of mine who can stop in a small shop and buy fresh tamales, crispy and golden. However, in New England, we are grateful to be able to get them canned. There are a number of brands of the canned chili con carne. If the kind you get is too mild, spike it up with more chili powder.

NEW ENGLAND BOILED DINNER

6-lb cut of corned beef, brisket or rump

Place in cold water to cover, add ½ clove garlic and 6 peppercorns.

Bring to boiling and cook slowly, skimming when needed. This takes about 4 hours as a rule. Test for tenderness with a fork. When tender, remove it and add to the stock the following:

> 6 carrots
> 3 large yellow turnips, cut in halves or quarters
> 4 small parsnips
> 8 small peeled onions

Simmer 15 minutes, then add 6 medium potatotes, peeled and cut in quarters, and a head of cabbage cut in quarters.

When the vegetables are tender, return the corned beef to the pot and reheat.

Serve on a hot platter, garnished with parsley.

SERVES 6 – 8

Gild the lily, if you want it gilded, with horseradish sauce. (Beat sour cream with fresh grated horseradish or prepared bottled horseradish. If you use the prepared, add a little lemon juice.)

No doubt it was the New England boiled dinner that gave the early folk energy to fell trees, conquer the wilderness. It has been around a long time, possibly it stems from the English boiled mutton. It still warms the cockles of the heart on a snowy winter night.

CORNED BEEF AND CABBAGE

6-lb brisket or rump of beef
Onions, peeled
Carrots, peeled
Cabbage, cut in wedges

We like our own corned beef, and this is the way we fix it in the country. We put it for 36 hours in the brine, weighted down with a plate.

BRINE

Mix:

8 cups water
1 cup salt
3 tbsp sugar
6 peppercorns
1 clove garlic
2 bay leaves
2 tsp mixed spices
¼ tsp saltpeter dissolved in ½ cup warm water.

Place meat in cold water to cover, add ½ clove garlic and 6 peppercorns. Bring to boiling and then cook very slowly until tender, skimming when necessary. It takes about 5 hours to cook it well.

For the last ½ hour of cooking add onions and carrots, and for the last 20 minutes, wedges of cabbage.

SERVES 6–8

BAKED CORNED-BEEF HASH

2 cans corned-beef hash
²/₃ cup top milk
Pinch dry mustard

Mix the corned beef and milk and turn into a greased casserole, adding the mustard.

Put in medium oven (350°) and, when the milk is hot, stir it all with a fork once. Bake until bubbly (20 to 25 minutes).

SERVES 4

Could hardly be easier and tastes delicious. Takes about 2 minutes to pop it in the oven, while those unexpected guests divest themselves of hats and coats, and you mix the green salad while they sip their tomato juice or cocktails.

If they phone from the post office that they are coming, you may also serve them cornsticks, made of cornbread mix and baked with the hash. Or corn muffins, if you have no cornstick iron pans.

Put the catsup or chili sauce or Sauce Diable on the table.

Break out the special peaches for dessert and keep the coffee hot.

MARROW DUMPLINGS

Beef marrow enough to make ½ cup mashed
1 egg
1 cup soft bread crumbs
1 tbsp chopped parsley
Seasoned salt and pepper to taste

Remove the marrow with a thin knife. You need a 4-in. bone. Blend all ingredients well. Shape into small balls about the size of a walnut. Lay them on a flat pan and chill an hour; then cook, covered, about 5 minutes on top of beef stew or soup.

MAKES 8–10 marrow balls

This is an old-fashioned dish. My Viennese friend first made it for me, and, from then on, it was a question as to whether the marrow bones were ours or really had to go to the cockers and Irish.

QUICK BOILED DINNER

4 small potatoes, scrubbed
2 or 3 carrots, scrubbed and quartered
6 scallions
½ head young green cabbage, cut in quarters
1 12-oz can corned beef, sliced

Cook potatoes and carrots in boiling salted water until half tender — about 10 minutes. Then lay the cabbage quarters over the potatoes and carrots, next the scallions, and finally the corned beef. Cover and steam until the cabbage is tender. The beef, scallions and cabbage should not be down in the liquor but on top of the potatoes and carrots. Drain and serve on a warm platter, dressed with salt, pepper and melted butter or margarine.

For a sauce for the corned beef slices, use Western View Mustard Sauce, or combine 2 parts commercial sour cream with 1 part preserved mustard.

SERVES 2

I learned this from Louella Shouer, whose Quick and Easy Meals for Two *has been a classic for some time. The recipe has been popular enough to be copied in another publication, so here goes again. I especially like it in hot weather after cold dishes begin to pall, for it is a rib-sticking dish but does not heat up the kitchen as a regular boiled dinner does.*

SWEDISH MEATBALLS

1   lb top round ⎫
¼   lb veal   ⎬ Have butcher grind all this together
¼   lb pork   ⎭
1   large egg, beaten
3   slices stale white bread or toast soaked in warm
      milk
1   tbsp heavy cream
1   medium sized onion (grated)
    A few sprays of fresh parsley (chopped very very
      fine)
    Salt and pepper
    Pinch of sugar
    About ½ tsp allspice, powdered

Place all of this in mixing bowl, working everything in with your hands, until well mixed and very smooth. Do not hurry this procedure. The more you work it the smoother it is.

Put a chunk of butter into, preferably, an iron skillet. Form ingredients into small round balls about an inch in diameter. Brown in the butter, watching the flame so pan doesn't get too hot. As the meatballs are fried, take from pan and place in a casserole.

SERVES 4–6

You can make gravy from the residue in the pan. Stir in a little flour, a beef bouillon cube dissolved in boiling water, and a tablespoon of heavy cream.

LOUELLA'S SWEDISH MEATBALLS IN SOUR-CREAM SAUCE

2 cups bread cubes soaked in
   milk (½ cup is right)
1½ lbs ground beef
1 chopped medium onion
3 beaten eggs
2½ tsp salt

¼ tsp pepper
2 tsp ground nutmeg
2 tsp paprika
1 tsp dry mustard
1 tsp dried mixed herbs
¼ cup butter or margarine

Squeeze bread cubes dry, and add to the beef. Sauté the onion in 2 tablespoons butter or margarine, then add eggs and seasonings, and mix well with the beef.

Form into small balls (the size of a large walnut). Makes about 72 meatballs. Brown in a skillet with ¼ cup butter or margarine, turning to brown evenly on all sides. Keep warm in the oven while you make the sauce.

SAUCE

Add flour to the drippings in the skillet, using 1 tablespoon flour per tablespoon of fat. Add 2 teaspoons beef concentrate. Stir over low heat until thickened, then add 1 cup commercial sour cream. Reheat but do not boil or the cream will curdle. Pour over the meatballs and serve at once.

SERVES 4–6

Serve with noodles, a mixed vegetable salad, coffee.

SWEET AND SOUR MEATBALLS

1 lb ground beef	1 tsp salt
1 egg	2 tbsp chopped onion
1 tbsp cornstarch	Dash of pepper

Mix all ingredients together. Form into balls. Brown in oil. Set meatballs aside.

SWEET AND SOUR SAUCE

1 tbsp oil	3 tbsp vinegar
1 cup pineapple juice	6 tbsp water
3 tbsp cornstarch	1/2 cup sugar
1 tbsp soy sauce	

To the oil, add pineapple juice. Heat over low fire and add mixture of cornstarch, soy sauce, vinegar, water, and sugar. Cook until juice thickens, stirring constantly.

4 slices pineapple, cut in chunks
3 green peppers, cut in strips lengthwise

Add meatballs, pineapple, and green peppers. Heat thoroughly and serve on hot rice.

SERVES 4-6

I highly recommend this as a way to glorify the inevitable ground beef.

NORWEGIAN MEATBALLS

2 lbs ground round, lean ⎱
1 lb ground pork, lean ⎰ Have butcher grind all
1 lb ground veal   this together very fine.
4 eggs
½ cup flour
   Grated onion to taste (dehydrated onion is fine, about 2 tbsp). It must be *fine*.
1 tbsp ginger
   Salt and pepper

Make balls about size of walnut. With your hands mix the whole thing together. Have 2 iron skillets ready with some bacon drippings. The meat will make some of its own fat, so not too much fat to begin with. On a medium burner, brown on all sides. Shake the pan to help turn them, or use a regular dinner fork. A large tined fork will break them.

Remove each batch to a large casserole. When finished, make a roux with flour, adding a little drippings if necessary, and add equal parts of water (potato water is good) and canned consommé, making enough gravy to cover the meatballs. Cover, and bake slowly for 1½ hours.

Four pounds of meat makes 90 to 100 meatballs. Can be made smaller for cocktail bits. These can be kept a day or two in the refrigerator. They also freeze well.

DELUXE MEAT PATTIES

3 slices white bread	1 tsp salt
½ cup red wine	¾ tsp instant minced onion
½ cup water	1 lb ground beef
Dash of pepper	Dry bread crumbs

Soak bread in mixture of wine and water. Add seasonings and mix well. Add beef. Blend well. Form into patties. Roll in dry bread crumbs. Brown in butter.

This will yield about 10 patties, depending on the size you make.

I sometimes think America is founded on ground beef. This is a nice variation.

COFFEE ROAST

4, 6 or 8 lb lean roast (can be either cheap or expensive cut)

Onion	Garlic
Vinegar	Coffee

With a large knife make incisions clear through the meat. Open up incisions with your finger and fill halfway with onion chunks, then put in 1 clove garlic. Finish filling the incisions with onion chunks. Make as many incisions as meat will take. Place in a glass dish and pour 1 cup vinegar in the incisions (not one cup in each!). Cover with waxed paper and place in refrigerator overnight and until after lunch the next day.

Place meat and liquid in a frying pan and brown all sides until it's almost burned. Place browned meat in a pan with a lid and add 1 cup of extra strong coffee and 1 cup water. Cover pan with the lid and on a low burner let it cook at least 6 hours. Add water if needed. Remove meat and season. Thicken with flour to make gravy and serve.

SERVES 6–8, depending on size of roast

This is one of Smiley Burnette's specialties. His usual remark, after one of his gourmet meals has been thoroughly admired, is "Waal, I ain't mad at nobody."

SAUERBRATEN

4   lbs beef (rump or chuck or round)
1   pint vinegar
    Water
4   bay leaves
12 peppercorns
6   cloves
1   bunch carrots, cut in slivers
6   medium onions, sliced thin
1   tbsp sugar
12 gingersnaps
    Salt and pepper to taste

Wipe meat with a damp cloth and sprinkle with salt and pepper. Place in an earthen dish or crock and add vinegar and enough water to cover the meat. Add spices and let stand 5 days in a cold place (not freezing). Keep covered. Then put meat in a large kettle (preferably a Dutch oven) and brown well, turning often. Add carrots, onions and 1 cup of the spiced vinegar. Cook, covered, over a low heat about 3 hours or until meat is tender when pierced with a fork. Then add sugar and crumbled gingersnaps and cook 10 minutes more. If needed, add more of the vinegar.

SERVES 6

The gingersnaps don't make sense but they give a mysterious wonderful flavor. You may use wine vinegar if desired. Serve with wide noodles.

SUKIYAKI

1½ lbs round steak (fairly thick)
4 small white onions
2 bunches scallions or young leeks
2 green peppers, medium size
1 head celery (discard outer stalks)
1 can (medium size) sliced mushrooms
1 lb spinach
2 tbsp butter or margarine, or drippings

Slice the meat into thin bite-sized pieces, using a sharp knife. Cut across the grain and keep the slices ⅛ inch thick. Cut the onions into eighths, slice the scallions or leeks lengthwise, then crosswise into small pieces. Seed the peppers and slice thinly lengthwise. Cut the celery in small bits. Shred the spinach (washed and crisped).

SAUCE

½ cup soy sauce
1 bouillon cube dissolved in ½ cup boiling water
1 tbsp sugar
   Salt to taste

Blend the sauce ingredients.

Melt the fat in a heavy skillet or electric frying pan, add half the meat, and stir until browned evenly. Then add half the onions, peppers and celery, then half the sauce. Stir lightly. Cook over medium heat about 5 minutes. Then stir in half the scallions and the mushrooms (drained). Cook 1 minute. Add half the spinach and cook 1 minute.

Serve with hot fluffy rice.

Repeat the process for the second helpings.

SERVES 4

This is pre-eminently a table-cooked dish, but if you have no electric frying pan, you may do it in an iron or heavy aluminum skillet. For a buffet, the table may be set with bowls of the chopped vegetables and meat and sauce, and guests can help with the cooking, which is brief enough so they won't be bored!

This is not a traditional sukiyaki, which calls for bamboo shoots, bean curd, and so on. But it tastes delicious, is easy, and inexpensive.

The quick-cooking keeps the vegetables crisp, and the second help-ing cooks while guests consume the first. You may, also, do the chop-ping and slicing ahead of time, keeping the ingredients crisp in their own bowls covered with aluminum foil or waxed paper.

If you have no table-warmer to keep the rice hot, use a heavy casse-role dipped in very hot water. Put the rice in, and run it in the oven for a few minutes.

CHINESE PEPPER STEAK

1   lb round or flank steak cut in strips ⅛ inch thick
    Salt, pepper, paprika
2   tbsp salad oil
1   medium onion, chopped
1   clove garlic, minced
2   green peppers, diced
1   cup bouillon
1   cup drained canned tomatoes
1½ tbsp cornstarch
2   tsp soy sauce
¼   cup water

Sprinkle the meat slices with salt, pepper, paprika and sauté in the oil in a large heavy skillet with onion and garlic. Add peppers when steak is browned, pour the bouillon over and simmer, covered, for about 10 minutes. Then add the tomatoes and simmer 5 more minutes.

Meanwhile mix the cornstarch, soy sauce and water together, add to the meat mixture and stir until the sauce is thick and clear (a few minutes will do it).

SERVES 4

If you use flank steak, cut across the grain, not with it. Delicious! Serve with hot, fluffy rice, plenty of coffee or tea.

OLD COUNTRY DANISH ROLLEPULSE

1 large flank steak	Allspice
1 Bermuda onion	Brine
Black pepper, freshly ground	Suet, optional

Lay the steak flat and slice the onion, paper thin, over it. Grind the pepper over all until it is just black with it. Add light sprinkling of allspice. Roll tightly and secure with string. Wrap in cheesecloth and tie again. Soak in brine 10 days. After 10 days boil it in fresh water (no salt added) until tender. Place on a pie pan, put another pan on top and weight it down with a heavy rock. Let stand in a cool place (do not refrigerate) for at least 36 hours, then unwrap and slice like luncheon meat.

If you use the suet, lay thin slices on meat before adding the onions. For the brine, add salt to water until it is strong enough to float an egg.

SERVES 4-6

This recipe comes from Leadville, Colorado, from Mary Ann Paulsen, who says you aren't apt to find it outside of a Danish settlement. It is wonderful with dark bread, fresh pears, bleu cheese, and iced tea. She says no Scandinavian summer is complete without it, and yours won't be either, once you've tried it. In these days of quick cooking, it is nice to make a leisurely dish that is traditional. And, after all, during the 10 days, you just let it alone!

Rollepulse is pronounced *Rō-pilse*

HUNGARIAN STUFFED CABBAGE

3 to 4 lb cabbage
1 lb sauerkraut
1/3 cup uncooked rice
3/4 lb ground beef, pork or veal
1/2 cup finely chopped onion
1 clove garlic

1 egg, beaten
2 tsp salt
1/2 tsp pepper
   Pinch of Cayenne
2 cups tomato juice

Mix together rice, meat, onion (to which garlic has been added before chopping), egg. Season with salt, pepper and Cayenne.

To prepare the cabbage, cut out the core of a cabbage head and drop the head whole into a large kettle of rapidly boiling water. Cook until the large outer leaves come off easily; then pull off 12 of the largest. Drain the rest of the cabbage and chop it coarsely. Put half the chopped cabbage on the bottom of a heavy iron kettle together with 1/2 pound of sauerkraut.

Put a tablespoon of the meat mixture in the center of each of the large leaves, roll up, turn the ends under, and secure with toothpicks. Arrange in the kettle, and top with the remainder of the chopped cabbage, and another 1/2 pound of sauerkraut. Pour over all 2 cups tomato juice and enough water to almost cover the stuffed ieaves. Season with salt and pepper if more is needed, and 2 tablespoons of bacon drippings. Cover and cook 45 minutes.

SERVES 6

VEAL CUTLET VIENNESE

2 lbs veal cutlet, cut in serving pieces
1 or 2 eggs, beaten
   Flour and bread crumbs (1 part flour to 3 of crumbs)
   Butter or margarine
1 lemon, sliced thin
   Salt, paprika

Pound the cutlets until very thin, using a wooden mallet or the edge of a dinner plate. Dip into the egg, and then into the flour and crumbs. Season well with salt and paprika. Let stand about half an hour for the breading to settle comfortably to the meat. Then in a heavy skillet melt the butter or margarine and sauté the cutlets over a medium heat until golden (it takes only a few minutes for each side). Remove to a hot platter and lay a slice of lemon on each cutlet. Serve at once.

SERVES 4

When my Viennese friend first made this at Stillmeadow, I inquired as to what he needed for the gravy. "Gravy!" he shouted, "a sacrilege, have you NO lemons?" We had lemons. He was quite right, for the veal is so delicate that a gravy would mask the flavor. But you may always serve a casserole of macaroni and cheese as a side dish, plus a tossed salad with a little sour cream added to the basic French dressing. Comes out all right.

VIENNESE VEAL STEW

1½ lbs stewing veal	2	bouillon cubes
Flour or bread crumbs	¼	cup boiling water
Shortening		Juice of half a lemon
Chives	¼	tsp caraway seeds
Salt and pepper	1½	cups sour cream
Several juniper berries		

Roll the meat in flour or dried, powdered bread crumbs. Brown in the fat. Lift it into a pressure cooker or oven casserole. Dissolve the bouillon cubes in the boiling water and add with all the other ingredients to the pan from which the meat is removed. Cook for 5 minutes. Pour the gravy over the meat and cook for 15 minutes in a pressure cooker or 1½ hours in a moderate oven.

SERVES 4–6

If you feel as I do about caraway seeds, leave them out.

VEAL SCALLOPS VIENNESE

2 lbs boneless veal		Butter or margarine
2 beaten eggs		as needed
About ½ cup milk	1	lemon sliced thin
Seasonings	½	cup chopped parsley
Bread crumbs enough to dip pieces in	2	tsp capers

Have the butcher cut the veal in slices from the leg. Pound with a wooden mallet or the edge of a heavy plate until thin. Dip pieces in egg mixed with milk, then in bread crumbs. Season. Let stand about 30 minutes. Brown in the butter or margarine over a hot fire, turning once. This takes about 5 minutes. Remove the scallops to a warm platter and garnish with the lemon, capers and parsley.

SERVES 6

Serve with a bowl of buttered noodles and fresh string beans. If the slices of veal are too big, cut them in half to make the right size for individual servings.

SMILEY BURNETTE'S SPICED LEG OF LAMB

1 leg of lamb	⅛ lb butter or margarine
1 onion, sliced thin	2 bay leaves
1 tbsp salt	1 cup water
1 tbsp whole pepper	½ cup cider vinegar
1 tbsp allspice	1 pint plum jam

Crush the salt, pepper, allspice in a mortar or in a cloth. Roll the onion slices in the powder, make incisions in the lamb and insert the slices. Put the roast in the roaster with bay leaves, butter, and water, and sprinkle any powder left over the top. Roast 1 hour, covered. Then add the vinegar and spread the plum jam over the meat. Finish roasting uncovered, basting every 10 minutes or so, until the meat is tender when pierced with a fork. Remove to a heated platter and make the gravy.

GRAVY

Flour
1 cup port wine

Add flour to the drippings in the pan, using 2 tablespoons flour to 2 tablespoons drippings. Add the wine, stirring constantly. When the gravy is thickened, strain, and serve with the roast. (Or you may shake the wine and flour up in a covered jar, and add to the drippings, stirring until thickened.)

SERVES 6–8

This is designed to make those who simply hate lamb pass their plates for a second helping.

LAMB STEW

2 lbs shoulder or neck of lamb, cut in 2-inch cubes
1 medium onion, sliced thin
5 medium potatoes, peeled and quartered
¾ cup peas, cooked
1 cup tomato paste
1 cup meat stock
2 tbsp butter or margarine
1 cup sour cream

Melt butter or margarine in a heavy kettle and sauté the onion in it until golden. Season with salt, freshly ground pepper, and paprika, add the lamb and let it brown, stirring with a wooden spoon to brown the pieces evenly. Remove the meat to a soup kettle. Add tomato paste and meat stock to the fat and stir well until blended, then pour this over the lamb. Bring to a boil, then lower the heat, cover, and simmer gently for an hour or so. Add the potatoes for the last 25 minutes of cooking, and check the seasoning at this time. Add the peas for the final 5 minutes. Remove the meat and vegetables with a slotted spoon and gradually add the sour cream to the gravy, but do not let it boil. Pour the gravy over, and serve at once.

SERVES 4–5

CURRIED LAMB I

Cooked lamb (about 1 cup per person) cut in small pieces
1 large onion, cut up
½ cup raisins
½ tsp salt
⅓ tsp Worcestershire
  Pepper
2 bananas, cut in pieces
2 apples, cut in pieces
¼ cup flour
1 tsp curry powder

Cover lamb, onions, raisins, etc. (except apple and banana) with water and simmer at least one hour. During the last 15 minutes add apple and banana. Then mix flour, curry powder to a paste in water. Put with lamb and cook 20 minutes longer.

Serve with:

rice
chutney
crystallized ginger
unsalted peanuts or almonds
tart green salad or grapefruit salad

SERVES 6

This is almost better the second day than the first.

CURRIED LAMB II

2 to 3 cups cubed cooked lamb
1 large onion
2 tbsp butter
7 peppercorns
  Celery salt
1 tbsp curry powder
½ pint consommé or meat stock
1 cup cream, thickened with 1 tbsp flour mixed with
1 tbsp cold water

Chop onion and brown slowly in butter. Add peppercorns, celery salt, and curry powder. Mix well. Add consommé or meat stock and simmer slowly for 20 minutes. Add cream. Add meat and simmer 20 minutes more.

Serve in center of rice ring. Serve with any of the following: shredded cocoanut, chopped peanuts, chutney, chopped hard-cooked egg, chopped crisp bacon, chopped pickled onions, Bombay duck.

SERVES 4–6

Lamb adapts itself to curry, in my opinion, better than almost any other meat. You can add more curry for real curry addicts or use less for timid souls.

TACOS

Leftover roast lamb (a cup or more)
1 head lettuce
Salt and pepper
1 medium onion, chopped
1 can enchilada sauce
1 can tortillas (or fresh if you can get them)

Grind the lettuce in a food chopper or chop finely in a wooden bowl, having 3 or 4 cups shredded.

Grind the meat. Mix lettuce and meat and season well with salt and pepper. Add chopped onions and enchilada sauce—just enough to moisten.

Fold tortillas in half and fry lightly in a skillet with hot fat. Turn once. Take out and put the filling in each tortilla, folding the tortilla back to keep the filling in.

Drop in deep hot fat again, just long enough to heat.

If the remaining sauce is not enough to spoon over, add a can of tomato paste or some canned tomatoes, reheat and serve.

SERVES 3–4

IRISH STEW

½ lb lean lamb (breast, shoulder or neck)
½ lb veal (same cuts)
½ lb beef (same cuts)
½ lb lean salt pork
1 bunch of carrots
3 white turnips
2 big onions
2 stalks of celery
1 medium parsnip
6 potatoes

Ask the butcher to cut meats in small pieces. Put the meat in a deep, heavy kettle or Dutch oven, and add water to one-third depth of the meat.

Pare and slice carrots, turnips, onions, celery, and parsnip. Add to the meat a sample of each vegetable for flavoring. Simmer the rest of the vegetables separately until tender.

Thirty minutes before serving, season the gravy in the pan to taste, pare and add potatoes. Add the vegetables to the meat just long enough before serving to have them piping hot.

Place meat in a mound in the center of a hot platter. Arrange the vegetables around it. Pour the juice over it and serve.

SERVES 6

For a company meal, add dumplings.

ROAST VEAL

1 leg of veal
Salad oil
Lemon juice
Celery, parsley, onion, garlic salt
Juniper berries, if you can get them

Marinate the veal overnight in the salad oil and lemon juice (1 part lemon to 2 parts oil). In the morning, drain the marinade off, but do not toss it out. Make small incisions in the veal with a sharp knife and tuck in each incision a small bouquet, as it were, of celery leaves, parsley, onion slivers sprinkled with the garlic salt.

Roast, uncovered, in a slow (325°) oven. Add the juniper berries to the marinade and baste with this from time to time. The roast is done when the meat thermometer calls it just above Rare, or when a two-pronged fork pierces it and the juice runs out barely pink.

Now you may throw out the marinade. If you wish gravy, keep the roast hot while you add butter or margarine to the roaster, stir in flour (2 tablespoons flour to 2 tablespoons fat). You won't have any real drippings, so add chicken bouillon to the roux, stirring constantly.

Spike the gravy with a bit of liquid gravy maker.

SERVES 6–8, depending on size of roast

Veal is very happy with asparagus, new peas, spinach. And baked potatoes. Try Floating Island pudding, which is also delicate, for the dessert, but keep the coffee hot.

VERA WILKINS' VEAL CASSEROLE

    2 cups left over roast veal, sliced
    1 cup chopped celery
    ½ chopped green onions or scallions, tops and all
    ¼ cup chopped green pepper
    1 can condensed cream of chicken soup
    ½ cup milk
    1 can chow mein noodles
    1 4-oz can button mushrooms
    1 tsp soy sauce
    ½ tsp steak sauce or Worcestershire

Mix together the veal, celery, onions, green pepper. Add the milk to the chicken soup, then add to the meat mixture. Add all but ¼ can of the noodles, and the mushrooms, soy sauce, steak sauce. Taste for seasoning, add salt and pepper if needed.

   Put the mixture in a greased casserole, top with the extra noodles and bake in a moderate oven (350°) until bubbly.

SERVES 4–5

Serve with orange and onion salad or a tossed green salad, coffee and, for dessert, nothing heavier than a custard.

MARGUERITE'S SAUSAGE AND SCALLOPED POTATOES

    6 medium potatoes
       Link sausages, 12 or more
       Milk
       Salt, pepper, flour

Wash and peel potatoes. Slice very thin. Take a baking pan at least 2 inches deep and fill it three-fourths full with layers of the potatoes, sprinkling each layer with salt, pepper, and a little flour. Nearly cover with milk. Put in a moderate oven (350°) for 30 minutes, covered. Remove cover, place link sausages in pairs over the top. Place again in the oven and bake, uncovered, 20 to 25 minutes longer, or until the sausage is done.

SERVES 4–6

SWEDISH MEAT RING

1	envelope unflavored gelatin	1	slice onion, cut up
¼	cup cold water	2	tbsp lemon juice
½	lb liverwurst	½	tsp salt
½	medium green pepper, chopped fine	2	tsp sugar
		½	tsp dry mustard
1½	cup tomato juice	6	stuffed olives

Add gelatin to water, heat over low fire until dissolved. Cut liverwurst in sizable chunks. Put in blender, add rest of ingredients, turn to high speed, blend. Use 1-quart ring mold, oiled. Garnish with more olives, etc. Chill several hours.

SERVES 4

BARBECUED PORK LOIN

1 pork loin (a whole loin weighs 10 to 14 lbs but can
    be cut to give 5–6 lbs)
  Salt and chili powder
4 tbsp vinegar
2 tbsp chili powder
3 tbsp brown sugar
1 tsp dry mustard

Rub the pork well all over with salt and chili powder. Roast about 1½ hours or until nearly tender, while half covered with water. Drain off ½ cup of liquid from the roast. Add to it the vinegar, chili powder, sugar, and mustard. Baste the loin frequently with this until it is tender and crusty on the outside. Serve hot or cold.

SERVES 6

This was a favorite of Jill's, whose devotion to pork was constant and fervent. Even when we went to a fancy French restaurant in the city, she would study the menu gravely for twenty minutes and then look up at the waiter and say, "I'd like pork chops, if you have them."

SAVORY PORK RING

3   cups left over pork roast, diced finely
1½ cups cornmeal (water-ground if possible)
⅓ cup sifted flour
1½ tsp salt
3   tsp baking powder
2   eggs, beaten
1¼ cups milk
¼ cup melted butter or margarine
1½ cups gravy

Sift the dry ingredients together. Add eggs and milk to butter or margarine, and pour over the dry mixture. Stir until moistened. Bake in a greased 9-inch ring mold at 400° or hot oven about 25 minutes. Test center with a straw; if it comes out clean, the cornbread is done.

Meanwhile heat the pork and gravy. Unmold the corn ring and put it on a hot platter. Fill the center with the pork and gravy.

SERVES 4

If you are short of gravy, use cream of mushroom or chicken soup, diluted with ⅓ can of water or milk.

PORK CHOPS AND CABBAGE

6   pork chops
1   large onion
1   large head fresh cabbage
    Milk
    Salt, pepper, paprika

Brown the pork chops, using a little butter or margarine if necessary. Slice the onion and add to the chops after you have turned them.

Arrange the chops in a large greased baking dish or casserole with the onion slices around them. Season well.

Slice the cabbage thinly with a sharp knife and pack it tightly on the chops, filling the casserole almost to the top (it will shrink). Pour over milk enough to barely cover. Add more salt, pepper, paprika. Bake, covered, for 45 to 60 minutes (depends on the cabbage) in a moderate oven (350°). Test with a fork for tenderness.

SERVES 4–6

Serve with baked potatoes, for the pork, onion, milk makes a gravy that begs for a baked potato.
    You may have some of the milk and cabbage left over. And next day's luncheon soup is ready!

POLISH HUNTER'S STEW

2 lbs cabbage, shredded	2 cups water
1 large can sauerkraut	1 lb Polish sausage
2 lbs pork chops (shoulder preferably)	1 8-oz can tomato sauce
	Salt, pepper to taste

Cook the cabbage, sauerkraut, chops and seasonings with the water in a deep kettle about an hour or more, until pork is tender. Remove bones and cut the meat in pieces. Cool. Peel the sausage and cut in bite-sized pieces and add with tomato sauce to the first mixture. Cover and cook until sausage is tender.

SERVES 6–8

This is best when you simmer it about an hour for the last step, so the flavors can blend and enhance one another. It is a rich dish, a meal in one, and if you want to serve anything other than crusty pieces of Italian bread for dipping, serve hot boiled potatoes. For delicate guests, have a bottle of soda mints at hand. It is worth it. Polish sausage, called Kielbasa or Kielbaski, is rich and elegant and sometimes hard to get. A highly spiced Italian sausage may do.

PORK ROAST AND SAUERKRAUT

3 lb shoulder of pork, boned
1 cup sauerkraut juice or vegetable stock
   Sauerkraut
   Flour, salt, pepper

Rub shoulder inside and out with salt and pepper. Fill the cavity with sauerkraut from which most of the liquor has been drained. Sew or skewer the edges together. Dredge with flour. Place in a dry pan in a hot oven for 15 minutes; then reduce to a moderate heat and add sauerkraut juice or vegetable stock. Cover and cook 1 hour and 10 minutes; then remove the cover and cook 20 minutes longer. Allow the stock to boil down somewhat after you remove the meat, and use it as gravy.

SERVES 4–5

Pork and sauerkraut have a friendship like roast goose and applesauce. This is fine for a cold winter night when snow piles against the windowpanes.

PORK CHOPS WITH SOUR CREAM

4 pork chops, preferably loin
   Flour, seasonings for dredging
½ cup water
2 tbsp vinegar
1 tbsp sugar
1 small bay leaf or ½ large one
½ cup sour cream

Dredge the chops in the flour and brown slightly in fat. Combine the remaining ingredients and heat over a moderate heat. Arrange the chops in a shallow baking dish and pour the liquid over them. Cover tightly and bake in a moderate oven (350°) about an hour, or until tender.

SERVES 4

The first time I had this dish came about when the butcher sent me the meat package with a note on it: "I am sorry I didn't have the lean chops you like, so here are four at a very low price." I trimmed off as much of the fat as I could, used a bit of it for the browning, and baked them. All I can say is the very low priced pork chops were melting good.

STILLMEADOW SPARERIBS

4	lbs spareribs cut in serving-size pieces.	1	tbsp prepared mustard
1	large onion, diced	1/4	cup vinegar
1/2	cup drippings (*see below*)	1	tsp salt
1/2	cup catsup	1/4	tsp pepper
1	pint tomato juice	2	bay leaves
2	tsp chili powder	1	tbsp Worcestershire
		2 1/2	cups boiling water

Salt and pepper the ribs, dredge with flour and broil until brown. Turn once.

Drain 1/2 cup of the drippings from the broiler pan and put in a large skillet. Brown the onion in the drippings, add the rest of the ingredients and simmer 5 minutes.

Place the ribs in a large casserole or baking pan, pour the sauce over, cover (use aluminum foil if your pan has no cover) and bake 1 1/2 hours.

SERVES 4

This is one of the top buffet-dinner dishes. Can be made the day before and reheated. Serve with crusty French bread and a green salad.

SPARERIBS WITH SAUERKRAUT

2 qts sauerkraut   6 small onions
Spareribs (allow 1 lb per person. A pair
    should serve 4)

Place the sauerkraut in a mound in the middle of a baking pan. Imbed onions in the kraut. Lay the racks of ribs over the mound, and bake each side until brown, basting with the kraut juice from time to time.

SERVES 4–6

This was the standard way of preparing spareribs a generation ago in the Middle West.

This is good served with mashed potatoes or with potatoes which have been peeled and browned in the same pan as the roast for the last 45 minutes of the cooking. This latter method saves preparation time and means one less pan to wash.

FRIED SALT PORK

Slice wafer thin, cover with cold water. Set on low heat but do not boil. Drain off water. Flour both sides.

This can be fried without fat if started at first on low heat. Turn only once if possible. Cook to delicate brown on both sides.

On bitter winter nights at Stillmeadow in the early days, we used to favor a supper of fried salt pork, cream gravy, and baked potatoes. Eaten in front of the applewood fire, it tasted just right. It also helped our budget, usually sinking for the third time.

ANNE'S PORK CHOPS WITH KIDNEY BEANS

8   thin pork chops (any cut)
1   tbsp salt
¼   cup brown sugar
½   cup chili sauce
2   tbsp vinegar
1   tbsp steak sauce
2   onions, finely chopped
½   cup water
1   or 2 cans baked kidney beans

Brown chops in skillet, adding a little cooking oil if necessary. Combine all remaining ingredients except kidney beans. Pour over chops, simmer 5 minutes. Heat the kidney beans to boiling, pour in oven casserole. Top with chops, pour sauce over.

Bake in 400° oven 25 to 30 minutes. (Canned *baked* kidney beans are not available everywhere. Ordinary canned kidney beans can be substituted, but drain most of liquid from beans. Use ½ cup of this liquid instead of water in the sauce, discard the rest. Increase all sauce ingredients if the mixture seems bland to taste before baking. A little horseradish adds something, too.)

SERVES 4

TAMALE PARTY PIE

2 lbs ground lean beef or pork
2 large onions, diced
    Salt and pepper to taste
1½ cups cornmeal
1½ cups milk
1½ tsp salt
1 No. 2½ can tomatoes
1 can cream-style corn (15½ oz or 1 lb)
1 can (8½ oz) ripe olives, sliced
2 tbsp chili powder

Brown the meat and onions, adding fat if the meat is really lean. Add salt and pepper. Simmer 40 minutes, stirring occasionally.

Meanwhile mix cornmeal, milk and salt in a big kettle. Add tomatoes and cook slowly about 30 minutes, stirring often. Then add corn, olives, chili powder and mix well.

Combine meat and cornmeal mixture and place in a greased casserole or baking dish. Bake at 300° for 1½ hours or until it begins to draw away from the sides of the pan.

MAKES 12 PORTIONS

You may make this the day before and reheat. And greet the guests with a smile.

HAM BANANA BAKE

4   slices boiled ham
4   bananas, peeled
1½ tbsp melted butter
    Prepared mustard

Spread the ham slices lightly with mustard, then wrap the slices around the bananas. Brush the ends of bananas with butter. Place the rolls in a greased shallow baking dish and pour cheese sauce over. Bake in a moderate oven (350°) about 30 minutes or until bananas are tender. Serve at once.

CHEESE SAUCE

1½ tbsp butter
1½ tbsp flour
¾   cup milk
1½ cups grated Cheddar or
    American cheese

Melt butter in a saucepan, add flour and stir until smooth. Slowly add milk; then add cheese and cook, stirring, until sauce is smooth and thickened.

SERVES 4

You may use canned cheese soup if you prefer. Dilute with ½ cup top milk. This is best with rather firm bananas.

LOIS KLAKRING'S CHICKEN AND HAM CASSEROLE

6   equal slices each of cooked
    chicken and ham
1   onion, minced
    Butter or margarine
½   cup sliced mushrooms
    Paprika, salt
¾   cup hot cream
    Grated Parmesan cheese

Cook onion in butter or margarine until golden, add mushrooms, paprika and salt. (If you have no fresh mushrooms, substitute canned, drained.) Simmer 5 minutes for fresh mushrooms; 2 minutes for canned.

Turn mixture into a greased casserole, put in ham; then place chicken on ham. Pour the hot cream over, and sprinkle with the cheese. Bake in a hot oven (400°) until bubbly and brown.

SERVES 4–6

If you use an oblong flattish casserole, you will have an easier time serving.

MIDSUMMER HAM BUFFET

  1 canned cooked ham
  1 pkg lemon gelatin
    Pimiento strips for garnish
    Parsley

Remove the juices from the canned ham, and wipe it dry with a paper towel. Place it on a rack over a platter. Prepare the gelatin according to directions on the package and let it cool until it is beginning to set. Pour a layer over the ham, let cool in the refrigerator until it is firm, then pour the remaining gelatin over and chill until glazed. Just before it is jellied, add strips of pimiento, and sprigs of parsley for decoration.

For easy serving for company, slice the ham when you have dried it, then tie it together with a fine string. The slices will slide neatly on the plate. Remove the string as you serve.

Since this is cold, serve one hot dish with it. I favor a casserole of baked beans, bubbly and spicy. A mixed green salad, and garlic toasted French bread, plus the coffee complete the buffet.

Honeydew melon wedges garnished with mint sprigs dipped in powdered sugar are my last word on this one. With ham, try for a dessert that will not be sweet or rich.

STILLMEADOW SAVORY HAM PIE

1 ½ or 2 cups cooked leftover ham, diced
4 tbsp onion, diced
4 tbsp green pepper, diced
4 tbsp butter or margarine
6 tbsp flour
1 can condensed chicken or celery or mushroom
    soup
1 ⅓ cups milk
1 tbsp lemon juice (fresh, frozen, canned)

Cook onion and pepper in the fat until golden, stir in flour and, when it is bubbly, add milk and soup. Stir until smooth, add lemon juice and ham and put into a deep greased casserole.

Top with a crust made of the following:

> 1½ cups prepared biscuit mix
> 6 tbsp milk
> ½ cup grated Cheddar cheese
>   (or Swiss if you prefer)

Mix cheese and prepared biscuit mix and stir in milk to form a soft dough. Roll out or pat in shape on a floured board. Cut with a doughnut cutter. Lay on top of the ham mixture and tuck bits of pimiento in the small holes left by the cutter. Bake in a hot oven (450°) until the top is crusty and brown.

SERVES 4–6

This is a rib-sticking winter-night dish. Needs a tossed green salad with a lemon juice-oil dressing, and a fruit compote for dessert. Plenty of coffee.

CREAMED SWEETBREADS

1 lb sweetbreads
2 tbsp butter
2 tbsp flour
1 cup cold milk or half milk
    and half cream

To prepare the sweetbreads, cover with boiling water with 1 teaspoon salt and 2 tablespoons lemon juice added. Simmer 20 minutes, then drain and drop in cold water to cool quickly. Remove membrane and tubes.

Melt the butter, blend in flour and add the milk, stirring until smooth and creamy. Season with salt and pepper to taste and add the sweetbreads. You may add Worcestershire if you like. Serve on toast points or in individual baking dishes.

SERVES 4

For a company dish, sprinkle toasted slivered almonds on top.

CREAMED SWEETBREADS WITH CHIPPED BEEF

3 tbsp butter
1 pair sweetbreads
¼ lb chipped beef
¼ cup flour
3 cups milk

Dice parboiled sweetbreads. Melt butter in a heavy saucepan. Add sweetbreads and chipped beef. Brown for 3 to 4 minutes. Sprinkle with flour and stir while adding milk. Continue stirring and cooking slowly until sauce is thickened. Serve on toast.

SERVES 2

BRAISED SWEETBREADS

3 pair sweetbreads	2 sprigs parsley
Juice of ½ lemon	½ cup dry white table wine
3 tbsp butter or margarine	1 cup chicken broth (fresh or
1 onion, chopped	made with a cube or
1 carrot, diced	canned)
1 bay leaf	

Soak the sweetbreads in ice water for about an hour, then plunge them in salted boiling water to which lemon juice has been added. Cook 15 minutes, remove, run cold water over at once. When cool, discard the tough membranes.

In an oven casserole, on a spreader, melt the butter or margarine, add the vegetables and seasonings and cook until the carrots turn golden. Sprinkle a little flour over them, add the sweetbreads, wine and chicken broth. Bring to a boil, then cover the casserole and put in a moderate oven (350°) for about half an hour. Turn them once or twice and test with a fork for tenderness.

Remove the sweetbreads to a hot platter, strain the juices and add a tablespoon or two of sherry if desired.

Reheat the sauce just until it is good and hot, and pour over.

SERVES 3–5 according to how you like sweetbreads

Most sweetbreads are overcooked. If they are young and tender, they need not be parboiled as long.

KIDNEYS WITH MUSTARD SAUCE

2 veal kidneys or 4–6 lamb kidneys
Butter for sautéeing

Peel the fat from the kidneys and cut away the filament with a very sharp knife, being careful not to cut into the meat itself. Sauté them whole in hot butter for 7 or 8 minutes, turning frequently. They should not get brown, as overcooking toughens them.

MUSTARD SAUCE

2 tbsp Dijon mustard
1 tbsp butter
2 shallots or scallions or young leeks diced
2 stalks parsley, coarsely chopped
½ cup dry vermouth
Juice of half a lemon
Seasoned salt and pepper to taste

Blend the butter and mustard together until creamy. Remove the kidneys from the pan and put the shallots in. Cook a couple of minutes, then pour the vermouth in and let it cook until the liquid is reduced a third. Slice kidneys in thin slices crosswise and season them. Add to the pan and add the mustard butter mix, then stir in the lemon juice. As soon as the sauce is heated, serve at once.

SERVES 4

The kidneys should be faintly pink when you slice them. If some juice runs out, add it to the sauce. Serve with hot French bread or toast points. A green salad with plain French dressing is best, as the kidneys are rich.

WHOLE COOKED TONGUE

1 large tongue, 4–5 lbs	2 bay leaves
Water to cover	1 small onion, chopped.
¼ cup cider vinegar	1 carrot, diced
2 tbsp brown sugar	1 celery stalk, cut in pieces,
2 or 3 allspice	with leaves
4 cloves	

Wash the tongue under cold running water. Put in a heavy kettle with water to cover. Add remaining ingredients and bring to a boil, then simmer 2 or 3 hours. It should be tender when pierced with a fork. Cool in the liquor. Remove skin and gristle and small bones at base. To skin, run a sharp knife down the middle, cutting through the rough skin, then pull skin away.

MAKES 24 thin slices

This is good to have on hand for a cold platter or sandwiches or in salads. Cold tongue curry is my favorite (see recipe). You may serve it hot with raisin sauce or heated in some of the stock.

STUFFED CABBAGE

1 large cabbage	1 can tomatoes
1½ lbs round steak, ground	2 small cans tomato paste
½ lb lean pork, ground	3 tbsp vinegar
1 cup cooked rice	2 tbsp brown sugar
1 large onion, minced	10 bay leaves
Sage, salt, pepper	3 ginger snaps

Boil cabbage, head down, in water to cover for a few minutes. Separate leaves, starting at stem end. Mix together meats, rice, onion, sage, salt, pepper, and 3 tablespoons tomato paste. Fill each leaf with a generous helping, fold like an envelope, and lay in a large casserole. When all meat has been used, cover cabbage rolls with tomatoes, paste, 1 paste can of water, vinegar, brown sugar, bay leaves, and gingersnaps. Cook, covered, 3 to 4 hours.

SERVES 6–8

COLD TONGUE CURRY

1 cup cooked beef tongue, sliced thin (or
   1 7½-oz can of tongue)
1 envelope unflavored gelatin
1 cup cold water
1 can cream of mushroom soup
1¼ tsp curry powder
1 tsp lemon juice
   Salt, paprika
3 hard-cooked eggs, sliced
   Green pepper rings, sliced stuffed
    olives for garnish

Stir the curry into ½ cup of the water, then sprinkle the gelatin over the top. After 5 minutes dissolve over boiling water.

Combine remaining ½ cup water with the soup, lemon juice, seasonings. Stir in the gelatin. Let cool until beginning to set. Then pour a layer of the gelatin in a mold or flat baking dish (such as you use for au gratin recipes). Arrange the sliced eggs on the gelatin. Set in the refrigerator a few minutes, then arrange the sliced tongue for the second layer, pour over the remaining gelatin and set until firm. Unmold at serving time, and garnish with pepper rings and olives.

SERVES 4–6

A side bowl of mayonnaise with 1 teaspoon of mustard added makes a fine complement.

For a company one-dish dinner, arrange sliced fresh tomatoes and cucumbers around the curry.

TRANSYLVANIAN LAYERED CABBAGE

1½ cups rice
1½ lbs ground beef
1 lb ground pork
1 onion, chopped fine
  Bacon drippings
1 egg
½ cup milk
2 cans sauerkraut

½ green pepper, chopped fine
1 pint sour cream
1 pint cottage cheese
  Chopped parsley
  Freshly ground black pepper
  Paprika
  Salt

Steam rice and put aside. Sauté pork and beef with chopped onions in bacon drippings for 5 minutes, or till slightly cooked. Salt and pepper to taste. Beat egg in milk and pour into simmering meat. Sauté 5 more minutes. Put meat mixture aside. Squeeze sauerkraut dry, then rinse in cold water and squeeze out once more. Sauté in bacon drippings with green pepper until slightly brown. Take *large* casserole and add layer of rice, meat, sauerkraut, sour cream, and cottage cheese in that order. Sprinkle each layer with chopped parsley, paprika, ground pepper, and salt. Bake uncovered in a 350° oven for 30 minutes.

SERVES 8–10

Fowl

CHICKEN DINNER FOR SUNDAY HAS BEEN A TRADITION IN most of our country until recently. In the small town in the Midwest where I grew up, I spent part of the church service thinking of food. The pews were hard and uncomfortable and the sermons were long, the prayers as long as most sermons of today. By the time we finally reached home, I was in a state of starvation. Then came the chicken, fricasseed, with creamy light dumplings and a bowl of golden gravy with giblets sparking it. And also fluffy mashed potatoes and whatever vegetables were in season. Or it might be a savory roast chicken. Fried chicken was reserved for times when Mama could be in the kitchen instead of in church.

Fried chicken was for suppers and picnics. Who ever had a picnic without a basket of fried chicken covered with a damask napkin? Broilers were a treat because most farmers preferred to keep their chickens until they had paid their way with new-laid eggs. Rock Cornish hens had not been invented, and I never heard of squab until I

159

moved to Virginia. But we had plump, range-fed chicken raised in the good clean sun and not in wire cages.

Turkeys were for Thanksgiving and Christmas. They had plenty of dark meat, which has much more flavor, and they were stuffed with old-fashioned bread stuffing. It is convenient to be able to buy frozen turkey any time of year and nothing graces a buffet like a crisply brown turkey resting on a bed of watercress. But some of the magic has gone just because it is always around.

Duckling was scarce and goose was a rare treat. Wild game was plentiful and was shared with the neighbors. I have never been able to eat it, or venison either, although there is a fine moral distinction between eating a tame duckling and a wild duck.

There are, I imagine, hundreds of ways to prepare fowl, but I have my favorite recipes, and I never grow tired of chicken.

CHICKEN ROYALE

2½ to 3 lb fryer, cut up
¼ cup flour
½ tsp salt
¼ tsp pepper
1 tsp paprika
¼ cup butter
1 can cream of chicken soup
1 tbsp white wine

Combine flour, salt, pepper and paprika. Coat chicken pieces thoroughly. Brown in butter. Place skin side down in shallow roasting pan. Bake uncovered at 400° about 30 minutes.

Combine soup and wine. Heat. Turn chicken, pour soup mixture over and continue baking about 15 minutes. Make gravy by adding any leftover seasoned flour and water to pan juices and blend to desired thickness.

SERVES 4

ARROZ CON POLLO

1 5- to 6-lb stewing chicken, disjointed
1 thread of saffron
2 cloves garlic
   Olive oil or lard
2 medium-sized diced onions
4 large tomatoes, cut in pieces
3 tbsp chopped parsley
¼ tsp Cayenne pepper

1 cup raw green peas
½ cup carrots, sliced thin
4 artichoke hearts, cut in quarters
2 cups rice
2 large red or green peppers, seeded and sliced thin
4 cups chicken broth

This is a Latin dish, so the seasoning is all-important. Place chicken in Dutch oven or other deep, heavy kettle, covering it with at least 2½ quarts of water. Bring to boil, then reduce the flame to a simmer.

Soak saffron in 3 tablespoons boiling water until water is well colored. Dice and brown garlic cloves in olive oil or lard. Remove garlic and discard it. Now brown in the same fat the diced onions. Add tomatoes, parsley, Cayenne pepper, and the saffron water. When heated together, add these ingredients to the chicken and continue to simmer it. When the chicken is almost tender add peas, carrots and artichoke hearts.

Wash and drain rice and put in a large saucepan with peppers. Cover with chicken broth from the chicken, seasoning the broth to taste with added salt and pepper. If the broth is absorbed before the rice is tender add more broth, but it should all be absorbed, and the rice only moist when it is done.

Place the rice in the center of a deep platter, mound the chicken and vegetables over it, and serve the extra broth in a gravy boat or tureen instead of gravy.

A handful of pimiento-stuffed green olives may be added to the rice along with the peppers if you want a more exotic flavor.

SERVES 4–6

CHICKEN SPECIAL

4   chicken breasts
     Butter
1   pkg cream of leek soup
1½ cups milk or half-and-half
1   can mushrooms (optional)

Brown the chicken breasts in butter until golden, in an electric skillet or the old iron one. Combine soup and milk or half-and-half; heat just to boiling, stirring constantly, to make a sauce. Pour over chicken and simmer for 30 minutes, stirring occasionally. If needed, stir in another half cup of milk or half-and-half. Or dump in a can of mushrooms and their liquor. Simmer 15 minutes longer or until the chicken is butter-tender.

SERVES 4

This is a stand-by for me. I keep frozen breasts in the freezer and the packages of soup on the emergency shelf. I can add more of the chicken if unexpected company comes, and open another package of the soup. Also this dish can simmer a long while and just be better, so you can serve any time. It's what I call a restful menu with salad and rice or noodles.

CHICKEN CACCIATORE

2   frying chickens (around 3 lbs each)
¼ cup flour
     Salt and pepper
½ cup olive oil or salad oil (or half each)
1   large onion, chopped
1   carrot, chopped
1   clove minced garlic
1   can tomato purée (No. 2½)
½ cup dry white wine
2   tbsp chopped parsley

Disjoint chickens, dredge with seasoned flour, and brown in the oil. Add onion, carrot, garlic, and when onion is transparent, add tomato purée and wine. Cover and simmer about an hour, or until chicken is tender. Add parsley and test for seasoning.

SERVES 6

This is perfect for an electric skillet which goes to the table for serving.

When using olive oil, be sure it is mild and fresh-tasting.

This recipe may be varied by using canned tomatoes, and adding chopped green pepper (¼ to ½ cup).

Either fluffy rice or broad noodles are in order.

CHICKEN CACCIATORE À LA STILLMEADOW

1 young roasting chicken, cut in
   pieces
1 beaten egg
   Flour
   Salt
   Pepper
   Basil
   Thyme
   Bacon fat or other cooking fat
1 No. 2 can tomatoes
1 tbsp finely diced onion
   Grated Parmesan cheese

Roll chicken pieces in beaten egg and then in flour which has been seasoned with salt, pepper and a little basil and thyme. Brown in fat in a skillet. Place in an earthenware pot and pour tomatoes over the chicken. Add onion and stir it in slightly. Top with a liberal amount of cheese and bake in a moderate oven for 1½ hours, or until the chicken is tender.

SERVES 4–6

If I were on a desert island and had only one thing to eat, I would undoubtedly choose chicken. I could survive on just chicken. Of course it would taste better cooked — as, for instance, Cacciatore.

CZECH BAKED CHICKEN WITH SOUR CREAM

1 roasting chicken (cut into individual servings)
Flour
1 egg, beaten
3 tbsp water
Fine bread crumbs
4 tbsp melted butter or cooking oil
Salt
Pepper
Paprika
1 pint sour cream

Wipe chicken with damp cloth and roll in flour. Dip into beaten egg to which water has been added, then into bread crumbs. Brown on all sides in melted butter or oil and transfer to baking pan. Season with salt, pepper and paprika. Bake at 375° for 30 minutes; then with a tablespoon put a little sour cream on each piece. Do this 3 more times at 15-minute intervals while baking, or until all the cream is used. Bake slowly for another 25 minutes – a total of 1 hour and 40 minutes.

The number this serves depends on the size of the chicken. I like to use a 2-pound fryer sometimes, which serves 4.

HELEN'S PARTY CHICKEN

1 frying chicken (2½ lbs)
1 pkg dehydrated onion soup
Rice
Chicken broth

Arrange chicken pieces in a large casserole. Sprinkle onion soup over. Then add uncooked rice to cover chicken well. Pour over enough chicken broth to cover well (about 2 cups). Put in medium oven (325°) and bake 2 or 3 hours. Add more broth if needed.

Use regular or long-grain rice, not instant.

SERVES 4

This dish has many variations. You may use chicken breasts (thawed, if frozen). Mushrooms and sliced pimiento may be added.

HAWAIIAN CHICKEN

1 cut-up frying chicken, 2 – 3 lbs
1 egg, slightly beaten
1 cup fine bread or cracker crumbs
1 tsp salt
¼ tsp thyme
¼ tsp marjoram
½ tsp paprika

Mix crumbs with seasonings. Dip chicken in egg, then in the crumb mixture. Fry in ¼-in.-deep hot fat in skillet until brown. (Electric skillet is perfect for this.)

Drain off excess fat.

SAUCE

1 cup pineapple juice
½ cup water
2 tbsp lemon juice
¼ tsp curry powder (I use more
      than this)
1 tbsp cornstarch
1 tbsp sugar
1 cup pineapple bits
   Slivered almonds

Combine the juices, cornstarch, curry and sugar. Cook until blended. Add the pineapple bits. Pour over the chicken, cover and cook slowly in oven or electric skillet (325° to 350°) for 30 minutes.

Arrange chicken on hot platter, pour the sauce over, and sprinkle with sliced blanched almonds.

SERVES 4

You can fry the chicken ahead of time, make the sauce, and combine for the baking while the guests sip their tomato juice or drinks.

JELLIED CHICKEN

2 2½-lb chickens
   White pepper to taste
   Bouquet garni.
   Seasoned salt
1 envelope unflavored gelatin

Cook chickens gently in water to cover with the bouquet garni in a cheesecloth bag. For the bouquet use a bay leaf, a few sprigs parsley and celery tips, a few shreds of carrot, and a minced leek. You may vary this according to what you like and have. When the chickens are tender, cool in the stock and then lift them out and slice the meat in thin slices. Arrange them in a mold, alternating the white and dark meat.

Put the bones, necks, and wings back in the stock and boil gently for half an hour or so. Strain the stock and add the gelatin dissolved in ¼ cup cold water. Pour over the chicken and set in the refrigerator until jellied.

SERVES 6–8

This may be made the day before and is fine for a company luncheon. Garnish with ripe olives, pimiento slices, watercress or parsley.

JILL'S BARBECUED CHICKEN

As chicken is grilling over open fire, baste with this sauce:

⅔	cup margarine	1	tsp chili powder
	cooking oil	1	tsp Worcestershire
⅔	cup water	2	tsp flour
1½	tbsp lemon juice	2	tsp meat sauce
1½	tsp salt		Dash of tabasco
1	tsp mustard		

Blend dry ingredients and stir into melted fat and liquids. Cook several minutes.

The charcoal should have burned down to a white ash before the chicken goes on. Turn the chicken frequently. A clean paintbrush (one you do not use to paint woodwork with) makes a good dipping and spreading tool for the sauce.

PAELLA

2 broilers, cut up
  Scant half cup olive oil or half
    salad oil and half butter or
    margarine
4 small onions, chopped
2 cups rice
1 quart chicken broth
2 dozen cherrystone clams

2 dozen shrimp
6 slices Italian sausage
2 cloves garlic
3 or 4 slivers saffron
2 oz sherry
  Seasoning
  Grated Parmesan cheese

In a Dutch oven or very heavy large kettle sauté onions and chicken in the oil. When chicken is nicely browned, add the rice and stir until the rice begins to dry out. Add 1 cup of the boiling broth. When it is all absorbed, add more broth. Simmer until chicken and rice are fairly tender, then add the clams in the shells and the unshelled shrimp and the sausage.

Mash the garlic with the saffron and stir in about a cup of the broth. Let it stand a few minutes, then strain broth into the pot, add sherry and seasoning. Cook 5 minutes or until clam shells open and shrimp are pink, then sprinkle cheese on top and run under the broiler a few more minutes.

SERVES 6–8

I first had this in a Basque restaurant in lower Manhattan. I kept going back trying to figure out how to make it. Unfortunately they never made it the same way twice. Sometimes there were mussels in it, shiny and blue-black and rich. Sometimes there was diced ham. There might be pimientos or ripe olives. There was always a green salad and hard crusty bread and quite dreadful black coffee. It was all gay and wonderful.

ANNE'S CHICKEN WITH BLEU CHEESE

1 fryer, in serving pieces
   Flour
   Salt and pepper
   Butter and cooking oil
2 to 3 oz bleu cheese
½ pint sour cream
   Large clove garlic

Shake chicken pieces in paper bag with flour which has been seasoned with salt and pepper. Brown quickly in large skillet in equal parts butter and oil. Transfer to oven casserole with lid. Pour off most of butter-oil from skillet: add bleu cheese, stir until melted, then add sour cream and crushed garlic. Heat almost to boiling, stirring to scrape up glaze from pan. Season to taste with salt and pepper. Pour over chicken, cover, bake at 325° until tender, about 40 minutes depending on size. (This sauce is excellent over rice.)

I am a cheese addict, but I like bleu cheese better in things than just in chunks on crackers. I love bleu cheese dressing, as in Kay's salad dressing and in Louella's Goop, both of which are somewhere in this book. And I like my Anne's chicken with it too.

BRUNSWICK STEW

1 5-lb stewing chicken, cut in pieces
¼ lb salt pork, diced (or bacon)
   Salt, pepper
1 medium onion, diced
2 cups canned tomatoes (or four or five fresh, cut up)
2½ cups green lima beans, fresh or frozen
2½ cups canned or fresh corn kernels
3 potatoes, sliced thin
¼ lb butter
   Flour

Brown the chicken in the pork drippings, add a quart of water and simmer, covered, until the chicken is tender. (If you use your pressure cooker, follow directions for fricasseeing.) When chicken is tender, cool it enough to remove meat from the bones and cut in bite-sized pieces. Return to the kettle, add all the ingredients except corn and butter and flour. Cook until the vegetables are tender, then add corn and butter and cook about 5 minutes. Meanwhile blend about 4 tablespoons of flour with enough cold water to make a smooth mixture, and add to the stew to thicken it.

SERVES 8

I first had a variation of Brunswick Stew in Virginia and asked my hostess how it was made. "We just toss in whatever we have," she said vaguely. Some cooks add a can of condensed tomato soup; some, of course, add rabbit. It is company fare, served with a salad and hot biscuits.

CHICKEN EN GELÉE

> 4 chicken breasts
> 1 can chicken consommé (or 2 bouillon cubes
>   dissolved in 2 cups boiling water)
> 2 stalks celery
> 3 scallions
> 2 small carrots, diced
> 4 cups water
>   Seasoning to taste
> 2 envelopes unflavored gelatin
> 1½ cups each: cooked peas, lima beans, green beans,
>   carrots

Simmer the chicken breasts in the water and consommé with the scallions, celery, carrot and seasonings. When tender (45 to 50 minutes) take out the chicken and chill. Strain and chill the broth separately, removing the fat when it rises. Then soften the gelatin in 1 cup of the broth, heat until dissolved, and add to remaining broth (you need 4 cups of broth in all).

Now take the bones from the chicken breasts, slice the breasts and arrange in a deep platter or serving dish. (A large glass rectangular dish will do.) Cover the chicken with the vegetables, and, when the gelatin is chilled until almost thick, spoon it gently over.

Chill thoroughly.

SERVES 8

FAY'S BAKED BROILERS

Broilers, split, ½ to each person
Rice, cooked (¾ cup per person)
Butter or margarine
Salt, paprika, pepper, onion or garlic salt

Grease an oblong dish, or a roaster if you are having a party. Lay the cooked rice, seasoned, in a mound in the center. Lay the split broilers over the rice, skin side up. Dot well with butter or margarine, and bake in a slow oven (325°) until broilers are done. Turn once during baking and add a little more butter or margarine to the underside of the broilers.

Fay used to cook her rice the night before and put it in the roaster, then add the broilers when she came home from her radio job around five. She used a wood stove and never timed them, but somehow they were just ready when ten or twelve guests trooped in. I have tried it with poultry stuffing as well as with instant rice, and can recommend it. The chicken juices drip down and give that extra special flavor. The dish is ready to serve when a fork slides into the breast without bringing any rosy juice back with it. From 30 to 45 minutes does it.

This is a godsend for a buffet party because you can turn the oven low and the chicken and rice do not dry up. We favor it for guests who may arrive an hour late or may, on the other hand, turn up before we expect them!

Serve a grapefruit and avocado salad with this and cooked frozen peas with a can of sliced mushrooms added.

DIJON BROILED CHICKEN

1 broiler, 1½ lbs	½ tsp thyme
⅓ cup Dijon mustard	1½ tbsp chopped scallions
5 tbsp butter	1½ tbsp bread crumbs
Dash of tabasco	

Flatten the chicken. If you are good with a knife, remove the backbone by cutting along each side with the knife. Mix the mustard, butter, scallions, and seasonings, and spread over the chicken. Then put the crumbs over, crumbing the underside first. Lay the chicken skin side down and broil 10 minutes. Turn and broil 10 minutes on the other side, basting with the juices. Turn again and broil until tender and golden brown. The time depends on the size of the broiler, about 30 to 35 minutes for a 1½-pound broiler.

SERVES 2

You may get this ready to broil ahead of time or even partly cook it. Serve with fresh baby peas and hot biscuits for a gourmet and, oh, so easy dinner.

ERMA VANEK'S CHICKEN PAPRIKASH

> 1 4 – 5 lb fowl, cut up
>   Butter or margarine as needed
> 1 large onion
> 3 tbsp paprika
> 1 pint sour cream

In a Dutch oven or deep kettle, brown 1 large diced onion. When it is golden (but not brown) add 3 tablespoons paprika (the sweet Hungarian paprika if possible). Add the chicken, cover tightly, and when it begins to brown, add ½ cup water to make the steam, and cook until tender.

Add water if needed later.

When the chicken is tender, add 1 pint container sour cream. Do not let boil, or the cream separates.

DUMPLINGS

Put 1 cup lukewarm water in a small mixing bowl. Break 2 eggs in and stir. Add the liquid to 2 cups flour sifted with 1 teaspoon salt.

Stir until it makes a soft dough – when it pulls away from the side of the bowl, it is ready.

Have a kettle of boiling water ready, and drop the dough into it in spoonfuls. Dip the spoon in the water after each dumpling to keep them from sticking together. Use a dessert or soup spoon so the dumplings will be small.

Cook dumplings about 7 minutes, then drain in a colander and add to the chicken. You may test the dumplings for doneness by breaking one in two.

SERVES 4 – 6, depending on the size of the fowl

STILLMEADOW FRIED CHICKEN

½ frying chicken to each person (you may use larger
    than usual for this method)
Eggs, beaten lightly (1 egg to each fryer)
Milk (1 tbsp to an egg)
Flour and seasoned bread crumbs (these come in a
    package), half of each (¾ cup to each fryer)
Butter or margarine (2 tbsp to each fryer)

Add the milk to the beaten eggs. Wipe the chicken with a clean damp
cloth. Dip in the egg and milk. Dip in the flour and crumbs. Dip lightly
again in the liquid to set the crumb mixture. Let rest while you heat the
heavy skillet or electric frying pan with the butter or margarine. Dip
again in the crumb and flour mix, and when the butter or margarine is
bubbling hot (this is the best way I can describe it) lay the chicken
pieces in.

Brown until golden, lift with tongs or a spatula (do not pierce with a
fork and let those juices run out) turn and brown the other side. Then
turn the heat low and continue to cook for 30 to 40 minutes. If the
chicken shows signs of getting dry, cover the pan. Add a little salad oil
if needed.

Serve on a hot platter, and I do mean hot.

*This is a combination of Maryland fried chicken, Virginia fried
chicken, and New England fried chicken. It is not according to any
one rule. Also the covering is controversial. But it happens to work for
me.*

GRAVY

For this, the chicken stays hot in the oven on a heat-proof platter. I stir
in flour, 1 tablespoon, to 1 tablespoon of the drippings and cracklings
left in the pan. I then add the broth from having cooked the neck, the
giblets, a bit of celery top, and a slice of onion. If this turns out to be
short of liquid, I add thin cream or top milk. I do not let cream boil, this
is fatal. But when it simmers and is ready to boil, the gravy is done.

Fried chicken and cream gravy such as this needs tiny hot biscuits (I
use a mix) because a split biscuit takes so well to extra gravy.

*Serve a non-starchy vegetable such as spinach or asparagus or
broiled tomatoes with this, a very crisp green salad with nothing but*

*oil and vinegar on the side. And who wants dessert? Just reach for
one more bite of chicken.*

*I sometimes, when hurried, do the seasoned-flour version. I shake
the chicken up in a paper bag, praying it won't have a hole in it, with
plenty of flour, salt, pepper, paprika, a dash of onion salt. Then I
proceed as above.*

*I could never approximate my Virginia cook's fried chicken, but,
then, I never got the recipe. She said she just fried it, being careful.
But the Stillmeadow fried chicken never seems to have any leftovers,
so I shall have to settle for that.*

RUSSIAN HUNTER'S CHICKEN

1 fricassee chicken, 4–5 pounds	3 stalks celery
1 clove garlic	1 No. 2 can tomatoes
1 sliced onion	Salt, pepper, paprika,
1 minced green pepper	oregano
3 chopped carrots	Butter or margarine

Brown the garlic, onion, pepper, carrots, celery (chopped) in a heavy
skillet. Meanwhile brown the cut-up chicken in a Dutch oven or electric
frying pan, using the butter or margarine. When the chicken is golden
brown, pour the tomatoes over, add the remaining ingredients, seasonings. Cover tightly and cook until the chicken is about to fall from the
bones. Then remove the bones, lift the chicken meat to a warm platter
and pour the sauce over.

SERVES 4–6

*Serve with broad noodles, boiled, fluffy rice or whipped potatoes.
Green beans are good with it; but skip the salad. Needs no biscuits, as
everybody wants more noodles anyway. For dessert canned grapefruit sections laced with créme de menthe.*

*I have made this in my pressure cooker often. I follow the fricassee-
chicken directions, but I cut the timing by one-fourth.*

CHICKEN DIVAN

1   large chicken, boiled, sliced
4   bunches broccoli, cooked
½ cup melted butter or margarine
½   cup flour
2   cups milk, heated
1   cup whipped cream
½   tsp Worcestershire
1½ tbsp Parmesan cheese
1   jigger dry sherry
      Salt and pepper to taste
½   cup Hollandaise sauce

Lay broccoli in a greased large flat casserole and cover with slices of the chicken. In a separate pan melt the butter or margarine, blend in the flour and add the milk, stirring until smooth and thickened. Add the cream, seasonings, wine and cheese, and the Hollandaise.

Pour the sauce over the chicken, sprinkle Parmesan cheese on top and run the casserole in the oven until hot. Turn the broiler on to brown the cheese. Add a dash of extra sherry before serving if you like.

SERVES 10

MY OWN BROILERS

½ broiler per person
1   bottle garlic French dressing, as needed
      Butter or margarine

Marinate the broilers in the dressing for an hour or so. Drain. Place broilers on the broiler rack, but 4 inches from the unit. (This is unorthodox, I believe. Slower broiling makes for tenderness.)

Broil, turning once or twice and adding a little of the butter or margarine as needed. Baste once with the drained marinade. Broilers are done when the skin side turns golden brown and the underside is no longer pink. Take your time on this, many a broiler has been served with red juice still running out.

Serve on a hot platter garnished with toast triangles and sprigs of watercress, parsley, or bits of lettuce.

CHICKEN BORLANDIA

1 fowl, cut up
Flour, salt, pepper, paprika, powdered garlic
Shortening
Milk to half-cover the fowl
Baby carrots (the same as onions)
Baby onions (allow 2 or 3 per serving)
2 cans mushrooms (or 1 large can)
Parsley, chopped

Dredge the fowl in flour, salt, pepper, paprika, powdered garlic, in a paper bag. Sauté in the shortening until golden brown. Remove, place in a greased casserole. Add milk to half-cover the chicken. Bake in a moderate oven (350°). When the chicken browns, turn it, and add carrots, onions and mushrooms (drained).

Continue baking until the chicken is tender (test with a fork).

Sprinkle chopped parsley on top, and serve in the casserole.
Serve with a salad and crunchy bread.

SERVES 4–6, depending on the size of the fowl

"And there you are, or should be," says Barbara Borland. As a writer, gardener, housekeeper, hostess, and hiking companion for her husband, Hal, she chooses easy-to-fix dishes.

This freezes well, or can be made the day before.

CHICKEN WITH WINE

1 3-lb frying chicken, cut in quarters
2 tbsp butter or margarine
½ cup dry white table wine
1 can (medium) mushrooms
1 cup cream
Salt, pepper, paprika
1 tbsp orange juice

In a deep kettle, sauté the chicken in the butter until golden brown. Cover and cook slowly until tender (about 40 minutes), adding a little water if it gets dry. When the chicken is tender, keep it hot on a warm platter. Add the mushrooms to the juice in the kettle, and gradually add the wine. Stir cream in gradually, add seasonings and orange juice, and when hot and thick, pour over the chicken.

SERVES 4

TURKEY TETRAZZINI

4   tbsp butter or margarine
4   tbsp flour
2   cups well-seasoned turkey stock
½   lb fresh mushrooms, sliced
2   tbsp butter or margarine
2   tbsp sherry
1   cup table cream
2½   cups diced cooked turkey
½   lb spaghetti
½   cup Parmesan cheese, grated

Melt butter and blend in flour, cook until smooth. Add stock and again cook until smooth and thick, stirring constantly. Sauté the mushrooms in 2 tablespoons butter or margarine, and add to sauce along with the sherry and cream, and turkey.

Meanwhile, cook the spaghetti in boiling salted water until tender. Drain. In a greased 8-by-12-inch baking pan, put half the spaghetti. Cover with half the turkey mixture. Add the rest of the spaghetti and turkey. Top with cheese. Bake in a moderate oven (350°) until browned and bubbly. (It takes about 25 minutes.)

SERVES 6

TURKEY CROQUETTES

3 tbsp butter	2 cups finely diced turkey (left
1/3 cup flour	over from the holiday).
2 tsp grated onion	3/4 dry bread crumbs
1 tsp seasoned salt	1 egg
1 cup hot milk	Salad oil
1 egg yolk	

Melt butter in a saucepan. Take from heat and blend in flour. Gradually add milk and cook over medium heat. Add onion. When very thick (about 10 minutes) take from heat and stir in egg yolk. Cook about 2 minutes longer, stirring. Add turkey. Spread the mixture in a shallow pan and refrigerate at least 1½ hours. Then form into croquettes and roll in the crumbs. Chill again on a wire rack. Beat the egg with ¼ cup water and dip the croquettes in, roll again in crumbs and chill 30 minutes more. When ready to fry, heat oil in a heavy kettle, using enough to cover the croquettes. Heat to 300° on deep-frying thermometer or until a cube of bread browns quickly when dropped in. Fry croquettes a few at a time, drain on paper towels. Serve with leftover turkey gravy, or cream of mushroom soup diluted with ⅓ can of water.

SERVES 4-6

The packaged bread crumbs are easier to use. This sounds like a lot of chilling and rechilling, but you can make them ahead of time and fry at the last minute. Serve with broiled tomatoes or asparagus spears, cranberry sauce, brown-and-serve rolls, and coffee. Fruit dessert, please.

NEW YEAR'S TURKEY LOAF

1   cup spaghetti
1   qt water
2   cups diced turkey
¼ cup melted butter or turkey fat
1½ cups milk
3   beaten eggs
¼ cup chopped green pepper and pimiento

Break spaghetti into small pieces and cook in 1 quart boiling salted water, for 7 minutes. Drain and rinse quickly in hot water. Mix spaghetti with diced turkey, then stir in melted butter or turkey fat, milk, eggs, pepper, and pimiento. Pack into a loaf pan, top with crumbs and some dabs of butter, and bake at 325° for 45 minutes. Serve with a can of hot undiluted mushroom soup.

SERVES 4–6

Leftover turkey can seem to be a chore, but try it this way and nobody complains.

ROAST DUCKLING

Wipe with a damp clean cloth and place duckling on a rack in shallow open roasting pan, breast up.

Stuff wishbone cavity lightly, and fasten neck skin to back with skewer. Stuff body cavity, and close openings with skewers or cord. Tie drumsticks to body with a cord.

Roast in a slow oven (325°). Do not add water, and do not sear. Do not cover or baste. Spoon extra fat from the pan as it drips down.

Turn duckling, when almost done, to brown the underparts. A 5-pound duckling takes 2½ to 3 hours' roasting. Always test for doneness by moving the drumstick; when it moves easily up and down, the meat is tender.

STUFFING

You may use quartered tart apples, halved onions, celery for the stuffing. Or you may use your favorite bread stuffing. In this case skimp on the melted butter or margarine, as the duckling has plenty of fat.

GRAVY

You may make a regular gravy with the chopped cooked giblets stirred in. Or you may prefer:

ORANGE SAUCE

2 tbsp butter or margarine	Grated rind of one orange
2 tbsp flour	Dash of salt
1 cup water	1 tbsp sugar (or more if you
¼ cup concentrated orange juice	want it very sweet)

Melt the fat over low heat, stir in flour and blend. Add the remaining ingredients and cook, stirring, until thickened.

Serve hot.

SERVES 4

HURRICANE DUCK

Leftover duck (or turkey or chicken)
1 box instant rice
1 can (1 large or 2 small) mushrooms
Diced green pepper and onion
Salt, pepper, paprika
1 can condensed mushroom or chicken soup

Remove all meat from the bones of the duckling. Meanwhile bring the water to a boil for the rice (follow the directions on the package) over your charcoal grill in a 1-quart kettle. Set the grill in your fireplace hearth. When the rice is added, cover and set on the hearth for 10 minutes. Meanwhile sauté onion and pepper in another kettle over the grill, adding butter or margarine as needed. Add the cut-up duck. Add the rice and stir lightly. Then add as much of the condensed soup as necessary to make duck hurricane creamy. If it is too thick, add a little fresh or canned milk.

Cook until the duck is bubbling.

SERVES according to how much duck you have and how many hungry people are waiting.

Adding a few ripe pitted olives, if you have them, is a fine idea. The hurricane duck will keep warm on the hearth while you boil enough water for instant coffee or tea. Serve with a tossed salad, if you have any greens, and fresh fruit for dessert, if you have any fresh fruit!

CORNISH HENS ROSÉ

2 Cornish hens
⅔ cup precooked rice
½ cup water
6 tbsp rosé wine
   Dash of pepper, nutmeg,
     allspice

¼ tsp salt
½ tsp sugar
2 tbsp raisins
2 tbsp butter or margarine
2 tbsp blanched, slivered
   almonds

Rinse hens, removing any excess fat and waste inside. Combine rice and water. Bring to a quick boil, fluffing with a fork. Add wine, seasonings and raisins. Cover, remove from heat and let stand 10 minutes. Melt butter, stir in almonds over low heat. Brown lightly, then add to rice mixture. Stuff lightly into hens.

BASTING SAUCE

2 tbsp rosé wine
1 tbsp butter or margarine
1 tsp lemon juice

Combine and brush hens with mixture.

Roast, uncovered, in a 450° oven for 15 minutes. Lower to 350° and roast ½ hour longer, basting once or twice.

GRAVY

½ tbsp butter or margarine
½ tbsp lemon juice
   Dash of Cayenne

4 tbsp currant jelly
2 whole cloves
¼ cup water

Combine, simmer 5 minutes. Strain. Add ¼ cup rosé wine. Add to pan juices. Thicken, if desired, with a little cornstarch.

SERVES 4

ROCK CORNISH GAME HEN

6 small game hens, cleaned, fresh or frozen
3 tbsp butter or margarine
3 tbsp olive oil
2 cups dry white table wine
 Salt and pepper to taste
6 shallots, chopped (or young green onion tops)
2 cups button mushrooms

Heat the oil and butter or margarine in a heavy pan. Brown the hens lightly, turning to brown evenly. Add wine and seasonings, cover, and cook for about 20 minutes (if frozen, cook until tender when pierced with a fork). Then add the shallots and mushrooms and cook 20 minutes longer.

Lay the birds on a hot platter and pour the sauce from the pan over them.

SERVES 6

CORNISH HENS MARSEILLE

3 tbsp butter
¼ tsp garlic salt
¼ tsp salt
⅛ tsp black pepper
2 tbsp crumbs
2 Cornish hens, split
½ cup dry white wine
1 medium-sized tomato,
      seeded, peeled and diced
3 scallions, chopped fine
½ cup sour cream

Blend the first 5 ingredients and spread over the hens. Place hens in a shallow open pan and roast for 30 minutes in a hot oven (400°). Then pour the wine over and continue cooking 20 to 25 minutes, basting from time to time. Add the tomato and scallions during cooking. Remove hens from pan and place on a warm platter. Blend the sour cream with the pan juices and pour over.

SERVES 2–4

I like this way of cooking Rock Cornish hens because it keeps them from being too dry and brings out the delicate flavor. Serve with fluffy rice and a green salad. If you are serving four, add something like spoon bread, because those hens are never very big.

Vegetables

IN THE WHOLE WORLD OF COOKERY, NOTHING IS MORE IM-
portant than vegetables. For some reason, many of the most expensive
restaurants do not serve vegetables tempting enough to bother with. I
have often eaten in places where the lobster bisque is a dream, the
entree delectable, the salad crisp and tangy, the dessert a triumph. But
the vegetable might as well have been left in the kitchen. I do not know
whether this is because those gourmet chefs don't waste their talent on
string beans and beets or whether the vegetables are cooked ahead and
reheated while that French sauce is being flamed. I just know it is so.

When we had our first vegetable garden, my education began, because we planted enough vegetables to furnish the state of Connecticut. We canned them, we froze them, and we ate them day after day all
season long. So I began to learn to cook them in different ways and to
cook them with care.

Before that, I had spent many hours in city markets trying to find
vegetables that were edible. I tried all the varieties of canned vegetables

too, and began to work my way through frozen ones. But my love affair with vegetables began when the first sun-ripened tomatoes came to the kitchen from the garden. I am not so concerned with all the minerals and vitamins in them as how good they taste. If you cook them properly, the minerals stay there anyway.

If you have canned vegetables, they can be made interesting. I drain the juice from the can and add seasonings (canned vegetables have very little) and reduce the juice about half by simmering. Then I add the vegetables, butter, seasoned pepper and salt (check as you go along on this). For peas and beans, I use a little thin cream, and chopped canned mushrooms or grated onion. A dash of sugar helps lima beans and corn. Rosemary gives string beans a nice lift, and a mint leaf does peas no harm.

Cook frozen vegetables covered, on low heat. If the directions call for added liquid, I cut the amount called for. The frost in the vegetables will provide more than you think. When I add liquid, I seldom use water, but, instead, chicken or beef broth. I use half a bouillon cube in half a cup or so of water. Spinach is better thawed before cooking if you have time. I often stir a little horseradish in this or a half cup of cream of mushroom soup.

If you have tired corn, you can make it taste better by adding milk to the water you cook it in and a spoonful of sugar to replace the sugar lost because the corn was around too long. If you can possibly get corn just picked, run, don't walk, to the boiling kettle of salted water and cook it about 3 or 4 minutes. Butter it lavishly with melted butter (a butter brush helps).

Serve vegetables so they look attractive. Use paprika on pale ones, chopped parsley on tomatoes, and broiled mushroom caps on almost any (the canned caps are excellent). I sometimes stir sour cream in string beans or add some cottage cheese. Try to get a color contrast in the vegetables you are serving; the eye is a stern critic. Mashed potatoes and cauliflower together have no charm, but with scarlet tomatoes or emerald peppers they look inviting.

Always use as little liquid as possible; remember the vegetables will cook in the steam and keep crisper. If you drown them, you lose the flavor and texture. Winter carrots tend to have a musty taste, but sliced thin and cooked in chicken broth and seasonings, they are improved.

Never pay any attention to people who say they hate vegetables. Just cook vegetables with imagination and put them on the table and see what happens!

HELEN'S ASPARAGUS SUPREME

2 cans asparagus stalks   1 cup grated Parmesan cheese
2 cans large green peas   3 egg yolks, beaten
2 tbsp butter   3 egg whites, beaten stiff
2 tbsp flour   Cracker crumbs (about 1 cup)

Drain the vegetables, saving the juice. Melt 2 tablespoons butter in a saucepan. Blend in 2 tablespoons flour and slowly add vegetable juice, using about 2 cups. If there is not enough juice, make up the amount with top milk. Place the asparagus and peas in alternate layers in a greased shallow casserole. Add beaten egg yolks to the sauce, then fold in beaten whites. Pour the sauce in the casserole, lifting the vegetables up with a spatula to let the sauce spread around them. Sprinkle half the crumbs in the casserole as you add the sauce, then top with the remaining half. Season to taste. Bake in a moderate (350°) oven about 25 minutes, or until bubbly and brown on top.

SERVES 4–6

This is an elegant dish for a luncheon with hot biscuits and a green salad. The trick is not to stir the vegetables and sauce together as it breaks the asparagus tips.

BANANA SCALLOPS

4   bananas
1/2 cup fine corn crumbs or cornmeal
1½ tsp salt
1   egg, slightly beaten, or
1/4 cup undiluted evaporated milk or thin cream
    Melted oil or butter

Add salt to egg or milk. Slice peeled bananas crosswise into 1-inch-thick pieces. Dip into egg or milk, then roll in crumbs, coating well. Heat oil or fat in a heavy frying pan. Have it about an inch deep. Heat until a cube of bread browns in 40 seconds. Fry about 2 minutes, until brown and tender.

SERVES 4

I use half salad oil and half butter for the frying.

PINTO BEANS

2 cups dry pinto beans	1 bud garlic
4 cups cold water	7 tbsp chili powder
½ lb salt pork (cut in 2-inch dice)	2 tbsp flour
	Salt to taste

Put the beans into a large heavy kettle with the water, salt pork, garlic, and 1 teaspoon of the chili powder. Bring to a boil and simmer gently 4 hours, adding more water if the beans tend to get dry. Taste and add more salt if needed. Continue to simmer until the beans have swelled and are tender. Thirty minutes before serving blend the flour and remaining chili powder with 3 tablespoons water from the bean pot and add to the pot to thicken the sauce.

SERVES 4–6

This dish is even better the next day—that is, if you have any left over.

RANCHO BAKED BEANS

2 cups chopped onion
1 lb ground beef
¼ tsp salt
1 cup tomato catsup
2 tbsp prepared mustard
2 tsp vinegar
1 large can pork and beans in tomato sauce
1 can (1 lb) kidney beans, drained.

Brown beef and onions, add salt, catsup, mustard, vinegar. Mix well. Add pork and beans and kidney beans. Pour in 2-quart casserole or 9″ × 13″ dish. Bake at 400° for 30 minutes.

SERVES 8

This is a meal in one dish and it is so easy to have the makings on hand.
"Well, of course we didn't expect to stay for supper—we only just dropped in . . ."

MARGARET'S BEAN-POT BEANS

1 lb Old York California beans. Soak in plenty of water overnight. Drain. Put into boiling water plus a *small* pinch of soda. Boil just till skins crack when you blow on 'em.

While beans are boiling, put into the bean pot:

> 1   small onion
> ⅓ cup molasses
> ½ tsp ground mustard
> 1   big tbsp brown (or white) sugar
>   *Scant* ¼ tsp salt and some hunks of salt pork.

Drain beans, put in pot, fill pot with boiling water. Bake at about 300° for 8 hours adding hot water as it boils down. (If you use yellow-eye or any other kind of bean, the cooking time will be shorter.)

SERVES 4–6

Margaret Stanger lives up a hill in a small Cape Cod house. A round table under a wide window is set with a red-checked cloth, charming ware, and the bean pot, bubbling over with rich juices. A fire in the fireplace casts a warm glow on Early American pine and maple as supper is served.

"Now let me tell you a story," says Margaret — and the evening is merry indeed.

BRAISED CELERY

> 1   bunch celery
>   Butter or margarine
> ½ cup chicken stock, or 1 chicken bouillon
>   cube dissolved in ½ cup boiling water

Wash and separate the celery stalks. Cut in 3-in. pieces. Sauté gently in the butter or margarine until just beginning to brown. Add the stock, season with freshly ground pepper, cover, and cook until the celery is tender.

SERVES 4–6

Celery is a dieter's delight, but raw stalks do get tiresome.

GREEN BEANS WITH SWISS CHEESE SAUCE

1   tbsp butter
1   tbsp flour
1/2 tsp each salt and sugar
1/8 tsp pepper
1/4 cup milk
1/2 tsp grated onion
1/2 cup sour cream

2   cans (1 lb each) small
    whole green beans,
    drained
1 1/2 cups shredded Swiss cheese
1/3 cup cornflake crumbs
2   tbsp melted butter

In a small pan melt butter and thoroughly blend in flour, salt, sugar, and pepper; cook, stirring until bubbly. Blend in milk. Remove from the heat and stir in the onion and sour cream till well mixed. Combine sauce with green beans (drained) and cheese and turn into buttered 1 1/2-quart casserole. Combine cornflake crumbs with melted butter and spread on top. Bake in hot oven (400°) for 20 minutes. Good with beef or lamb roast.

SERVES 4 nicely

Some people say they don't like canned vegetables. Try them with this.

CONNIE'S KIDNEY BEAN CASSEROLE

2   No. 2 cans kidney beans,
    drained
3   small onions, cut fine
1   small can tomato paste

1/4 cup chopped ham
    Bacon strips
1/2 green pepper, chopped
1   cup red wine (Burgundy)

Mix the beans with the onions, green pepper, ham and tomato paste. Pour over the red wine. Place the mixture in a greased casserole and lay the bacon strips over. Bake about 30 minutes in a moderate (350°) oven.

SERVES 4

If you can get the Almaden Mountain Red wine it is especially good. Connie serves this with hot French rolls and a green salad and plenty of coffee.

CHILI BEANS

1 cup pinto beans
  Cold water to cover
  Water for boiling.
  Medium-sized piece of salt pork

Soak beans overnight in cold water. In the morning drain the beans, add water to cover. Add salt pork. Bring to a boil, reduce heat and simmer 5 or 6 hours. Keep water just at a boil if possible. When the beans are almost tender let the water boil down. Put the beans in a warm serving dish and pour over the hot chili sauce (see basic chili sauce recipe, page 240).

SERVES 4

Add a tossed green salad and hot coffee for a good supper on a winter night.

BARBECUED CORN CASSEROLE

2 large cans whole-kernel corn, drained,
    or an equal amount of frozen
8 frankfurters
1 8-oz can Spanish tomato sauce
¼ cup lemon juice
4 tbsp diced onion
1 tsp dry mustard
Salt and pepper to taste
Dash of garlic salt

Season the corn with salt and pepper and spread in the bottom of a greased casserole or baking dish. Prick the frankfurters with a fork and arrange on the corn. Mix the remaining ingredients and bring to boiling point. Pour over the frankfurters. Bake in a moderate oven (350°) for 25 to 30 minutes.

SERVES 6

CORN PUDDING

3 cups corn, fresh, cooked or canned
2 eggs
2 cups top milk
¼ cup sugar
¼ cup fine bread or cracker crumbs
½ tsp salt
⅛ tsp pepper

Beat eggs slightly, and then beat in top milk. Add sugar, bread or cracker crumbs, salt, pepper and corn. Mix and pour into a greased baking dish. Set in a pan of water and bake until it sets and the tip of a knife inserted in it comes out clean. This will be 40 to 50 minutes at 325°.

SERVES 4 or you can squeeze it to 5

My mother made this often because canned corn was always available in our little town. In those days we ate what was in season supplemented with canned corn, peas, beans, and tomatoes. Corn pudding was very good in winter when cabbage, carrots, and squash got pretty tiresome. It's even better if you use fresh corn but actually not too much better.

SUMMER CASSEROLE

2 medium onions sliced
1 medium or 2 small zucchini
   squash
1 cup diced celery

2 medium sliced tomatoes
1 can condensed cheese soup
   Seasoning to taste
⅓ cup water or broth

In a greased casserole layer the vegetables. Add water and seasoning to the soup and pour over the vegetables. Top with buttered crumbs and bake in a moderate oven (325°) until bubbling.

SERVES 4

This may be expanded or reduced according to the size of the vegetables. If the tomatoes are not fully ripe, you may need an extra one. Go easy on the salt, as the cheese soup is fairly salty, but use plenty of seasoned pepper or freshly grated pepper.

CONNECTICUT CORN PUDDING

2 cups corn (canned, frozen or fresh)
6 strips bacon, fried until crisp and drained
½ green pepper, diced
1 small onion, diced
½ cup soft bread crumbs
2 eggs, beaten
2 cups top milk
1 tsp salt
½ cup buttered crumbs

Drain bacon on a paper towel. Then sauté the pepper and onion in 2 tablespoons of the bacon drippings. Add corn, bread crumbs, eggs, milk, seasoning and bacon broken in bits. Stir together and pour into a greased 1½-quart casserole. Top with buttered crumbs and bake in a moderate oven (375°) for about 40 minutes.

SERVES 6

This is a good supper dish, served with broiled tomatoes, a green salad, buttermilk biscuits (buy ready to bake), and coffee.

CURRIED CORN AND PEAS

1 pkg frozen whole kernel corn
1 pkg frozen peas
½ cup water
3 tbsp butter
½ tsp curry powder
   Seasoned salt and pepper to taste

Put the vegetables in a heavy saucepan and add the water. When water boils, cover, and cook the vegetables until tender but not soft. Add butter, curry, and salt and pepper.

SERVES 4–6

You may have to add more water if the vegetables seem dry. This dish is a nice way to vary those frozen vegetables which do get monotonous in midwinter.

BAKED STUFFED CUCUMBERS

1　large cucumber
½ cup milk
½ cup water
　　Stuffing (your choice of: buttered bread crumbs
　　　topped with cheese; creamed finnan haddie;
　　　leftover meat chopped together with a small
　　　onion and moistened with a little cream sauce;
　　　or leftover fish treated the same way).

Split cucumber lengthwise, remove the seeds, and steam closely covered until half tender. Remove from the steamer well before the pieces are soft. Fill center cavity with stuffing. Top with buttered crumbs. Place in a baking pan and pour milk and water around the cucumbers. Bake in a hot oven for 20 minutes. Serve on a hot platter deep enough to hold the milk in which they have baked.

Jill and I used to make a whole supper of these and it took 4 cucumbers to serve the two of us. I do not know who started the idea that cucumbers have to be eaten raw, but it was a mistake.

SAUTÉED EGGPLANT

1　medium eggplant
2　eggs, slightly beaten
　　Flour
　　Salt, pepper, paprika

Slice the eggplant without peeling in slices about ¼ inch thick. Dip the slices alternately in the egg and the flour, and season well.

Sauté in a heavy skillet with butter or margarine or bacon drippings. Turn once. When golden brown and tender to a fork, they are done.

Allow 2 or 3 slices per person according to how big the circumference of the slices.

There are many delicious ways to cook this purple fruit of the garden from stuffed, Creole, to Eggplant Caviar. But at Stillmeadow we serve it this way, since this is the only way I am not allergic (slightly) to it.

EGGPLANT CAVIAR

(Backlajannaya Ickra)

1 large eggplant
4 large onions, chopped fine and browned in vegetable oil
1 green pepper, chopped
2 tbsp chopped green leaves of dill
Juice of half a lemon
1 tbsp sugar
1 small can tomato paste
Salt and pepper
2 tbsp salad oil

Prick eggplant with a fork in a few places and bake for 2 hours in a medium hot oven. When ready, peel off the skin and chop the eggplant fine or run it through a meat grinder. Add onions, green pepper, dill, lemon juice, sugar, tomato paste, salt and pepper to taste, and salad oil. Mix it up, put in a greased casserole and bake, uncovered, in medium oven for 1 hour. Serve cold as an appetizer, relish, or filling for sandwiches. Delicious on dark pumpernickel.

SERVES 6-8

I first had this in the Russian Village near Southbury. It was a wild winter night and the wind howled the way wolves do in Russian plays. Three of us spoke nothing but plain common English, but we understood the beauty of the old Russian songs the rest sang because the language of the heart is universal. We also understood how elegant the dinner was from the eggplant caviar to a dessert like an ice palace.

EGGPLANT STUFFED PEPPERS

1   large eggplant, or 3 small ones
6   eggs, well beaten
½ cup iceberg lettuce, finely shredded
1   tsp poultry dressing
1   tsp allspice
1   tsp salt
3   tbsp olive oil
     Speck of red pepper
3   tbsp milk
½ cup Parmesan cheese, grated
½ cup sharp Cheddar cheese, grated
10 to 12 saltines, finely crushed
8 to 10 green peppers, seeded and cut in half

Wash and dice eggplant. Boil until just soft. Drain and chop. Beat eggs and add rest of ingredients. Mix, add to chopped eggplant and mix well. Add another crushed cracker or two to absorb any excess liquid. Heap pepper shells with eggplant mixture, arrange in shallow baking pan. Dribble more olive oil over all and bake in 375° oven about one hour.

SERVES 4

HARVARD BEETS

1   13½-oz can beets, sliced or diced, drained
½ cup sugar
½ tbsp cornstarch
½ cup vinegar

Mix sugar and cornstarch and add to vinegar. Boil together for 5 minutes. Pour over beets, and let stand in a warm place for at least 30 minutes. Reheat before serving.

SERVES 4

I don't know whether Harvard invented this or not. It does not fit with my image of Harvard. But whoever invented it deserves a medal.

BIBI'S BROCCOLI SOUFFLÉ

1½ cups chopped cooked broccoli, or asparagus, or
    spinach
3   eggs
1½ cups mild cheese, diced or grated
2   tbsp butter or margarine
2   tbsp flour
¾   cup milk
1   tsp chopped onion

Make cream sauce with butter or margarine, flour, milk. Add onion and cheese, stir until cheese melts. Add beaten egg yolks and vegetable. Fold in stiffly beaten whites of eggs. Turn into a greased casserole or baking dish, and bake in a moderate oven (350°) about an hour. Since this is like a custard, it helps to put the dish in a pan of hot water in the oven. It is done when it begins to draw away from the side of the casserole or when a knife inserted in the center comes out clean.

SERVES 4–6

With a grilled ham steak, this makes company fare. Add fresh, chilled, sliced tomatoes bedded on lettuce and drizzled with garlic French dressing for the last word.

NEW CABBAGE SPECIAL

2   cups finely shredded green cabbage
¾ cup top milk
2   tsp butter
¼ tsp salt (or more)
¼ tsp seasoned pepper

Combine ingredients in the top of a double boiler. Cover and cook over hot water about 15 minutes or until tender.

SERVES 2

Try this on someone who says cabbage doesn't agree with him/her.

SWEET AND SOUR CABBAGE

1 qt red cabbage	4 tbsp brown sugar
2 tart apples	2 tbsp wine vinegar
2 tbsp butter, bacon fat, or	2 tbsp flour
margarine	Salt and pepper to taste

Shred the cabbage fine, add salt and pepper, and the apples sliced. Heat fat in heavy skillet and add cabbage and apples. Pour boiling water over to cover and cook until tender. Sprinkle the flour over and add sugar and vinegar. Let simmer a little longer.

SERVES 4–6

This was a favorite dish in Wisconsin when I was growing up. Dinner with a German farm family always meant a huge dish of sweet and sour cabbage along with fresh ham roast, mashed potatoes, six or seven kinds of jellies and preserves and relishes, and hot light rolls and at least two kinds of pie.

CAULIFLOWER CASSEROLE

1   medium head cauliflower
½ cup dairy sour cream
½ cup shredded sharp process American cheese
1   tsp toasted sesame seeds
Salt and pepper.

Break the cauliflower into flowerets and cook them, covered, in a small amount of boiling water with ½ tsp salt. Cook until tender, about 8 to 10 minutes, and drain well. Put half the cauliflower in a greased 1-quart casserole, season with salt and pepper. Spread with half of the sour cream and half of the cheese. Add rest of the cauliflower and top with the remaining sour cream and cheese and the sesame seeds. Bake at 350° (moderate oven) for 10 minutes or until browned.

To toast sesame seeds place in shallow pan at 350° for 10 minutes, shaking the pan now and then.

SERVES 4

MELANZANA AL PREZZEMOLO

1 large eggplant
1 cup oil
2 cloves garlic
  Large bunch parsley
  Salt to taste

Slice and cube eggplant. Sauté split garlic cloves in oil, add chopped parsley and eggplant, and stir 15 minutes. As the eggplant shrinks in cooking there will be room for it all in the frying pan! No more oil need be added since eggplant makes its own juices.

SERVES 4

This is served in Italy as an entree by itself. It can be served as a main dish with rice. Simply boil rice in lots of water for 19 minutes. Garnish with sprigs of parsley or with paprika.

BARBECUED LIMA BEANS

Soak 2 cups dried lima beans in cold water to cover overnight. Drain, cover with fresh cold water and cook until tender with ¼ pound diced salt pork, or an end of bacon.
Drain, reserving 1½ cups of the liquor.

1	sliced onion	1½ tsp chili powder	
1	clove garlic	1	tsp salt
¼	cup fat or drippings	1	can tomato soup diluted
1½ tbsp dry mustard			with half a can of water
2	tbsp Worcestershire	⅓	cup vinegar

Brown onion and garlic in fat. Add remaining ingredients and the liquor from the beans. Simmer 5 minutes. Place beans and sauce in a deep casserole, top with thin slices of salt pork, and bake in a hot oven (375°) for 30 minutes, adding more bean liquor if needed.

SERVES 6

This is a perfect main hot dish for a buffet. Thin sliced cold ham and salad do no harm. Lemon bisque adds the last touch.

STUFFED MUSHROOMS

1 lb medium-sized fresh mush-
    rooms (about 12)
1 cup finely chopped pecans
3 tbsp chopped parsley
¼ cup softened butter
1 clove garlic, crushed
    Dash of thyme
    Salt and pepper to taste
½ cup heavy cream.

Stem the mushrooms and wipe with a damp cloth. Place them in a shallow casserole hollow side up. Chop the stems and mix with the other ingredients except cream. Fill the mushroom caps with the stuffing, then pour the cream over. Bake in a moderate oven (350°) for 25 minutes or until tender.

SERVES 4

MUSHROOM CASSEROLE

1½ lbs fresh mushrooms
½   cup water
     Bread crumbs or prepared stuffing
⅔   cup grated Parmesan cheese
5   tbsp olive oil
     Seasoned salt, pepper, garlic salt

Stem the mushrooms and chop stems. Steam stems and caps in the water for 10 minutes, or until mushrooms are fairly tender. Strain. Mix stems with remaining ingredients. Lay caps in a greased casserole and put the stem mixture over. Bake in a moderate oven (350°) 30 minutes or until crumbs are brown.

SERVES 6

If you are fortunate enough to live near a mushroom grower and can buy baskets of the cream-colored beauties, this is a good way to use extras. Such mushrooms do not need washing, just wipe with a damp cloth. If you have run-of-the-market mushrooms, wash them quickly in running cold water. They will turn dark if left in water.

ONION PIE

8 onions sliced thin   ⅓ cup milk
3 tbsp shortening   1 egg
2 cups flour   ½ cup thin cream
2 tsp baking-powder   Seasoning
½ tsp salt   6 or 7 broiled bacon strips
⅓ cup shortening

Cook onions in shortening until golden but not brown. Meanwhile sift the dry ingredients together, cut in the ⅓ cup shortening, work it in until the texture is like coarse cornmeal. Moisten with the milk. Mix into a ball and knead on a floured board. Roll out and fit the dough into a 10-in. pie pan.

Spread the onions over when slightly cool, and season with salt and pepper.

Beat the egg with the cream and pour over all.

Bake 20 minutes at 450° (hot oven), or until the pie is slightly brown on top and the biscuit well done. Sprinkle bacon over the top and serve.

SERVES 4–6

This makes a one-dish luncheon with a green salad and coffee. If you want dessert, make it a light one.

GLAZED ONIONS

12 large onions, peeled   ⅔ cup honey
½ cup melted butter   ⅓ cup catsup

Parboil the onions in boiling, salted water until partly tender. Place them in a shallow baking dish (glass if you have it). Blend the remaining ingredients and pour over the onions.

Bake in a moderate oven (350°) until the onions are tender (test with a fork) and the glaze is thick and almost candied. Baste frequently.

SERVES 8–10

This is what we always serve with the Thanksgiving turkey and the Easter ham. I have known even non-onion eaters to take a second on this dish.

SUPPER ONIONS

1 large onion per person
Prepared poultry stuffing
1 cup or more consommé or bouillon, as needed
Milk
Butter or margarine, melted

Peel the onions and with an apple-corer or a grapefruit knife remove the centers (save for soups or salads). Pack prepared stuffing well into the centers. Brush the onions with milk. Spoon a small amount of the butter or margarine in the centers of the onions, then place the onions in a greased shallow baking pan. Pour the consommé or bouillon around them. Bake in a slow oven (325°) until the onions are tender when pierced with a fork. Baste occasionally.

You may sprinkle grated Parmesan cheese on the tops just before the onions are done. Serve with broiled bacon or Canadian bacon, a green salad, and hot crusty poppy-seed rolls.

FRENCH PEAS

2   lbs fresh peas (2¼ cups)
½ cup lettuce (cut in pieces)
½ tbsp shallots or onions, cut fine
1   tsp sugar
1½ tbsp butter

Bruise peas slightly with your hands. Put in a saucepan and cover with cold water. Bring to a boil, add lettuce, shallots, and seasonings. Cover. Cook about 20 minutes, or until peas are tender.

SERVES 4

This recipe is particularly useful when the peas are just any old market peas. Don't mash them to a pulp, just run your hands through and squeeze a few times. This breaks the tough shell and lets the flavor in.

KING'S ARMS CREAMED CELERY

1 bunch celery
Cream sauce
Chopped pecans

Separate, clean the celery, cut in bite-size pieces and cook in boiling, salted water until tender. Meanwhile make the cream sauce (see CREAM SAUCE). Place the celery in a greased casserole, pour the sauce over, and add chopped pecans (use ½ cup to a cup of cream sauce).

Top with buttered bread crumbs. Bake in a moderate oven (350°) until browned on top.

The amount is variable. 2 cups of cooked celery to 1 cup of cream sauce serves 4–6, but celery stalks differ. I first had this in Williamsburg and begged the recipe from the chef. He told me pecan halves would do equally well, and I tried it, and he was right! At King's Arms this was served with fried chicken, a tossed salad, hot cornsticks, and the Green Gage Plum Ice Cream.

SPINACH TIMBALES

4 slices bacon, diced
3½ cups cooked spinach
       (fresh, frozen, or canned)
3 eggs, slightly beaten
   Salt and pepper to taste

Fry bacon until crisp and add the drained spinach. Then add eggs and seasonings. Turn into greased custard cups or ramekins and bake in a moderate oven (350°) until set. This takes around 35 minutes, according to the size of your containers. Unmold and serve with cheese, or with a cream sauce, or with cream of mushroom soup, heated and diluted with half a can of milk.

SERVES 6

COUNTRY-FRIED POTATOES

½ cup diced salt pork
1 tbsp onion, finely diced
6 raw potatoes, thinly sliced.
   Salt and pepper

Place salt pork in a frying pan over a low flame and fry until a golden brown. Remove the pork from the pan. Add onion and potatoes. Fry until tender and lightly browned. Season with salt and pepper and serve.

SERVES 4–6

At Stillmeadow, we like a real Sunday breakfast. Sometimes is is creamed finnan haddie, sometimes fried tomatoes and broiled bacon. It may also be waffles or pancakes or fillets of flounder, crisp and golden brown. But country-fried potatoes with paper-thin slices of sugar-cured ham may be the best.

I note the diet experts have come right back to the old-fashioned New England rib-sticking breakfasts. Country folk have always known a day's work goes better with a hearty breakfast. Lunch can be buttermilk und a sandwich, but none of this black coffee and orange juice to start the day off.

POTATOES CHANTILLY

4 cups hot mashed potatoes
½ cup heavy cream, whipped
⅓ cup grated cheese (Parmesan is best)

Spread mashed potatoes in a shallow buttered casserole. Spread whipped cream on top and sprinkle with cheese. Bake in a hot oven (400°) for 10 to 15 minutes, or until cheese is melted and top brown.

SERVES 6

This is a nice variation of mashed potatoes and is especially good with cold sliced roast beef or ham.

SCALLOPED POTATOES SUPREME

1   medium-sized potato per person, sliced thin
4   link sausages per person
½ onion per person, thinly sliced
    Flour
    Milk to cover
    Grated Swiss, Parmesan or Cheddar cheese
    Seasonings – salt, pepper, paprika

Use a flat baking dish, preferably glass. Grease it well. Arrange a layer of sliced potatoes in the bottom, next a layer of onion. Season this layer with salt, plenty of freshly ground pepper, paprika. Sprinkle flour over. Sprinkle some of the grated cheese over. Add another layer of potatoes, onions, seasonings and cheese, and a dusting of flour. When the final layer is in the dish, pour the milk over, to barely cover the top layer (heated milk will hurry up cooking time).

Bake in a moderate (350°) oven, covered. Meanwhile partly cook the sausages, just to get some of the fat out, but not all of it. When the potatoes have baked 25 minutes, arrange the drained sausages on top, remove the cover, and finish baking. When the potatoes are tender, it is done.

You may speed this up by boiling the potatoes and onions a few minutes in boiling salted water. This is an elegant dish, because the sausage flavors the whole. Serve with almost any vegetable such as peas, green beans or asparagus.

GRANDMOTHER'S CREAMED POTATOES

Boil potatoes, but not until soft. Place in refrigerator overnight. Peel and slice very thin into a heavy skillet. Salt well and dredge with flour. Add cream to top of slices, but do not cover. Dot with butter. Cook over medium heat (no stirring) until shiny. Add pepper to taste.

Cream should not be thick. Allow one potato per person.

This recipe comes from my friend Mildred Morse, and it was her grandmother's special trick with potatoes. It's good!

RHODE ISLAND SUPPER POTATOES

5   medium potatoes, peeled and sliced thin
½ cup melted butter or margarine
1½ tsp Worcestershire
1¾ tsp salt
¼ tsp paprika

Cook potato slices in boiling salted water for 5 minutes. Drain, and spread them out in a greased baking pan. Pour over the butter or margarine mixed with the seasonings. Bake in a moderately hot oven (375°) until the potatoes are tender, basting frequently with the sauce.

SERVES 4

Serve with thinly sliced cold rare roast beef or sliced boiled ham or cold cuts. Orange and onion salad is a good accompaniment. (Slice oranges and onions thin, arrange on lettuce leaves, dress with plain French dressing.)

POTATO OVALS

6 potatoes	4 tbsp milk
2 tbsp butter	1½ tsp salt
2 tbsp grated onion	Pepper
2 egg yolks, beaten	

Cook potatoes until tender and force through a ricer. Add butter, onion, egg yolks, milk, salt and pepper. Form into oval balls, roll in a little flour, and place around a roast 20 minutes before it is taken from the oven. When nicely browned, remove and serve with the meat.

SERVES 4–6

This is a great help during times when potatoes are poor. It seems to me they are poor most of the time lately, limp and woody. When we raised our own, I never made potato ovals. I scrubbed the potatoes and laid them around the roast and basted them with drippings occasionally and they were crusty outside and flaky-tender inside.

POTATO PANCAKES

8 medium potatoes peeled and grated
Bouillon or beef stock
2 eggs
1 cup all-purpose flour, or more as needed
Salt, pepper, paprika to taste
Butter, margarine, or bacon drippings

Soak the grated potatoes in ice water for a few minutes, then drain and dry well on paper towels. Measure the pulp (the amount will vary according to the size of the potatoes).

Add an equal amount of bouillon or stock to the potatoes, then the eggs, slightly beaten, and the flour and seasonings. Beat well. (I hope you do have an electric beater.) Add more flour, beating constantly, until the batter has the consistency of regular pancake batter. Meanwhile heat the griddle with the fat on it and, when it is hot, drop the batter in spoonfuls on the griddle. Turn once to brown evenly.

SERVES 6

This is a lovely Sunday brunch dish. Crisp bacon or tiny sausages go well with it. A classic served with pot roast.

SWEET POTATO BALLS

2 cups hot mashed sweet potatoes
¼ cup pineapple juice
Crushed cornflakes

Add pineapple juice to potatoes. Beat until smooth; then form into balls the size of a small egg. Roll these in crushed cornflakes, place in a buttered shallow pan and bake in a medium oven for 25 minutes.

SERVES 4-6

The pineapple juice takes away the too-sweet taste of the potatoes.

CANDIED SWEET POTATOES

6 medium sweet potatoes   5 tbsp butter
1 cup syrup   Dash of salt

Cook the sweet potatoes in boiling salted water until nearly done. Peel them and slice lengthwise. Put in a flat greased baking dish so there will be only one layer. Meanwhile heat syrup, butter and salt, and pour over the potatoes. Bake in a moderate oven (350°) until the syrup is candied and the potatoes tender. It takes about an hour.

SERVES 6

I use a commercial canned syrup, but not the pure maple type. This is a good dish with baked ham or roast pork.

SWEET POTATO SOUFFLÉ

2 cups sweet potatoes, cooked and mashed
4 eggs, separated
½ cup milk
¼ cup rum or brandy
4 tbsp butter or margarine
    Salt, Cayenne
1½ tsp grated orange rind

Heat the milk, add the rum or brandy and the butter or margarine. Beat this mixture into the potatoes, adding the seasonings. Beat the egg yolks and add them. Fold in the egg whites, stiffly beaten.

Turn the mixture into a greased casserole. Bake in a hot oven (400°) for 25 minutes or until the soufflé is delicately browned. Serve at once.

SERVES 4–6

If you have an electric mixer, this is especially easy. If you haven't, beat the potatoes with a wooden spoon, then with a rotary beater after adding the liquid. Serve with sliced cold chicken or turkey, fresh or frozen asparagus dressed with butter (no Hollandaise this time). No sweet dessert either, but a bowl of fruit with the inevitable coffee.

BOILED SWEET PEPPERS

Peppers are versatile. They are usually used to add flavor or appearance to other foods, but they may be served as a vegetable, and as such they stand on their own merit.

Remove the stem end, the seeds, and the stringy white veins. Slice into 1/4-in. strips or rounds. Drop in a little boiling salted water and cook 8 minutes, or until tender. Drain, and shake in the pan with melted butter. Season with salt and pepper.

CURRIED ONIONS AND RICE

3 large onions	Pinch of mace or nutmeg
1½ cups cooked rice	½ tsp salt
¾ cup evaporated milk	3 tbsp melted butter
¼ tsp curry powder	

Slice onions 1/4 in. thick. Cook until tender. Drain. Add remaining ingredients and mix well. Put in greased casserole. Bake. If made ahead, do not add curry till ready to serve, and bake in moderate (350°) oven until bubbly.

SERVES 6

PARSNIP PATTIES

2 cups parsnips, boiled and mashed	2 tbsp flour
	½ tsp salt
1 egg, beaten	⅛ tsp pepper
¼ cup milk	2 tbsp margarine

Combine parsnips, egg, milk, flour, salt, pepper, and margarine, and beat until smooth. Shape into 10 patties, sprinkle lightly with 3 tablespoons flour, and brown in drippings.

SERVES 4

People who won't eat parsnips will eat these and ask what they are.

AUSTRIAN POTATOES

6 medium potatoes
3 tbsp shortening or bacon fat
2 cups cottage cheese
3 tbsp thick sour cream
2 eggs, beaten
1 tsp salt

Wash and peel potatoes, and slice thin. Fry gently in shortening or bacon fat until tender and golden; then turn into a baking dish. Mix together the cottage cheese, sour cream, beaten eggs and salt and pour over the potatoes. Bake in a slow oven (275°) for about 10 minutes, or until the mixture has set.

SHOULD SERVE 6, but has been known to serve only 3

Cottage cheese and sour cream have an affinity for potatoes. Just plain baked potatoes taste better with either spooned over. Don't cut baked potatoes open with a knife, squeeze them gently until they fall open.

ONION PILAF

3 cups rice
¼ lb butter, margarine, or Crisco
1 medium onion, sliced thin
6 cups broth (chicken, lamb or beef)
  Salt and pepper

Melt butter in heavy skillet, add rice. Braise well until butter bubbles. Fry onion in separate pan until golden. Mix with rice. Add broth and seasoning. Stir well. Bake covered at 375° to 400° for 30 minutes. Stir well. Bake 10 minutes more.

SERVES 6

Jill used to make this in the electric skillet unless the oven was on for something else. Keep heat low if you do and add more moisture if needed.

SAVORY SUMMER SQUASH

Summer squash
¼ cup grated cheese, Cheddar or American
3   tbsp grated onion
Salt, pepper, paprika

Slice the squash thin. You should not have to peel it unless it is tough. In that case, remove the center seed portions, too.

Arrange the slices in a greased baking pan, slightly overlapping them. Dot generously with butter or margarine, then sprinkle onion and cheese over.

Add seasonings. Broil 4 inches from the broiler unit until the squash is nicely browned and tender.

A MEDIUM squash serves 4

STUFFED SUMMER SQUASH

Pattypan squash (sometimes called Cimling)
Salt, pepper, paprika
Stuffing

Use the young small Pattypan squash. Scrub them, and put whole in boiling, salted water. Cook until the shell is slightly soft. Remove from water, and cool slightly. Then remove a round section from the stem end and scrape out the seeds. Season the inside of the squash shell with salt, pepper, paprika. Fill with the stuffing and bake in a hot oven about 20 minutes, or until the squash is tender to a fork and the stuffing bubbles.

STUFFING

Use prepared poultry stuffing moistened with top milk (or creamed tuna, or creamed chicken, or creamed peas with mushrooms). Dot with butter or margarine, and sprinkle grated Parmesan cheese on top.

If you must use squash larger than a butter plate, pour a little milk in the baking dish to help tenderize the shell.

This makes a perfect luncheon dish with fresh fruit salad and hot corn muffins and coffee.

FRIED TOMATOES

Ripe or green tomatoes, washed and cut in half
Flour or cornmeal, enough to dredge tomato slices
Salt and pepper
Bacon fat, or butter, or margarine, or cooking oil

Add seasonings to flour or cornmeal and dredge the tomato halves in it. Heat the fat until it is hot but not burning. (A heavy skillet is best.)

Fry the tomatoes, turning once. When they are tender to a fork and browning, remove them from the fire and lay them on a hot platter. Keep warm while you make the gravy.

Stir 2 tablespoons flour into the drippings (or more, according to number you are serving). Add 1 cup top milk or evaporated milk and stir until the gravy boils up and is smooth. Pour over the tomatoes.

If you use green tomatoes, unripe, add a dusting of sugar after you flour them.

Serve on toast triangles.

ALLOW two tomatoes per person. The gravy amounts above make gravy for 2–3 people. Increase amount according to how many you are serving.

For a supper one-dish meal, fry bacon until crisp, remove bacon, and fry the tomatoes. Make the gravy, lay the tomatoes on a hot platter, pour gravy over, top with the crisp bacon.

SPINACH AND COTTAGE CHEESE

¼ cup butter	2 pkgs frozen spinach
½ tsp ground turmeric	⅔ cup creamy cottage cheese
1 tsp ground coriander	1 tbsp sour cream
1 tsp salt	

Melt butter, add spices, cook 5 minutes. Add spinach, cover, cook until thawed and hot. Beat cheese and cream to curds. Add and cook.

SERVES 8

You'll be perfectly safe in serving this to non-spinach eaters. Don't overcook. Spinach shouldn't be mushy unless you go all the way and cream it the way the French do.

FRIED TOMATO BAKE

> Fried tomatoes, 1 medium (or 2 small) to a person
> Butter or margarine
> Buttered crumbs
> Parsley, chopped
> Salt, pepper

Fry the tomatoes (see recipe p. 212). Arrange them in layers in a deep greased casserole or baking dish. Top with buttered crumbs, dot with butter or margarine. Bake in a hot oven (400°) for 20 minutes, or until bubbly. Add parsley 5 minutes before you take from the oven.

This is a lifesaver for the last-minute cook. Who wants to stand watching frying tomatoes (and you cannot leave them a minute) when guests are in the living room having fun? Who wants to take time to fry tomatoes when getting in late from work? Well, not I. These may be fried the night before and put in the casserole ready to bake. Just take them from the refrigerator in time to warm the casserole, if it is glass or earthenware, before subjecting it to the hot oven. You will find that the tomatoes, served carefully, give the illusion of being just fried, and the dish is far, far better than any stewed tomato I have ever met.

SPINACH DE LUXE

> 1 box frozen chopped spinach
> ½ can condensed cream of mushroom soup

Cook the spinach as directed on the package, and, when it is nearly done, stir in the soup. Heat until it bubbles, stirring constantly.

SERVES 2-3

I take a stand on cooking frozen spinach. It should be partially thawed. Otherwise part of it is overcooked before the center has dreamed of thawing. It's easy enough to move that frozen spinach to the lower part of your refrigerator in the morning or the night before. But put a pan under it, as I have yet to find the frozen food of any category that won't leak through the package in time.

This is a very easy but glorified version of creamed spinach and the slight aura of mushroom does no harm at all.

SCALLOPED TOMATOES

1 No. 2 can tomatoes	1 tsp salt
3 strips crumbled broiled bacon	1/8 tsp pepper
1/2 cup diced onions	1 tbsp sugar
1/2 cup grated cheese	Bread crumbs
	Butter or margarine

Turn tomatoes into a buttered casserole. Stir in bacon, onions and cheese. Add salt, pepper, and sugar. Top with bread crumbs and dots of butter. Bake 30 minutes in a moderate oven (350°).

SERVES 4

It is a sad day when garden-ripened tomatoes go by. Those small, rubbery golf balls put up in cellophane have only one use, which is that you can save the cellophane. Canned tomatoes, however, are better than they used to be, and this is a good way to have them.

FLUFFY YELLOW TURNIPS

2 tbsp butter or margarine
1 small onion, finely minced
2 tbsp flour
1 large yellow turnip, about 3 cups, mashed
1/8 tsp pepper
1 tsp salt
2 tbsp brown sugar
2 eggs, separated

Sauté onions in butter until tender but not brown. Add flour and blend well. Peel and cut up turnip. Simmer until tender and mash. Add onion mixture and seasonings to mashed turnip. Blend in beaten egg yolks. Beat egg whites until stiff but not dry. Fold into turnip mixture and pour into 1½-quart buttered casserole. Bake uncovered at 375° for 40 minutes.

SERVES 4–6

Turnips are much maligned. Try them like this and see what happens.

TURNIPS À LA SHIRLEY

1   large yellow turnip
2   tsp brown sugar
½   cup grated Parmesan cheese
    Salt and pepper
1   can beef consommé

Pare and quarter the turnip, then slice the sections in ¼-in. slices. Put in layers in a deep greased casserole, sprinkling sugar and seasonings and cheese between layers. Pour over a can of beef consommé, undiluted. Place casserole in a moderate oven (350°) and bake, covered, for an hour; then bake uncovered until the turnip is fork tender (about half an hour).

SERVES 4–6, depending on size of the turnip

At the end of winter, this is a guaranteed lift for supper on a bleak night. Even people who absolutely deplore turnips will ask for a third helping of "whatever that is in the casserole."

BAKED ZUCCHINI

Zucchini   Parmesan cheese, grated
Ripe tomatoes   Buttered crumbs
Onion, diced   Salt, pepper, paprika
Butter or margarine

Slice the zucchini thin (do not peel). Remove stems from tomatoes and slice them. Arrange a layer of the zucchini slices in a greased casserole or baking pan. Season well. Sprinkle diced onion over. Lay slices of tomatoes on top of the zucchini, and season again. Add more diced onion. Repeat the process so you have 4 layers. Sprinkle the top layer generously with the cheese. Cover and bake 20 to 25 minutes in a medium hot oven (375°).

ALLOW 1 small zucchini (about the size of a large ripe cucumber) to 2 persons. Allow at least 1 tomato to 2 persons.

If you use a rectangular baking pan, make a cover of aluminum foil.
  This is fine with grilled chops, a relish tray of crisp carrot sticks, cucumber sticks, celery, or whatever you have that gives a crisp texture to complement the casserole.

MISS EDDY'S WALNUT CROQUETTES

2 eggs, slightly beaten
3 tbsp cream
1 cup soft bread crumbs
1 cup hot riced or mashed potatoes
1 cup finely ground walnuts
1 tsp each: salt, grated onion, grated celery

Mix eggs, cream, and crumbs.

In another bowl mix potatoes (no butter or cream when you mash them), walnuts, seasonings. Work into first mixture, making a stiff mass. Divide into 8 equal parts and shape into balls.

Roll in more soft bread crumbs (1½ cups is enough), then in beaten egg, then in crumbs. Fry in deep fat at 375° until the croquettes are golden brown. Makes 8.

Miss Eddy was a gentle lavender-and-lace old lady, a French scholar and teacher. She used to have me for lunch and treat me as a grown-up although I was in the pigtail age. Her walnut croquettes were my favorite luncheon dish. She had salad with them and fine China tea.

WILTED LETTUCE WITH SAUSAGE DRESSING

8 sausage links
1 head Boston lettuce
2 tbsp vinegar
2 tsp sugar
½ tsp salt

Sauté sausages over low heat until brown. Drain on absorbent paper and cut in 1-inch lengths.

Pour off all but 6 tablespoons sausage fat. Add vinegar, salt and sugar, and heat to boiling. Pour over the lettuce, broken into bit-size pieces.

Add sausages last and toss gently. Serve immediately.

SERVES 4

RICE

I have probably served more gummy, gluey rice in my life than would be needed to cement a house foundation. I have spent a good many hours scrubbing rice from ruined pans too. By the time I got the rice off, so was the bottom of my kettle.

Fluffy, dry rice is as important as a smooth cream sauce or a gravy without lumps. It is a foundation dish for everything from casseroles to puddings. And when I began to cook, I assumed that anybody could cook rice. But when I began to entertain, some of my most nervous moments were concerned with whether the rice would be *all right* this time. Sometimes the kernels would be separate, tender, and dry. Sometimes they stuck together and to the pan better than postage stamps ever stick to an envelope.

For a time, I lowered my battle flag in the bottom of the last kettle I threw in the garbage, and settled for noodles, macaroni and spaghetti. But then I came back to try again. I have now cooked rice in a pressure cooker, a fancy electric double-boiler unit, a big kettle, a covered heavy skillet.

I also have used Minute Rice, which is a help for a hurry-up meal, and belongs on every kitchen shelf, beside the long-grain California and the brown rice.

Herewith my favorite ways to cook rice:

BAKED CURRIED RICE

1½	cups raw rice	¾	tsp curry powder
2	tbsp butter or margarine	3	cups boiling water
2	tsp salt		

Place the first four ingredients in a baking dish big enough for 8 cups. Better grease it first. Pour boiling water over, mix lightly with a fork, and cover.

Bake in hot oven (425°) about 25 minutes.

Uncover, fluff rice with fork, top with a bit more butter or margarine (or Parmesan cheese if you are worrying about the calories).

SERVES 6

This is an easy way to save current or fuel if you have a roasting chicken in the oven anyway.

BOILED RICE

1 cup uncooked long-grain rice
2¼ cups fresh water
1 teaspoon salt, or seasoned salt
1 teaspoon lemon juice (fresh, frozen, canned)

Bring the water to a rolling boil in a large kettle. Add seasoning and lemon juice. Now gently shake in the rice. When it is all in, stir once with a fork, and, when it begins to simmer again, turn the heat *low*, and cover the kettle tightly.

Cook over low heat for 25 minutes.

SERVES 4–6

If you want very dry rice, remove the cover during the last 5 minutes of cooking. (I always do this anyway, just in case all the water is absorbed and you know what.) Turn off the heat, shake the kettle over the burner a couple of minutes, add butter or margarine, and if you cannot serve at once, keep warm in the oven.

We like to dust the top with curry powder.

HUNTERS' WILD RICE

1 cup wild rice
½ cup diced celery
½ cup diced onion
2 cans mushroom soup (undiluted)

Do *not* wash rice. Put it in about 3 cups boiling water, stir until it is boiling again, and cook it 15 minutes in all. Strain.

Cook onion and celery in not more than a cup of water until soft. Ten minutes will do it.

Combine rice, onions and celery and 1 can mushroom soup. Put this in a shallow pyrex dish (or casserole) and over the mixture spread the other can of soup, like a topping.

Bake at 350° for an hour. The mixture can be prepared way in advance of baking.

SERVES 4–6

This is both elegant and easy.

MRS. MOORE'S SWEDISH RICE

1 cup rice	1½ tsp salt
2 cups cold water	2 tbsp sugar
3 cups milk	3 eggs, beaten
¼ lb butter or margarine	

Wash rice and put in the top of a double boiler with cold water. Cook over hot water for 1 hour, or until all the water has been absorbed. Add milk, and cook again until all of this has been absorbed. This also takes about 1 hour.

Now add butter or margarine, salt, and sugar. Fold beaten eggs into the mixture. Bake 40 minutes at 350° in a buttered casserole.

SERVES 4–6

This reminds me of Oberlin, Ohio, on a still summer night. The moon was just rising and the air had that special heavy sweetness that you get in the Middle West. We had been to the usual Commencement festivities and my feet hurt. Mrs. Moore had a cold buffet supper for a few faculty members and us and with it she had this one hot dish. I ate four helpings and felt marvellously restored.

SPANISH RICE

1 cup raw rice
6 slices bacon, cut fine
1 medium onion, diced
2½ cups canned tomatoes
   Salt, pepper, paprika
1 clove garlic, crushed
2 green peppers, minced

In a heavy kettle sauté the bacon until crisp. Remove bacon. Add rice and cook, stirring, until it begins to brown. Then add the onion and continue to cook, stirring until the onion is golden. Add the bacon, and the rest of the ingredients.

Cover and cook slowly until the rice is tender (40 minutes to 1 hour). Keep the heat low. If necessary add more tomato toward the end of the cooking time.

SERVES 4

RICE PILAF

1   box long-grain or brown or regular white rice
1   medium onion, diced
1   clove garlic, minced
    Butter, or margarine, or olive oil, or salad oil
    Chicken broth or consommé as needed
½   teaspoon saffron, soaked in ½ cup warm water 30
        minutes

Melt the fat in a heavy skillet (iron or cast aluminum, preferably). When it is hot, add onion and garlic and cook until the onion is golden. Now add the rice and cook, stirring with a wooden spoon until the grains are beginning to brown. Add more fat if the rice begins to burn. Meanwhile bring the broth to a boil, and then pour over the rice. You will need to cover the rice about 1½ inches. Add saffron. Cover the skillet, reduce the heat to very low, and cook until the broth has all been absorbed and the rice is tender. Now taste for seasoning and add salt if necessary (the broth may be salty enough).

SERVES 6

This has a rich nutty flavor and is delicious with chicken or lamb or shrimp.

Salads

A SALAD MAY BE A WHOLE MEAL OR JUST THE ADDED TOUCH.
I have noticed that businessmen who have to eat out a lot, seldom view
a salad with applause. But when a really good salad is served them,
they ask for seconds. One or two of my men friends specialize in salads
and salad dressings as their contribution to the family cuisine. When a
man puts his mind on it, his salad is usually superb — partly because the
little woman is doing the meat, sauces, desserts, popovers, and setting
the table, while he just concentrates on the salad bowl.

The salad is only as good as the salad greens, which should be crisp
and chilled. They should be washed under cold running water, drained,
wrapped in a clean towel or put in a plastic bag and stored in the refrigerator. If you have limp store greens, soak them in ice water for a short
time before washing. When you make the salad, tear the greens in
pieces by hand.

I used to be a nervous salad maker because I was always making the
salad at the last minute just as everything else was ready for the table
and the guests were at the door. Now I have learned that I can make
the salad ahead of time; yes, I mean it. I fix the greens, tear them in
pieces and put them in a plastic bag with a rubber band around the top.

I make the dressing and put it in a bottle in the refrigerator. I slice the onions, peppers, or whatever, and wrap them separately in plastic. I rub the salad bowl with garlic and put it in the refrigerator (mine is a good big one). Then, at the last minute, I put everything together, pour the dressing over, stir lightly, and there it is, ready to eat.

There are many kinds of salad greens, and I like several in the same salad, such as chicory, oak leaf lettuce, young spinach, and Boston lettuce.

The commercial salad dressings are now very good, and you can always add a touch of sour cream or a pinch of dry mustard to them. Chopped onion, minced celery leaves, crumbled cheese, and sieved hard-cooked egg yolks are good additions.

For green salads or chef's salad I use a wooden bowl, but for fruit salads I use an earthenware or glass bowl. The wooden bowl always has a breath of garlic in it. I do not wash the wooden bowl with hot water and soap, Heaven forbid! I wipe it out with a damp paper towel and occasionally rub it with mild olive oil. When the handles of the wooden servers begin to get skiddy, I dip them in suds and wipe hastily.

As I think it over, it seems to me salads can be made of almost anything except pie, cake, or ice cream. Slivers of chicken, ham, turkey, salami, Swiss cheese, raw or cooked vegetables – all are suitable. I like to toss a few of the black Italian olives in any but a sweet salad.

For fruit salads, I use some fruit juice in the dressing and lemon juice instead of vinegar.

I like salads served in small individual bowls, wooden or earthenware, rather than on a flat plate, but I don't quite know why.

I've put in my favorite recipes, which you may vary in any number of ways.

SALAD BUFFET

1 lb shrimp	2 tbsp diced green pepper
Salt, parsley, celery leaves, peppercorns	2 cups diced celery
	1 diced alligator pear
2 heads fresh lettuce, pulled in pieces	2 shredded carrots
	2 tbsp diced onion

Cook the shrimp in boiling salted water with parsley, celery, peppercorns. Cook 25 minutes, drain, shell, devein. (You may substitute frozen canned shrimp.) Toss the lettuce with the next five ingredients and then add the shrimp. (Chill it if fresh.)

DRESSING

1 cup mayonnaise	6 drops tabasco
4 tbsp catsup	½ tsp pepper
2 tbsp chili sauce	½ tbsp salt
1 tbsp prepared mustard	2 tbsp vinegar

Mix well, and pour over the salad.

Rub a large bowl with a clove of garlic, arrange whole lettuce leaves in it, then add the salad. Garnish with tomato wedges dipped in sharp French dressing and 1 alligator pear, peeled and sliced, dipped in French dressing or lemon juice.

SERVES 4–6

With hot French bread, a meal for the men.

CAESAR SALAD

20 or so cubes of bread	Dry mustard, pepper, salt
Olive oil and garlic	6 tbsp olive oil
2 heads romaine (or lettuce)	4 tbsp tarragon vinegar
Watercress	2 eggs
½ cup Blue cheese, crumbled	1 tsp capers
(or grated Parmesan)	

Set bread cubes in a flat pan in a slow oven (200°) until browned, then sprinkle olive oil seasoned with garlic over them and shake until they are coated. Put aside to drain.

Tear the greens in small pieces, add cheese and seasonings. Now add olive oil and vinegar. Break the eggs, which have been coddled, over the salad. (Bring a pan of water to a boil, remove from heat and add eggs. Let them stand 8 minutes.) Add the capers and toss enough to mix the salad. Just before serving add the croutons.

SERVES 4

You may use ready-made croutons which come in packages. You may add anchovies with the capers if you like.

LOUELLA'S JELLIED CUCUMBER SALAD
WITH SHRIMPS

3   pkgs cooked frozen shrimp (or 4 5½-oz cans, or
      equal amount fresh)
3   large or 4 medium cucumbers, peeled, seeded and
      grated (You need 4 cups of pulp and juice)
2   envelopes unflavored gelatin
½   cup cold water
1½ cups boiling water
1   tbsp salt
½   tsp hot Mexican pepper sauce
¼   tsp pepper
    Juice of 2 lemons
2   medium onions grated
    Mayonnaise
    Chili sauce

Soften gelatin in cold water, add the boiling water and stir until thoroughly dissolved. Add seasonings and lemon juice. Let cool, then add the cucumber and onions. Taste for seasoning. Add a few drops of green coloring if necessary. Pour into a 6-cup ring mold and chill until set. Turn out on a round platter. Mix shrimp with mayonnaise and add chili sauce enough to make it pink. Pile shrimp in the center of the cucumber jelly.

SERVES 10

Especially fine for a hot August night when company comes.

MOTHER'S SHRIMP SALAD

Combine canned shrimp with finely shredded cabbage in the proportion of 1 cup of shrimp to 2 cups of cabbage. Toss with French dressing.

This makes an excellent luncheon dish with hot soup and rolls.

CURRIED CHICKEN SALAD

2¾ qts diced chicken (the meat from 3 chickens)
3 cups finely diced celery
½ cup minced onion

2 tbsp curry powder
½ cup cream
3 cups mayonnaise
Salt and pepper

Chicken should be cut as for any good chicken salad — not too big. Add celery and onion to chicken. Blend curry powder with cream and stir into mayonnaise. Mix the dressing with the chicken, celery and onion. Season very lightly with pepper. Season to taste with salt and pepper. Arrange on a bed of lettuce and garnish with sliced stuffed olives or tomato slices.

SERVES 10

This is a chicken salad to serve when you are entertaining the most important guest and feel all fluttery about the whole thing. Just steady yourself and make this salad. I serve it on an ironstone platter (a fish platter is what it is) and garnish it with canned artichoke hearts, big satiny ripe olives, crisp lettuce and watercress, and it does no harm to lay a few slivers of pimiento on top of the salad itself.

RUTH SANFORD'S CURRY RING

3 cups cooked rice
2 tbsp butter or margarine
3 tbsp curry
Mayonnaise enough to hold together the rice

Melt butter or margarine, stir in curry and simmer a minute or more. Blend into rice. Add mayonnaise and pack in a ring mold. Set in refrigerator overnight.

Turn out on a platter, and fill the center with chilled cooked jumbo shrimp or cut-up cooked lobster. Serve with a dressing combining sour cream and mayonnaise in equal parts.

Chutney as a side dish is a must.

SERVES 4–6

This is tops for a party luncheon. Serve tiny hot biscuits and coffee. Fruit compote for dessert.

PARTY CHICKEN SALAD

1 large chicken, cooked
1 large cucumber, peeled and chopped
1 cup walnut meats, chopped
1 can French peas, drained
3 cups celery, diced
   Mayonnaise

Remove the meat from the chicken and cut in pieces, but do not dice. Add the rest of the ingredients and mix lightly with mayonnaise. Use just enough mayonnaise to give a good consistency but not sloppy. Turn into a bowl and chill thoroughly. When ready to serve, place the salad on a chilled platter with crisp lettuce around it. Garnish with strips of pimiento, or chopped ripe olives, or green pepper rings, or tomato slices, or watercress.

SERVES 6–8 or more, according to the size of the chicken

You may use frozen chicken breasts for extra elegance. If so, steam them until tender, adding a little dry white wine while cooking.

SHRIMP MACARONI SALAD

1 cup cooked shrimp (or 1 large-size can)
1 cup diced celery
2 cups cooked elbow macaroni
4 hard-cooked eggs, cut fine
1 tsp seasoned salt
1 tsp seasoned pepper
3/4 cup mayonnaise
   Watercress, or parsley, or tomato wedges,
     or sliced cucumber, for garnish

Mix the first four ingredients gently. Sprinkle seasoning over and add mayonnaise. Chill.

SERVES 6

You may use lobster or tuna, or a combination of them, with the shrimp.

TWENTY-FOUR-HOUR SALAD

2 eggs, beaten
4 tbsp vinegar
4 tbsp sugar
2 tbsp butter
2 cups white cherries, cut in half
2 oranges (Remove rind and membranes. Cut
    oranges in pieces.)
2 cups pineapple chunks, canned or fresh
2 cups marshmallows, cut in pieces with scissors
1 cup cream

Put the eggs in the top of a double boiler over boiling water. Add vinegar and sugar, beating constantly until thick and smooth. Remove from heat, add butter, and let cool.

When cool, fold in cream, whipped until stiff, and the fruits. Chill in refrigerator overnight.

SERVES 12

This recipe was sent to me by my friend Elizabeth Baker and she admits it is very rich, but delicious, which it certainly is. You may always go on a diet the day after the party.

MACARONI SALAD

3 cups cooked macaroni
    (elbow)
French dressing
1 tbsp chopped green pepper
2 tbsp diced celery
1 tsp finely diced onion
Salt and pepper
Mayonnaise

Marinate the macaroni in French dressing for several hours, then add the green pepper and onion. Season to taste and stir in a little mayonnaise. Sprinkle paprika over the top and serve very cold.

SERVES 4

If you use the regular macaroni, break it in pieces before cooking. I really like the flavor better, but the elbow is easier.

This can be varied by the addition of diced chicken or whole shrimp. It is good with thin slices of ham.

PINEAPPLE-CHEESE SALAD

¾ cup sugar
½ cup syrup from canned pineapple
1 tbsp gelatin
¼ cup cold water
1 cup drained, crushed pineapple
1 cup grated American cheese (or 1 cup cottage cheese)
1 cup heavy cream

Dissolve sugar in syrup, using low heat. Add gelatin which has been softened in cold water, and stir until it has dissolved. When this mixture has been chilled until partially set, add pineapple, cheese, and heavy cream which has been whipped until stiff, but not dry. Chill until firm.

SERVES 6 if they are not too ravenous

This is nice for bridge luncheons or when the committee meets. I don't advise it for men, but I could be wrong. The men I know prefer things like salami or slivers of ham in their salads.

HOT POTATO SALAD

6 cups cooked potatoes, sliced thin
1 cup finely chopped onion
2 tbsp minced parsley
⅔ cup vinegar
⅓ cup hot water
1 tsp sugar
1 beaten egg
⅓ cup salad oil
2 tsp salt (level)
   Pepper to taste
1½ tsp monosodium glutamate

Combine onion, potatoes, parsley. Combine water and vinegar and heat to boiling, then add sugar.

Add hot mixture slowly to egg, then add oil and seasonings. Beat with a rotary beater and, when well blended, pour over the potato-and-onion mixture. Stir gently and let stand in a warm place 15 minutes.

SERVES 6–8

If the potatoes are cold, set the salad in a warm oven or over a pan of hot water until the potatoes are heated through.

WHARTON'S FOUR-BEAN SALAD

1   can green beans, drained
1   can golden wax beans, drained
1   can garbanzos (or chick peas), drained
1   can red kidney beans, drained
1   large onion, thinly sliced
1   large green pepper, thinly sliced
½ cup vinegar (I use wine vinegar)
½ cup sugar (I skimp on this)
½ cup salad oil
    Salt
    Freshly ground pepper

Drain beans, saving liquids for soup. Add onion and pepper to beans in a large bowl; mix well. Make dressing of vinegar, sugar, and salad oil. Pour dressing over salad mixture and let stand overnight in the refrigerator. Before serving, add salt and pepper.

SERVES 6

This is good for a buffet, and a nice change from hot beans baked all day—although beans, any old way, are elegant to me.

GERMAN POTATO SALAD

2 cups cooked potatoes	1 tsp sugar
1 large onion, or 2 medium	Seasoned salt and pepper to
1 tbsp olive or salad oil	taste
1 tbsp tarragon vinegar	5 slices bacon

Dice potatoes while still warm and add the onion, grated or minced. Mix oil, vinegar, sugar and seasonings, and pour over potatoes. Then add the bacon, in small bits, along with the hot bacon fat. Serve warm.

SERVES 4–6

This will still not taste the way it does in a German restaurant. I have eaten German potato salad all over the country, and my final conclusion is that it needs to be made by the tubful to be just right. But there are never any leftovers with this version. Be sure the potatoes are not mushy. On the other hand, of course, if they are half raw . . .

MARTHA FITZGERALD'S POTATO SALAD

3 lbs potatoes, peeled and diced	½ tsp red pepper
8 tbsp olive oil	1 tsp prepared mustard
2 tbsp vinegar	2 tbsp chopped parsley
2 tsp salt	2 tbsp chopped onion
½ tsp freshly ground pepper	4 tbsp sherry

Cook the diced potatoes in boiling salted water until tender. Put in a warm bowl.

Mix the other items well and pour over the potatoes.

Serve hot, lukewarm, or cold.

SERVES 6–8

This is the cook's best friend in the matter of potato salads. It does not have to be made at the last minute. Standing only enhances the flavor. Perfect for picnics because you won't worry about keeping it icy cold.

MEXICAN SALAD

2 soft-ripe avocados	½ tsp salt
1 tsp lemon juice	1 small ripe tomato
½ tsp grated onion	2 drops tabasco sauce

Peel, seed and mash 2 avocados with lemon juice and grated onion and salt. Chop tomato very fine and add tabasco. Stir into the first mixture. Lay the avocado seeds in the mixture and chill.

Rub a bowl with garlic and arrange a bed of varied salad greens which have been tossed with French dressing. Pile the avocado mixture on top after removing the seeds, and decorate with pimiento-stuffed olives. If this cannot be served at once, leave the seeds imbedded in the salad to prevent discoloration. (I learned the trick from a Mexican friend, and it really works.)

Serve chilled in a bowl, with Hush Puppies, corn pone, or cornbread baked thin in a shallow pan.

SERVES 4

Or you can just serve two and not get into any trouble.

JELLIED SALAD

BASIC RECIPE

1   tbsp unflavored gelatin
½ cup cold water
1   cup boiling water, consommé, or juice.

Soak gelatin in cold water 5 minutes, then dissolve in the boiling water. This amount of jelly takes 1½ cups solid ingredients.

For sweet or fruit salads, add to basic recipe:

2   tbsp sugar
¼ tsp salt
¼ cup lemon juice

For vegetable or chicken or fish salads, add to basic recipe:

1   tbsp grated onion
¼ cup vinegar

Chill and when almost set, add the solid ingredients. Place in a wet mold and continue to chill until firm.

Jellied salads are my best friend during hot summer days. I make them the night before when the kitchen is cooler — or I think it is. They add just the right touch to a buffet too.

TOMATO CHEESE MOLD

1   tbsp unflavored gelatin (1 pkg)
½ cup cold water
1   can tomato soup, boiling

1   cup cottage cheese
½ cup heavy cream, whipped
½ cup mayonnaise

Soften the gelatin in the cold water, then add to the hot soup. Let cool. Beat in the cottage cheese. Fold in the cream and mayonnaise and pour in a ring mold which you have rinsed in cold water. Chill. Unmold on a round chop platter. Serve extra mayonnaise in a small bowl in the center, and garnish with crisp lettuce.

SERVES 6

This always calls for seconds.

EGGS IN ASPIC

8 eggs
2 envelopes unflavored gelatin
½ cup cold water
4 cups chicken broth (canned, or made with bouil-
        lon cubes if you have no fresh stock)
1 tbsp dried tarragon
½ cup liver paté or deviled ham
    Mayonnaise
    Dry mustard

Soak gelatin in cold water for 5 minutes. Meanwhile, heat the broth. Dissolve the gelatin in the broth. Cool. Then cover the bottom of a mold (or use 8 ramekins or custard cups) with a layer of the gelatin. Sprinkle the tarragon over.

Poach the eggs, trim the edges, and let them cool. When the gelatin is slightly firm, slip the eggs in carefully. Spread them lightly with the paté. Then spoon the remaining gelatin over and set in the refrigerator until firm. Turn out on a bed of shredded salad greens. Season mayonnaise with mustard to taste, and serve in a bowl with the aspic. Garnish with watercress.

SERVES 8

When my daughter tried this, she said the eggs kept floating and would not be pinned down. The secret is to let the gelatin set partially before adding the eggs.

LIME RING

1 pkg lime gelatin
1 cup cottage cheese
3 tbsp lemon juice or mild vinegar

Substitute the lemon juice or vinegar for 3 tablespoons of the water in which you would ordinarily dissolve the gelatin. Add the cottage cheese to the gelatin when it is just beginning to set. Mix lightly. Turn into a ring mold (rinse the mold with cold water). Chill until firm.

SERVES 6

This is so easy and so good. For a buffet try this at one end of the table, and the Tomato Cheese Mold at the other.

INDIVIDUAL ASPICS

3 cups chicken broth
1 cup tomato juice
4 envelopes unflavored gelatin

2 egg whites, beaten
Seasonings to taste
½ tsp sugar

Mix everything together and heat to boiling point, stirring constantly. Remove from heat and let cool. When the mixture is syrupy, put it into individual muffin cups or cooky molds. Chill until firmly set. When ready to serve, set the molds or cups on a towel wrung out of hot water. Turn out on a platter or individual plates.

MAKES 12 – 15 aspics

If you wish, you may add 2 tablespoons cognac after the aspic comes from the stove. For a buffet, this is easy and elegant. You may have a platter of cold meat, or chicken, or cold lobster, or salmon, and arrange the aspics around the edge. Garnish the platter with watercress or parsley. You may make the aspic the day before. The one problem is getting it out of the molds, but here you are on your own. A sharp pointed knife may help loosen the edges.

AVOCADO RING MOUSSE

2 pkgs lime jello
2 cups hot water
1 tbsp lemon juice
¾ cup salad dressing (I use
     Miracle Whip for this)
1 cup whipped cream

½ tsp salt
1 cup avocado put through a
     sieve
Lettuce
Grapefruit segments
Orange segments

Dissolve jello in hot water. Let cool and when it begins to thicken, add lemon juice, salad dressing, whipped cream salt, and avocado. Pour into buttered ring mold and let stand in refrigerator overnight.

To take from mold, dip mold in hot water briefly, then turn upside down quickly on a large round plate. Place lettuce in center and garnish with grapefruit and orange segments.

SERVES 6

This is an excellent summer luncheon salad and looks so cool!

LOBSTER MOUSSE

1 large can lobster
2/3 cup mayonnaise
1 tbsp unflavored gelatin
1 tbsp cold water

2 tbsp boiling water
1 cup heavy cream, whipped
Salt

Soften the gelatin in the cold water, add the boiling water and stir. Cool. Add to the whipped cream, then salt to taste. Stir well.

Spread a layer of cream over the bottom and sides of a greased mold. Set in the refrigerator until it begins to thicken slightly. Meanwhile mix the lobster and mayonnaise, and season to taste. Gently place the lobster mixture in the mold, and put the remaining cream over the top. Chill until firm.

SERVES 6–8

This may be made the day before, covered with aluminum foil and stored in the refrigerator.

FROZEN FRUIT SALAD

3 cups diced fruit (pineapple, peach, pear, melon balls, or whatever)
1/2 cup white grapes
1 banana, diced
1 tbsp unflavored gelatin
1/4 cup water
3 tbsp lemon juice
1 cup mayonnaise
1 cup cream, whipped (or see note under Chocolate Cream)

Soften the gelatin in the cold water, then dissolve over hot water. Combine the fruits and add lemon juice and gelatin. Put in the refrigerator until it begins to thicken. Then fold in mayonnaise and whipped cream. Turn into the biggest refrigerator tray and freeze in the freezing unit.

To serve, cut in squares and serve in lettuce cups with extra dressing.

SERVES 6–8

Canned fruit cocktail or frozen fruits may be used. But always have some fresh fruit with the canned.

FROSTED HAM SALAD LOAF

2 lbs lean ground fresh pork
1 lb ground smoked ham
3 eggs
   About ½ lb fine cracker crumbs
½ cup sliced stuffed olives
   Pepper
4 – 6 cups water
1 cup vinegar
   Horseradish sauce

Mix meat, eggs, cracker crumbs, olives, and pepper. Shape into a round loaf (if ham is mild add a little salt). Place loaf in clean white cotton sack or a square of white cloth. Tie ends securely with twine.

Now combine 4 to 6 cups hot water with 1 cup cider vinegar and bring to a rolling boil. Place loaf on rack in boiling liquid and boil gently for 2 hours over low heat. Remove loaf from cloth and chill thoroughly.

Just before serving spread top and sides with:

HORSERADISH SAUCE

1 3-oz pkg cream cheese
2 tbsp mayonnaise
1 tbsp cream
1 tsp horseradish
  Dash of tabasco

Blend well.

SERVES 6 – 8

Sauces and Salad Dressings

THE FRENCH HAVE A REPUTATION FOR SAUCES, AND SOME-
times I used to have the feeling that sauces were so difficult and took
so much time, there was no use trying. Actually a good sauce is not
hard to make if you follow directions. You cannot put a sauce on to
cook and go off and read the paper. A sauce is a delicate thing and requires watching. A burned sauce not only has to be thrown away but
you have a time cleaning the pan.

There is a new type of flour on the market which does not lump when
you add it. It is especially good for cream sauces and gravies.

And a French whisk is a help. This comes in several sizes, but I use
the small size. If you stir with a spoon, lumps tend to form on the spoon.
The whisk keeps the sauce smooth. Most hardware stores have these.

In sauces using flour, cook long enough so the flour will not taste
raw. Keep the heat low to prevent burning.

SPECIAL FRENCH DRESSING

1/2 cup red wine vinegar (or tarragon, or cider vinegar,
    if you wish)
1 cup olive oil (you may use part salad oil)
1 crushed clove garlic
4 tsp dry mustard
4 tsp salt
1/2 tsp paprika
    Freshly ground pepper to taste
    Pinch of Cayenne

Steep a pinch of salad herbs in the vinegar. Cool, mix vinegar and dry ingredients. Add the oil and shake.

For fruit salads, add a little sugar to the dry ingredients.

KAY'S SALAD DRESSING

1/2 lb bleu cheese
1 pint mayonnaise
1/2 pint light cream
1/4 cup milk
1/8 cup French dressing

Crumble the cheese and mix with the remaining ingredients.

This is a fine dressing for vegetable salads, tangy and smooth.

ROQUEFORT DRESSING

1/2 pkg blue cheese   Little tabasco sauce
    Cider vinegar to taste   Dash garlic salt
1 tsp Worcestershire   2/3 cup buttermilk
1 tsp horseradish   1 cup mayonnaise
1 tbsp catsup   Salt and pepper
1/2 tsp dry mustard

Crumble cheese and vinegar to soften. Mash with fork. Add other ingredients and put in quart jar. Shake well to blend. Use tabasco sauce and garlic salt to your taste. Store in refrigerator.

SMILEY BURNETTE'S REMOULADE SAUCE

1   cup mayonnaise
1   cup catsup
1   tsp Worcestershire
1   tsp prepared mustard
½ tsp salt
    Dash of tabasco
½ small onion, diced

Blend in an electric blender or beat with a rotary beater until smooth.

This is perfect for shrimp, crab, lobster. Or add sour cream for a special salad dressing. Or add cream cheese and stuff celery with it.

GREEN GODDESS DRESSING

1   cup mayonnaise
3   tbsp finely chopped chives
1   clove garlic (grated or
      pressed in garlic press)
1   tbsp lemon juice
3   tbsp tarragon vinegar

¼ cup chopped parsley
    Freshly ground pepper
    Seasoned salt
½ cup heavy cream
3   tbsp chopped anchovies

Put the ingredients in an electric blender and run at moderate speed about 20 seconds.

This is best with mixed greens.

PARTY BARBECUE SAUCE

2   tbsp chili powder
2   tbsp paprika
¼ tbsp Cayenne
1   tbsp prepared mustard
1   tbsp Worcestershire

1   pint cider vinegar
1   pint water
1   small onion diced
1   pint catsup

Place in a deep kettle and boil gently for 30 minutes. Stir constantly.

THIS is sauce enough for portions for 10 people

Use on hamburger, broiled chops, broiled chicken, ın barbecued sandwiches. Excellent added to baked beans for a picnic supper.

CORDON BLEU SOUR-CREAM DRESSING

2   tsp salt
3   tsp fresh pepper
1   tsp crushed garlic or ½ tsp garlic salt
1   tsp lemon juice
8   tbsp tarragon vinegar
4   tbsp cider vinegar
3½ cups sour cream
1   tsp dry mustard
½ tsp Worcestershire

Beat all together and use for salads.

Dione Lucas, that matchless cook, used this in a cooking class and I never forgot it. Of all the versions of sour-cream dressings, this is the most distinctive I have found.

MOTHER'S BOILED DRESSING

1 cup sugar	3 eggs, well-beaten
1 tbsp salt	1 cup sweet or sour cream
1 tbsp dry mustard	Large lump of butter
1 tbsp flour	1 cup vinegar
Pinch of red pepper	

Mix together sugar, salt, dry mustard, flour, and red pepper. Then add to these the well-beaten eggs, sweet or sour cream, and butter. Cook in a double boiler until thick; then remove from the fire and slowly beat in vinegar.

I used to eat this on bread, but it can also be used in potato salad, shrimp salad, fresh vegetable salad, or in deviled eggs. It is good to have on hand for almost anything, in fact.

BASIC CHILI SAUCE

3   tbsp butter or drippings
2   tbsp chili powder
2   cups or more water
1   tsp salt

Melt butter or drippings in a heavy skillet. Stir in chili powder and cook until blended, stirring constantly. Gradually add the water, letting it cook up each time. Add salt. It should cook 30 minutes or longer. Add water as needed.

This came from a Texas friend, and the first time I made it, the family went around gasping for a while. As my friend said, "You work up to it." So for beginners, I suggest cutting the chili powder by a third.

This is good with leftover vegetables heated in it, good on summer squash or string beans. And of course for chili beans.

BASIC CURRY SAUCE

1   small onion, sliced
1½ tbsp margarine
2   tsp flour
1   tbsp curry powder
1   tomato, sliced
1   pint soup stock

Sauté onion in melted margarine until slightly brown. Add flour and curry, stir. Add tomato, gradually stir in soup stock, salt and pepper, and bring to boil. Simmer 20 minutes.

One cup of sauce for leftover meat and vegetables.

MINT SAUCE

½ cup fresh mint, finely chopped
½ cup vinegar
1   tbsp sugar

Combine vinegar and mint and sugar, and heat over a medium heat for 5 minutes. Serve hot.

Serve with lamb or mutton.

CREAM SAUCE

2 tbsp butter or margarine
2 tbsp flour
1 cup warm milk
Salt, pepper, paprika to taste

Melt the butter or margarine over medium heat. Blend in the flour and stir until smooth, then add the milk gradually, and the seasonings, stirring constantly. When it is thick and smooth, it is done.

Use a French whisk if possible. There are only two tricks, keep the heat low, and stir. The flour should be cooked enough so the sauce will not taste of raw flour, and the slow cooking of butter and flour does it. Having the milk warm makes it blend easier.

SAUCE MORNAY

Make Cream Sauce according to the directions above. When it is done, lower the heat and gradually add:

2 tbsp butter or margarine
2 tbsp grated Parmesan cheese
2 tbsp grated Swiss or mild Cheddar
Dash of Cayenne

BEURRE NOIR
(Black Butter)

½ cup vinegar
1 bay leaf
1 cube butter
1 tbsp parsley, minced

Boil the vinegar and bay leaf until it is reduced to half. Cook the butter until deep brown. Remove bay leaf from the vinegar and combine vinegar and butter. Add the parsley.

Serve with eggs, sweetbreads, brains.

BÉCHAMEL SAUCE

2 cups milk
4 tbsp butter or margarine
½ small onion, finely minced
4 tbsp flour

Bring the milk to a boil in a double boiler. Meanwhile simmer the onion in the butter or margarine until golden but not brown. Stir in the flour, then gradually add the hot milk, and keep stirring until smooth. Simmer 15 minutes until the flour is well cooked, stirring now and then. Strain through a fine sieve and serve as desired.

You may use equal parts milk and stock (fish or vegetable) depending on how you are going to use the sauce.

GOURMET BÉCHAMEL SAUCE

Make the sauce as above, then add 1 beaten egg yolk and reheat but do not boil. (If eggs are pullet-size, add two yolks.)

BREAD SAUCE

1 medium onion studded with cloves
2 cups milk
   Dash of Cayenne
   Salt
1 cup fresh bread crumbs
   Butter or cream, if desired

Put the onion, milk and seasonings in a pan or double boiler. Bring to a boil, and boil 5 minutes. Remove the onion and clove.

Add the crumbs—use more if you need to thicken the milk. Correct the seasoning. Add a little butter or cream if you wish a rich sauce.

This is delicious with roast game, chicken or Rock Cornish game hens.

ORANGE GINGER SAUCE

1 cup orange juice
¼ cup sherry
¼ cup vinegar
¼ cup sugar
2 tbsp soy sauce
1 tbsp grated orange peel
1 tbsp fresh ginger, shredded
2 tbsp melted butter or margarine
2 tbsp cornstarch

Mix all ingredients and cook until thick and clear, stirring constantly.

Serve with pork or chicken.

CUCUMBER SAUCE

1 cucumber
½ tsp salt
2 tbsp vinegar
1 cup thick cultured sour cream
1 tbsp minced green onion or chives
   Pepper

Peel and remove seeds from the cucumber, then grate it. Add the salt and let stand in the refrigerator for an hour or more. Drain well. Combine with the vinegar, sour cream, onion, pepper. Taste for salt.

Serve with baked-fish dishes.

HORSERADISH SAUCE

2 cups tart applesauce
½ cup prepared bottled horseradish

Combine. Serve cold.

Serve with roast goose, duck, pork, or cold meats. If you are lucky enough to have fresh horseradish, add 2 tablespoons vinegar.

HOLLANDAISE SAUCE I

½ cup butter or margarine
4 egg yolks
¼ cup light cream
¼ cup lemon juice, fresh, frozen or canned
½ tsp salt
   Pinch of Cayenne

Heat the butter in the top of a double boiler, and set over boiling water when melted. Add the salt, Cayenne, and lemon juice to the egg yolks, and stir. (Don't beat the yolks.) Stir the yolk mixture into the hot butter, turn the heat down until the water in the bottom of the boiler is barely boiling.

Beat egg mixture with a rotary beater until thickened. Add the cream and continue to beat 2 minutes longer. Remove from heat.

This is so much easier than the traditional method of cutting ½ cup butter into 3 pieces and so on. Works, too.

HOLLANDAISE SAUCE II

3 egg yolks
   Lump of butter, size of an egg
¼ cup cold water
   Juice of half a lemon
   Salt to taste

Put all the ingredients in the top—have cold water in the bottom container—of the double boiler. Turn the heat on and stir until thick as the cold water comes to a boil. If too thick, add a little cold water.

This has come down in the family, said Katherine, as she copied it for me. It will never fail. If you like the sauce very thick, you will not want the extra water, but if you want it thinner (which I like for Broccoli) the added bit of water will do it. Katherine says Hollandaise always made her nervous until she began making it this way.

BLENDER HOLLANDAISE SAUCE

3   egg yolks, room temperature
1½ tbsp lemon juice
¾ cup butter or margarine
1   tbsp hot water
1   tsp mustard
    Salt and paprika

Put egg yolks and lemon juice in blender, add the hot water. Melt the butter or margarine until bubbly. Turn blender on high speed and pour the butter in evenly. Add seasonings and run blender about 30 seconds. This makes 2 cups sauce.

MILLIE'S GRAVY

2   tbsp drippings from roast meat
2   tbsp flour
1½ cups liquid
    Seasonings

Pour the fat and juices from the roasting pan (keep the roast warm in the oven). Scrape the crusty bits from the pan. Now measure in another pan 2 tablespoons of the drippings and add the scraped bits. Add liquid slowly as you heat and stir the gravy. Season to taste.

Millie's gravy is so good that when I go there for dinner, I tell her to have mashed potatoes and gravy, and never mind anything else. The secret is that she uses vegetable juices (or water in which vegetables have been cooked) for the liquid and that she makes the gravy in a separate pan. It takes more time, she says, but is smoother.

I make my gravy right in the roasting pan and it is true that with a large pan it is difficult to keep the whole mixture evenly stirred. I add 1 tablespoon or more of tomato sauce, juice from mushrooms (canned), and all sorts of seasonings, but I take my hat off to Millie. Her gravy is better than mine.

Gravy Maker, Worcestershire, a dash of soy sauce, Kitchen Bouquet—all are helpful, and if you are short on drippings, substitute half a can of beef bouillon for part of the liquid to intensify the flavor.

PEPPER SAUCE

12 sweet red peppers
1 hot red pepper
3 cups brown sugar
2 cups cider vinegar

Grind together sweet peppers and hot pepper and let them stand in salt water (1 tablespoon salt to 1 quart of water) for 30 minutes. Drain, add sugar and vinegar, and cook until thick, stirring frequently.

Grand with cold meat.

SAUCE FOR COLD LAMB

4 tbsp butter
2 tbsp vinegar
½ cup currant jelly
½ tsp mustard
Salt and pepper

Heat ingredients together and spoon over lamb.

You may heat the lamb slices in the sauce if you wish.

LOUELLA'S GOOP

¼ lb bleu cheese
½ cup softened butter
½ clove garlic, crushed
2 tbsp prepared mustard
Salt and pepper to taste

Put the cheese through a sieve (or use your blender). Cream the butter and garlic together, add the seasonings. Blend cheese and butter mixture together and spoon over hamburgers or steak.

This is a delicious way to glorify hamburger (or steak for that matter). It melts smoothly on the hamburgers and everyone takes an extra hamburger just for the sauce!

WESTERN VIEW MUSTARD SAUCE

2 egg yolks
½ cup sugar
2 tbsp dry mustard
1 tsp salt
1 large can evaporated milk or 1 pint thin cream
½ cup vinegar

Beat the egg yolks and stir in the sugar, mustard and salt. Add a little of the milk or cream to make a smooth mixture. Meanwhile heat the rest of the milk or cream in the top of a double boiler, but do not let it boil. When it is hot, add the egg mixture and stir constantly until it thickens. When it thickens, take from the fire, and stir in the vinegar slowly, then return to the stove and continue cooking until the sauce is creamy and thick. This takes about 5 minutes, and you must watch it at this point and stir.

Since it is extra good, you won't mind hanging over it briefly to be sure it doesn't boil up and separate.

Serve hot.

This is the best sauce for ham. Next day you can serve it cold on the leftover ham, and it is delicious on any cold sliced meat or in sandwiches. It is also good added to salad dressing.

RAISIN SAUCE

½ cup raisins (seedless are
    best)
½ cup brown sugar
½ tbsp dry mustard
½ tbsp flour
¼ cup cider vinegar
1¾ cups water

Mix the dry ingredients, then add the remaining. Simmer until thick and syrupy.

MAKES 1½ cups

This is for tongue (see Boiled Tongue recipe). It is good with ham too, although I like Western View Mustard Sauce better for ham.

MUSTARD CREAM GRAVY

2 tbsp flour
4 tsp dry mustard
⅔ cup butter
1½ cups boiling water
2 tsp Worcestershire
3 tbsp vinegar
   Salt

Mix flour and mustard and butter. Gradually stir in water, simmer, stirring until thick and smooth. Add other ingredients.

Especially good with fish or boiled beef.

HOT MUSTARD SAUCE

1 cup dry mustard   1 cup sugar
1 cup vinegar   2 eggs

Soak the vinegar and mustard overnight. Add the eggs well beaten, and the sugar. Cook until thick, stirring constantly. Remove from fire and stir while cooling until all steam has disappeared.

Serve this zestful sauce with fish or baked ham.

SHRIMP SAUCE

2 cans frozen cream of shrimp soup
½ lb sliced fresh mushrooms
2 tbsp butter
⅓ cup heavy cream
1 cup cooked shrimps, fresh or frozen
   Sherry

Heat the soup in the top of a double boiler over hot water, stirring until smooth. Sauté mushrooms in the butter about 5 minutes. Add mushrooms, cream, and shrimps to the soup. Do not let the sauce boil. Add sherry to taste (2 tbsp or so).

MAKES 3 cups sauce

There are endless uses for this, over rice or toast points, or on baked fish fillets, or in fish casseroles.

Breads

I ONCE HAD A FRIEND WHO LIVED IN A HOUSE THAT WAS haunted. She didn't mind at all, because the haunting was the smell of freshly baked bread which would suddenly fill the kitchen in the dead of night. What a nice way to be haunted! When the family troops in around suppertime, even a whiff of unghostly fresh bread or hot blueberry muffins or parsley cheese biscuits makes homecoming an event.

Modern store bread is, to me, barely edible. I take a dim view of all the good being taken from flour and then put back by additives. A few companies put out good flavorsome bread, but not nearly enough; spongy soggy loaves are the norm. The best bread is Anadama, and there are a couple of firms making whole wheat oven-baked bread. Otherwise you must make your own.

Oddly enough, the modern brown-and-serve rolls and the refrigerated biscuits and rolls are excellent, and if you are lucky you may get Italian, French or Portuguese bread. These have no artificial preservatives, so they must be eaten while fresh.

A very simple meal can be company fare if you bring in a basket of crusty popovers or hot baking-powder biscuits.

STARTER DOUGH

¼ cup milk
¾ cup water
2 tsp salad oil
2 tsp sugar
1½ tsp salt
1 pkg yeast
2⅓ cups flour, sifted (or Wondra unsifted)

Combine milk, ½ cup water and salad oil, and bring to a boil. Cool to lukewarm and add sugar and salt. Dissolve yeast in ¼ cup warm water. Add to cooled milk mixture. Stir in flour. Blend thoroughly. Cover, let stand in a warm place 12 to 18 hours to sour. This makes enough starter for 12 loaves of bread. It may be divided up and frozen. Bring it to room temperature before making the bread.

Recommended maximum storage time: 1 week in freezing compartment of refrigerator, 1 month in deep freeze.

This authentic recipe is treasured by my family. Jill's daughter and husband and two children always come for New Year's and bring, among other things, a plastic bag with a chunk of starter dough. In the afternoon, before New Year's Eve, Barbara vanishes in the kitchen while the children are building a snowman. I pay no attention because this is a surprise. Around eleven-thirty that night, when the small fry are tucked in and the cockers and Irish asleep and the fire burning low, Barbara vanishes again, and soon a fine and tantalizing smell drifts from the kitchen. At midnight, Val goes out to bring in the tray with hot crusty sourdough bread, cheeses, salami, smoked herring, and pepperoni, and this is the way we see the New Year in. It is a good tradition.

ALSATIAN SOURDOUGH FRENCH BREAD

1 pkg active dry yeast
¼ cup warm water
2½ tsp salt
4½ tsp sugar
½ cup milk
1 cup water
1½ tbsp shortening or salad oil
2 tbsp starter dough (see preceding recipe)
4½ cups flour

Dissolve yeast in warm water in large bowl, then add sugar and salt. Let rest while you bring 1 cup water, oil and milk to a boil in a saucepan. Cool to lukewarm. Pour milk mixture into yeast mixture and stir well. Pour slowly over the flour, mix all well. Add the starter dough and stir well.

Do not knead. Place dough, which will be soft, in greased bowl, cover with clean cloth and let stand in warm place until double in bulk. Turn onto floured board, sprinkle a little flour on top and on your hands. *Do not knead.* Cut in half with a sharp knife, flatten each half and roll into tapered loaf about 2″ × 16″. Place on greased baking sheet. Make ¼-in. deep diagonal cuts in loaves about 2 inches apart. Let rise uncovered until slightly more than double in bulk. Bake in preheated oven at 430° for 15 minutes; reduce heat to 345° and bake 15 or 20 minutes longer. Brush tops of loaves with milk and bake 5 more minutes.

BOSTON BROWN BREAD
(Grandmother Raybold's Recipe)

1 cup yellow cornmeal
1 cup graham flour
1 cup rye flour (2 cups cornmeal if no rye)
¾ cup molasses
1½ cups sour milk with 1 tsp soda and 1 tsp salt
1 cup raisins

Mix and sift dry ingredients and stir in the rest. Add raisins. Pour into tin cans, cover, and steam on a rack in a kettle of boiling water 2½ hours. Fill cans only ⅔ full.

ANADAMA BREAD

½ cup cornmeal	2 cups boiling water
2 tbsp shortening	2 yeast cakes
½ cup molasses	Flour to make stiff (about 6
3 tsp salt	cups)

Combine the first four ingredients and pour the boiling water over. Let cool until lukewarm, then crumble the yeast in and stir until well blended. Add the flour and knead lightly. Put in a greased bowl and let rise in a warm place until double in bulk. Knead again and divide the dough in two parts. Place in 2 greased bread pans and let rise again until almost double. Bake in moderate oven (375°) until the bread pulls away from the sides of the pans – 45 minutes to an hour – and the top is nicely brown.

MAKES 2 large loaves

The only place I have been able to get this bread is on Cape Cod, and when I go inland I take at least six loaves. It freezes well and will keep a short time in the refrigerator, but since it has no artificial preservative, it is not a bread you can keep around. On the other hand, it goes so fast that one seldom has any left to give to the birds. The origin of the name is a mystery. One theory is that an old sea dog used to say, "Anna Damner, where the bread?" I think this a most unlikely story.

CRAZY-QUILT BREAD

½ cup sugar	¾ tsp anise
1 egg	½ cup mixed candied fruits
1¼ cups milk	¾ cup chopped walnuts
3 cups Bisquick	

Heat oven to 350°. Mix sugar, egg, milk, and Bisquick. Beat vigorously 30 seconds. Batter will be slightly lumpy. Blend in anise, fruits, and nuts. Pour into well-greased loaf pan, 9″ × 5″ × 3″. Bake 45 to 50 minutes. Crack in top is typical. Cool before slicing.

I leave out the anise, but if you like anise, put it in.

HOECAKE

1 cup cornmeal
1 tsp salt
About ½ cup boiling water or milk
1 tsp molasses
1 tsp baking powder

Mix cornmeal and salt with enough boiling water or milk to make a stiff batter. Stir in molasses and baking powder. Bake slowly in drippings in a skillet. When browned on one side, place ½ teaspoon butter or margarine on each cake, turn and brown on the other side. Serve instead of hot bread.

I first had this in Ashland, Virginia, which was then a dreamy little town. The mockingbirds were singing and the air was honeysuckle sweet. My hostess did the hoecakes over the embers in an ancient fireplace. A time to remember forever.

BEE'S EASY BROWN BREAD

3 shredded wheat biscuits
3 cups boiling water
2 tbsp shortening
2 tsp salt

Pour boiling water over shredded wheat, shortening and salt. Cool.

Then add:

½ cup molasses
2 cakes (or pkgs) yeast dissolved in ¼ cup warm water
About 7 cups flour, white or whole wheat

Mix in very large bowl, just kneading enough so all is well mixed. Place in a greased bowl, cover, and let rise in a warm place for 2½ hours. Divide into 3 parts, shape into loaves and place in well-greased pans. Let rise again for 1½ hours. Bake in 350° oven 45 to 50 minutes.

Brown bread used to be a staple in most households, but nowadays a good many of us do not have time for it. This is easy and delicious.

GLADYS TABER'S NUT BREAD

1½ cups graham flour
2 cups white flour
2 tsp salt
4 tsp baking powder

1 cup light brown sugar
1½ cups milk
1 cup chopped nuts, raisins,
    dates or figs

Sift together graham flour, white flour, salt, baking powder, and sugar. Stir in milk and add nuts, raisins, dates or figs. Put into 2 buttered loaf pans, and allow to rise for 20 minutes. Bake for 45 minutes in a moderate oven (350°).

There are so many excellent coffee cakes, raisin breads, and so on, in the markets now that it may seem a waste of time to make nut bread. But it isn't hard and it is worth it.

CRANBERRY BREAD

2 cups flour
½ tsp salt
1½ tsp baking powder

½ tsp baking soda
1 cup sugar

Sift all together twice.

Then add:

1 orange, juice and grated rind
2 tbsp melted butter
Boiling water, ¾ cup
1 beaten egg
1 cup chopped nutmeats
1 cup whole cranberries, slightly cooked (or canned
    whole cranberries, which need no cooking)

Stir thoroughly, and bake in a well-greased bread pan (5″ by 9″) in a slow oven (325°) for an hour, or until bread draws away from side of the pan and a straw inserted in the center comes out clean. Store for 24 hours before cutting the bread.

This is delicious for tea, or toasted for breakfast, or as sandwiches spread with cream cheese.

CRANBERRY TEA BREAD

3   cups sifted all-purpose flour
4   tsp baking powder
1   tsp salt
1   egg, beaten slightly
1   cup milk
2   tbsp melted butter or margarine or Crisco
1   cup cranberries
¼   cup fine granulated sugar
½   cup chopped nut meats (walnuts or pecans)
1   tsp vanilla

Sift dry ingredients (the first 3) together. Add the milk and butter or margarine to the beaten egg and add to the dry ingredients. Stir until well blended. Put the cranberries through a food grinder or chop in electric blender. Add the sugar, nuts, and vanilla. Add to the batter and pour into a greased loaf pan 9″ by 5″ by 3″. Bake in a moderately hot oven (350°) for an hour or until the bread draws away from the sides of the pan and is browned on top.

This is good for tea sandwiches spread with softened cream cheese, or toasted for breakfast. Good just as is, too.

I first was introduced to cranberry bread on Cape Cod, where the cranberries ripen in the green bogs and come glowing like rubies from the pickers' scoops. The bread does them justice.

PEPE'S HOT CARAWAY SEED BREAD

¼ cup butter   ¾ cup milk
¾ cup sugar   1   tbsp caraway seeds
1   egg   ¾ tsp vanilla
1⅔ cups flour   ¼ tsp salt
1   tbsp baking powder

Melt butter, add sugar and egg. Then add flour, milk, salt, vanilla, baking powder, and caraway seeds. Bake in shallow pan in 350° oven about 30 minutes.

This is a rich bread and is grand for tea. A friend in Manila is the one from whom I got this recipe.

CRANBERRY-BANANA NUT BREAD

2 cups sifted flour
3 tsp baking powder
½ tsp salt
½ tsp cinnamon
1 cup fresh cranberries
1 cup sugar
1 tsp grated orange rind

1 cup very ripe banana, mashed
½ cup milk
4 tbsp butter or margarine
1 egg
1 cup coarsely chopped pecans

Measure flour, baking powder, salt, and cinnamon into sifter. Put cranberries through food chopper, using coarse knife, into medium-sized bowl; stir in sugar and orange rind. Combine bananas and milk in 2-cup measure. Cream butter or margarine until fluffy in large bowl; beat in egg; sift in dry ingredients, stirring until just blended. Stir in cranberry and banana-milk mixtures, and pecans. Pour into greased loaf pan, 9″ × 5″ × 3″ and bake in moderate oven (350°) 1 hour and 15 minutes, or until wooden pick inserted in center comes out clean. Cool for 5 minutes; turn out on wire rack and cool completely. Wrap in waxed paper, foil or transparent wrap. This bread slices and tastes best if stored for at least a day before serving.

MAKES one loaf

HUSH PUPPIES

1 cup cornmeal
1 tsp baking powder
½ tsp salt

1 medium onion, chopped fine
1 cup milk
Bacon grease

Sift together the dry ingredients and add onion. Add milk slowly until the dough is soft but easily handled. Shape into flat round cakes and fry in bacon grease, preferably in an iron frying pan. Or roll in small balls and drop into deep fat until brown and crisp.

This is one of the most controversial recipes I know of. People get violent on the subject of how Hush Puppies got their name and just how to make them in the real *way. Well, this is the way I learned in Virginia and I'll stay with it.*

WAYSIDE INN OATMEAL BREAD

1 pint (slow-cooking) oatmeal, uncooked
1 qt boiling water
2 tbsp lard or Crisco
1 tbsp salt
½ cup molasses
1 yeast cake (dissolved in ¼ cup lukewarm water)
7 cups bread flour

Add the lard or Crisco to the boiling water and pour over oatmeal. Stir lightly, and let stand for 2 hours.

Add salt, molasses and yeast cake, and gradually add flour, beating well until a soft dough is formed. Turn out on a pastry cloth or floured board and knead about five minutes, or until the dough is satiny. Place dough in greased bowl. Cover and let rise in warm place until doubled in bulk (about 2 hours), then punch down. Divide dough in three parts and put into greased 9″ × 5″ × 3″ bread pans. Let rise again and then bake at 425° for 1½ hours or until bread draws away from the sides of the pans and is browned on top.

MAKES three loaves

In summer, if it is hot, you may need an extra cup of flour.

BATTERBREAD

1 cup cornmeal (white, waterground)
1 tsp salt
¼ cup bacon grease
2⅔ cups boiling water.
1 cup milk
3 eggs

Combine cornmeal, salt, bacon fat, and boiling water. Stir well. Add milk and eggs. Beat with rotary beater until blended. Grease shallow baking dish well (10″ Pyrex pie plate). Cook in very hot oven (450°) for 45 minutes.

SERVES 6

SPOON BREAD

1   pint fresh milk
½ pint white cornmeal, sifted with
1   tsp salt and
½ tsp baking powder
2   eggs
    Butter or margarine (about half a stick), melted

Bring milk to a boil, then stir in the sifted meal, and cook until it forms a medium-thick mush. Break in the eggs, add the butter or margarine and beat well. Turn into a greased casserole (1-quart size) and bake in a hot oven (400°) about 20 minutes or until it puffs up and is delicately brown.

Serve immediately, before it falls!

SERVES 4–6

When I first had spoon bread in Virginia, I did not know whether to put it on my butter plate or on the dinner plate. I felt it might be a vegetable dish, and, on the other hand, might not. There are many versions of this, but the one we use at Stillmeadow never fails to please.

For the benefit of Northerners like me, I will say you spoon it onto your plate, drop a dab of butter on it, and eat it with a fork. It is one of the best Southern dishes.

Serve it with sausage, broiled tomatoes, a green salad. Or with chicken or pork or ham. Try a leftover spoonful for a bedtime snack.

SQUIRTS

Toast one side of a slice of bread. On the untoasted side place a mixture of fine chopped onions, mayonnaise, and Parmesan cheese. Place under the broiler until it is bubbling and brown crusts appear.

These are so easy to prepare that it doesn't seem right they should seem so elegant. Make plenty, because you will need them. I cut the bread in rounds with a small cooky cutter.

POPOVERS

1 cup flour
½ tsp salt
2 eggs
⅞ cup milk
1 tbsp melted butter

Sift flour and salt. Mix eggs, milk and butter and stir into dry ingredients. Beat until blended. Pour batter into muffin pans, filling them only a third full. Bake for 20 minutes in a hot oven (450°), then reduce heat to 350°and bake until popovers are brown and puffed up.

Iron muffin pans are best, but pyrex will do. Put oil or butter in pans and heat in hot oven for about 10 minutes. If you use the pyrex do not heat but rinse in hot water; then dry and then butter.

Take from pans at once.

MAKES 12 popovers

Popovers are transient. They fall in a short time, so plan to have them not quite done when guests begin to sit at the table. I have everything else for the meal on, and then whip out the popovers and run with them. They never sit long enough to fall once they are passed.

OLD HUNDRED BANANA BREAD

3 bananas   1 tsp baking powder
¼ cup shortening   ½ tsp salt
1 cup sugar   ½ cup chopped walnuts
1¾ cups flour   3 eggs
1 tsp soda

Blend mashed bananas, sugar and eggs, and shortening. Add nuts. Sift dry ingredients and add to mixture. Mix swiftly, pour in pan. Bake 30 minutes in slow oven (350°).

The bananas should not be green, just yellow, flecked with brown at the tip.

TOASTED LOAF

1 loaf unsliced bread, preferably day-old
Butter or margarine
Garlic salt or ½ clove crushed garlic

Remove the top from the loaf of bread and carefully scoop out the center, leaving ½-in. shell all around. (Use leftover bread for stuffing, crumbs, or whatever.) Mix butter or margarine and garlic, and spread over the inside of the loaf. Bake in a slow oven (300°) until the loaf is crisp and delicately brown but not hard.

Fill center with:

Hot sautéed lobster pieces, fried shrimp, or chicken.

Serve with a bowl of sauce to spoon over. For the sauce use a curry sauce, a Newburg sauce, or a rich cream sauce, according to what fits the filling best. Or use canned cream of mushroom or chicken soup diluted with half a can of milk, and heated.

It is preferable to serve the sauce separately to spoon over, so it does not soak into the casing. With a green tossed salad, this makes a meal. Add hot black coffee and a fruit compote for dessert.
* For a buffet party, make several loaves and fill with different ingredients. Arrange the loaves on a large ovenproof platter and keep hot until you serve. For most fillings, a dish of grated Parmesan cheese to sprinkle over is a help.*

BETTER CINNAMON TOAST

Cut slices of fresh bread diagonally. Fry slowly, add butter gradually until bread is golden brown. Drop bread into a bag of sugar and cinnamon and shake gently. Serve warm.

It is sublime.

CHEESE BREAD

¼ cup shortening
⅓ cup sugar
¾ cup milk, or a little more
1 egg
1 cup grated American or Cheddar cheese
2 cups flour, sifted with
3 tsp baking powder
    Dash of salt

Cream shortening and sugar. Beat the egg and add with the cheese. Mix well. Then add the flour, baking powder, and salt alternately with the milk to the first mixture. Turn into a greased 5″ × 9″ loaf pan and bake in a moderate oven (350°) for about an hour, or until a straw inserted in the center comes out clean.

If the cheese is very dry, you will need to add a little extra milk. The dough should come easily from the bowl, but not runny as pancake batter. Toasted, this is excellent for Sunday brunch with scrambled eggs. It makes fine sandwiches with deviled ham or crab-salad filling. It keeps well, and is good to have on hand.

CHEESE SHORTBREAD

¼ cup butter
1 pkg snappy cheese
½ cup flour

Cream butter and cheese and work in flour with the fingers. Place in icebox for at least 2 hours. Shape in thin molds the size of a 50-cent piece. Bake 5 minutes on cooky tin in a hot oven.

This makes a good pre-dinner snack and is also nice for a tea party as a pickup from the sweet cakes, mints, and so on.

ENGLISH MUFFINS

1 cup milk	1 tbsp water
1½ tsp salt	About 2¾ cups bread flour
1 tbsp sugar	2 tbsp butter or margarine,
1 cake yeast	softened

Scald milk and add salt and sugar. When lukewarm, add yeast dissolved in water and about half the flour. Allow to rise until double in bulk; add butter and remaining flour. Let rise again. Place on well-floured board and roll to ¾ inches in thickness and cut in rounds (about 2½ inches). When light, cook on griddle, using muffin rings, if available. When cool, split and toast.

MAKES 12 to 16

Instead of hot rolls or biscuits for dinner, try using English muffins split and spread with herb butter or cheese and paprika (use Parmesan grated cheese). If you don't make your own muffins, use the store ones, which will do.

DOUGHNUTS

2 tbsp shortening	3½ cups flour
¾ cup sugar	1 tsp salt
2 eggs, well beaten	5 tsp baking powder
¾ cup milk	2 tsp cinnamon

Cream shortening and sugar. Add eggs, milk, and then flour, salt, baking powder and cinnamon, sifted together. Mix until it holds together; then roll on a floured board and cut with a floured doughnut cutter. Dough should be ⅜-inch thick. Let stand 15 minutes to make it easier to handle. Fry in deep fat medium hot (375°). Drain on brown paper.

Doughnut dough should be just as soft as you can handle. Never fry too many at once: let each doughnut have room to cook. Turn only once while frying, when they rise to the top. Drain on brown paper and shake in a sack filled a third full of powdered sugar.

This is a true doughnut, not the rounds of stiff cake you can buy. It's worth the effort.

SMILEY BURNETTE'S BUTTERMILK PANCAKES

2 cups flour	1 tbsp sugar
2 cups buttermilk	½ tsp salt
1 tsp soda	1 egg
1 tsp baking powder	

Mix in a blender, or beat well with a rotary beater. If it seems too thick, add more buttermilk until it is of pouring consistency. Some buttermilk is heavier, and this batter should not be stiff.

Pour into a narrow-topped bottle such as a milk bottle and let stand overnight in the refrigerator. In the morning, shake up well, and pour on a hot griddle.

If you use an ordinary griddle, grease it well. If you use an electric frying pan, melt a little butter in it first.

Cook the pancakes until the edges are lacy; then turn and cook just until the underside is full of bubbles.

Serve with maple sugar, honey butter, or powdered sugar.

SERVES 6

HOT-WATER PASTRY

1½ cups cake flour
½ cup shortening, preferably lard
¼ cup boiling water
½ tsp baking powder
½ tsp salt

Place the shortening in a bowl and pour the boiling water over it. Beat until the mixture is creamy.

Sift the flour, salt, and baking powder together, and combine with the liquid ingredients, mixing well. The dough should form a soft ball. Place in the refrigerator, covered, and chill until firm.

MAKES a two-crust 8-inch pie

If you have a pastry cloth, roll out on that. Or roll between two layers of waxed paper.

Desserts, Cakes, Cookies

DESSERTS BEGIN WITH *D* AS DIET DOES. MY FEELING TOWARD both is lukewarm, but I have some beloved friends who do not consider they have had a meal unless it ends with a fabulous dessert. It is a pleasure to make a good dessert for Ted or Steve, for instance, because they look so *HAPPY* when they see it. Now and then I like something like strawberry shortcake as a meal by itself, but I really prefer a light dessert and an easy one.

Here are a few suggestions from my daughter, Connie, who wants a little something sweet at dinner's end, to add to her Easy Desserts which you will find in the following pages:

1) Add sauterne to canned pears, after draining and chilling the pears. Let stand overnight in the wine.

2) Dredge a bowl of sliced bananas and ripe blackberries with sweetened lime juice.

3) Stir some chopped-up candied ginger into applesauce and put in an ice tray. Freeze in the freezing compartment of your refrigerator. Cut in squares at serving time and garnish with Maraschino cherries.

I like a bowl of fresh fruit and a platter of cheeses with crisp crackers. I serve fruit cool but not chilled. I think it loses flavor if it is cold, and pears and apples make my teeth ache if they are icy.

If you use whipped cream for toppings, here is a tip. Whip cream until it stands in peaks and drop by spoonfuls on foil or aluminum pans. Freeze. Wrap in plastic and store.

Serve cheeses at room temperature and use natural cheese for dessert, not processed.

Most pies are better served slightly warm. The juices of fruit pies will stiffen if too cold.

If you serve after-dinner coffee, liqueur or dessert wine, also serve a bowl of nuts in the shell.

CHERRIES JUBILEE

1 large can black cherries (about 2 cups)	1 tbsp cornstarch
	1 cup juice
1 tbsp sugar	½ cup brandy

Drain the cherries, reserving the juice. Mix sugar and cornstarch and add gradually 1 cup of the juice. Cook over slow heat about 5 minutes, then add the cherries. Warm the brandy, pour it over the cherries and ignite it. Spoon the juice in the pan over the cherries and serve the dish aflame.

SERVES 6

This is a favorite chafing dish dessert. It may be served over vanilla ice cream if you like. Be sure the brandy is warm or it won't light!

MELON SUPREME

1 ripe canteloupe
Sauterne, or any dry white table wine

Cut out a hole in one end of the melon and scoop the seeds out with an iced-tea spoon. Pour 1 cup of wine (as needed, according to the size of the melon) in the hole. Replace the plug. Chill 4 hours. Cut in wedges to serve. Garnish with mint sprigs dipped in powdered sugar.

SERVES 4

You may arrange the wedges in a circle and fill the center with white grapes or other fresh fruit.

BAKED APPLES JUBILEE

6 large baking apples, peeled and cored
1 cup mincemeat
½ cup brown sugar (a little more if the apples are tart)
1½ cups dry white wine
1 tsp granulated sugar to each apple
3 tsp brandy or rum
1 lump of sugar
2 tbsp brandy

Fill the centers of the apples with mincemeat and arrange them in a baking dish. Spread the brown sugar over. Pour 1 cup wine in the pan, and bake in a moderate oven (350°) until the apples are tender. Put the apples in a warm serving dish. Add the rest of the mincemeat and wine to the juices in the pan and cook 5 minutes, then pour over the apples. Sprinkle the granulated sugar and ½ teaspoon brandy on each apple. Then put the lump of sugar in a ladle, add the 2 tablespoons brandy warmed, ignite and pour it burning over the apples.

You may pass a bowl of plain thick cream if you like.

SERVES 6 elegantly

If you are not fond of brandy or rum, this is still a good dessert. And now that mincemeat comes in cans, you can make this dessert easily.

AMBROSIA

1 ripe pineapple
6 oranges
2 cups grated cocoanut

Peel and slice the pineapple. Peel oranges and cut in small pieces. Put the fruit in a chilled bowl and sprinkle the cocoanut over. Add powdered sugar if the fruit is not sweet enough.

SERVES 6

You may add a dash of sherry or cointreau if you wish. This was a very special treat when I was growing up, because a ripe pineapple was an event. Canned pineapple just isn't the same, partly because the texture is different. This is a fine dessert for a roast beef dinner.

CONNIE'S EASY DESSERTS

CLARET STRAWBERRIES

Box of fresh strawberries, wash and hull
Sugar
Claret

Sprinkle sugar over berries, cover with claret. Chill for at least an hour, stirring occasionally.

SERVES 2–4

LEFTOVER HONEYDEW WITH WINE

Wedge of honeydew melon
1 ripe peach, peeled and diced
½ cup blackberries
2 tbsp powdered sugar
½ cup dry white wine

Dice melon and combine with peach and berries, then add sugar and wine. Chill.

SERVES 2–4

And now you have leftover blackberries, says Connie. Use them for breakfast!

SHERRY GELATIN

2 envelopes unflavored gelatin
½ cup cold water
¾ cup boiling water.
1 cup orange juice
¼ cup lemon juice (plus some grated peel)
¾ cup sugar
1 cup sherry

Soak gelatin in cold water, dissolve in the boiling water, then add remaining ingredients. Chill in your prettiest mold.

SERVES 4

BAKED FRESH PEARS

2 firm pears, peeled and cored
Cloves
¼ cup sugar
½ cup water
Grated cocoanut

Stud the pears with cloves and put them in a shallow baking dish. Mix sugar and water and pour over. Cover and bake in a moderate oven (375°) about 40 minutes. Just before serving, sprinkle with cocoanut.

SERVES 2

GLAZED FRESH PEACHES

2 fresh peaches, preferably freestone, peeled and halved

¼ cup honey
Chopped nuts

Heat the honey and dip the peaches in, then lay them gently in an ice tray from your refrigerator. Chill but do not freeze. Garnish with the nuts before serving.

SERVES 2

FROSTED GRAPES

Seedless grapes
Egg white, beaten
Powdered sugar
Orange or tangerine segments

Snip grapes into small clusters and dip each in the egg white. When almost dry, dip in the powdered sugar. Chill. Serve with the orange or tangerine segments in glass or crystal dishes.

PLAN on two or three clusters per person

SWEDISH RÖDGRÖT

Use fresh raspberry juice, adding a little currant jelly if too sweet. Cook 4 cups of the fruit juice and thicken with 3 tablespoons of cornstarch dissolved in a little water. Cook until it is thick as gravy and pour in a low bowl. Do not chill. Cover the top with ground almonds and heavy cream. You may add sugar to the juice if you need. It is really a fruit cream, very rich and yet delicate.

Alfred Lunt gave me this recipe while he was busily kneading cardamon bread in his kitchen in New York. It was the only time I ever met him, and I was unable to utter one sensible word. I just nodded my head when he asked a question. But I managed to get the recipe and to eat three slices of the hot bread.

CONNIE'S COMPOTE DE LUXE

1   cup sour cream
1   cup canned mandarin
      oranges, drained
1   cup canned pineapple
      chunks
½ cup miniature marshmallows
½ cup grated cocoanut
1   3-oz pkg toasted almonds
4 or 5 fresh strawberries

Mix first five ingredients together and put in the refrigerator overnight. When ready to serve, add the almonds and top each serving with a strawberry.

SERVES 4

As Connie says, this sounds rather awful but tastes delicious. I like it because, except for the sour cream, everything comes from that emergency shelf.

SPANISH CREAM

1   envelope plain gelatin
¼ cup cold water
2   cups milk
2   egg yolks, beaten
½ cup sugar
⅛ tsp salt
2   egg whites
1   tsp vanilla or lemon extract, port or sherry

Soften gelatin in cold water. Scald milk and dissolve gelatin in it. Mix beaten egg yolks with sugar and salt. Blend the egg mixture with 1 cup scalded milk; then add the rest of the milk and stir in top of double boiler over hot water until the mixture begins to thicken. Do not let it cook too long or it will curdle. Cool slightly before folding in the beaten whites of 2 eggs. Flavor with vanilla, lemon extract, port or sherry. Pour into a wet mold and chill.

SERVES 4–6

My mother used to make this for faculty dinners. It reminds me of hot summer days, women in flowered frocks, moonlit lawns, and the gleam of candlelight (which Father hated) on the best damask cloth.

GINGER POACHED PEARS

6 ripe firm pears
1 cup water
1 cup sugar
2½ tsp lemon juice
  Pinch of salt
1 tsp vanilla
4 or 5 pieces preserved or candied ginger cut in slivers

Peel the pears but leave the stems on. In a saucepan combine remaining ingredients except ginger and bring to a boil. Add the pears and simmer, covered, for about 25 minutes, or until tender. If the pears are large, cook 3 at a time in the syrup. Put the pears in a shallow serving dish, pour the syrup over and lay the ginger in a star-shaped design in the center so there will be a sliver or two for each serving.
  Chill and serve cold.

SERVES 6

CHOCOLATE SOUFFLÉ

5 egg yolks, beaten until thick
¾ cup sugar
¼ tsp salt
1 tsp vanilla
2½ squares bitter chocolate (melted)
1 cup toasted almonds (shredded)
5 egg whites, beaten stiffly

Beat egg yolks and gradually add sugar, salt and vanilla. Stir in melted chocolate and almonds. Fold in the stiffly beaten egg whites. Turn into a greased baking pan, set in a dish of hot water, and bake 35 minutes in a moderate oven (350°).

SERVES 4–6

This is a delicate and handsome dessert. I only make it when I know my guests will be punctual. A soufflé cannot be warmed over or kept an hour or so!

SWEDISH APPLE PIE

1½ cups apples (diced)   Dash salt
½ cup nut meats   2 tsp baking powder
½ cup flour   1 egg, beaten
¾ cup sugar   1 tsp vanilla

Mix together flour, sugar, salt and baking powder and add to apples and nuts. Beat egg and vanilla. Mix all together. Spread on well-oiled 9-in. pie plate. Bake 25 minutes at 350°.

Serve warm with vanilla ice cream plain — or with whipped cream.

SERVES 4 to 6

You don't have to bother with pastry for this, and it makes a dessert that isn't too heavy.

CHERRY CHEESE PIE

2 cups finely crushed graham cracker crumbs
⅓ cup granulated sugar
½ cup melted butter or margarine
1 pkg dessert-topping mix
1 8-oz pkg cream cheese, softened
1 can (1 lb 5 oz) cherry pie filling mix

Make pie the day before, as follows:

1. Start heating oven to 375°. In bowl combine crushed graham crackers and sugar; mix in butter with fork until mixture is crumbly.
2. Press mixture to bottom and sides of 10-in. pie plate. Bake about 10 minutes, or until crust is golden. Cool.
3. In small bowl make up dessert-topping mix according to directions on label. Then, with electric mixer, beat in softened cream cheese. Pile lightly in crumb crust, just inside outer edge, making a ring about 2½-in. wide.
4. Open pie-filling can and pour into center of pie.

Refrigerate and serve the next day.

SERVES 6–8

Elegant and delicious.

JAMES' FRENCH APPLE PIE

CRUST

1 pkg cream cheese
½ cup butter
1 cup flour

Place cheese and butter in a measuring cup. Let stand until soft. Mix butter and cheese with flour. Mix lightly with tips of fingers only. Finally form into a ball and let stand in the refrigerator for 20 minutes. Then roll out as you do any pie crust. This makes top crust for 8-in. pie. There is no bottom crust.

FILLING

6 medium-tart apples, peeled and thinly sliced
1 cup sugar
½ tsp cinnamon
¼ cup raisins
Butter (size of a walnut)
Juice of a half lemon
1 jigger brandy

Mix apples with sugar, cinnamon, raisins, and butter. Pour lemon juice and brandy over all and let stand for 15 minutes. Place apples directly in pie pan. Put on the pastry top, prick, and bake 20 minutes in a medium oven (350°).

SERVES 6–8

James is not French, but he is the best cook of anything in any language. He is a gentle Negro I have known for years. But when he told me this was simple, I found it wasn't for me. Rolling the crust is a problem on account of that cream cheese. But how delicious it is when you manage it!

CREAM SYLLABUB
(or Posset) 16th Century

½ pint double cream
3 oz sugar
2 tbsp sherry
1 tbsp brandy
1 tbsp lemon juice

Beat well together. Chill. Serve in glasses.

SERVES 2–3

CRÈME BRÛLÉE

2 cups cream
4 egg yolks, well beaten
Maple or brown sugar

Bring the cream to boiling point, stirring, and boil 1 minute. Take it from the fire and pour very slowly over egg yolks, beating constantly. Stir and cook 5 minutes in a double boiler. Place the cream in a buttered baking dish. Chill well. Then cover with a layer of maple sugar or brown sugar and run it under the broiler until the sugar is caramelized. Chill again and serve cold.

SERVES 4

This is elegant and easy to make.

HAZEL'S LIME MERINGUE PIE

1 baked pastry shell, 9-in.
1 cup sugar
¼ cup cornstarch
Pinch of salt
1½ cups boiling water
3 eggs separated
⅓ cup fresh lime juice
Rind of 1 lime, grated

Mix sugar, cornstarch and salt, and put in the top of a double boiler. Add boiling water slowly, stirring constantly. When blended, place over hot but not boiling water in the lower unit of the boiler. Cook until thick and smooth.

Meanwhile beat the egg yolks, add a little of the mixture from the double boiler, stirring constantly; then return to the double boiler and cook for 2 or 3 minutes. Remove from heat and stir in the lime juice and grated rind. Blend thoroughly. Cool slightly.

Pour into pastry shell. Beat the egg whites and pile lightly on top of the pie. Bake in a medium oven (325°) until the meringue begins to brown.

This is from the Hazel of Ted Key's inimitable cartoons, and Hazel ought to know what is delicious.

EMMA GOLDMAN'S STRAWBERRY GLAZE PIE

1   pastry shell for a 9-in. pie, baked
2   pkgs frozen strawberries, thawed
1/3 cup granulated sugar
3   tbsp cornstarch
1¼ cups strawberry juice
     Custard (*see below*)

Strain the berries. Make the custard and pour into the pie shell when partly cooled.

Meanwhile make the glaze, as follows. Mix sugar, cornstarch and juice, and cook over low heat, stirring constantly, until thick and smooth.

Lay the berries over the custard, then pour the glaze over. Chill in refrigerator. Before serving, top with whipped cream.

CUSTARD

3 egg yolks   2½ tbsp cornstarch
1/3 cup sugar 1 tbsp butter
1/4 tsp salt   2 cups scalded milk

Beat egg yolks, then gradually beat in sugar, salt, cornstarch, butter. Pour the milk over. Cook over boiling water in a double boiler, stirring until thick and smooth. Cool. Use half of this for the pie, reserve the rest for another day.

SERVES 5

It could not be richer, or more delicious. Serve it after a mixed grill (no potatoes, please) with coffee, extra black.

HOLIDAY RUM PIE

15–20 graham crackers
¼ lb butter
⅓ (scant) cup sugar

Roll the crackers until they are fine, melt the butter, and add butter and sugar to the crumbs. Work together with fingertips until it holds together. Line a pie tin (8 in.) with this, pressing down firmly.

FILLING

2 large eggs
½ cup sugar
1 tbsp rum
4 small pkgs cream cheese

Beat the eggs, add the sugar. Add the rum to the cream cheese and, if the cheese is very stiff, add a teaspoon of cream. Combine the two mixtures and beat until creamy. Pour into the crust and bake in a medium oven (350°) for 25 minutes.

TOPPING

1 cup commercial sour cream
3 tbsp sugar
1 tbsp rum

Mix well together and spread on top of the pie. Return to the oven a few minutes to heat the cream.

SERVES 4–5

This is a fine dessert for a winter buffet. Good with country ham, broccoli soufflé, a green salad, coffee.

IRIS FLANARY'S RAW APPLE CAKE

1½ cups finely grated raw
    apple
2 tbsp water
½ cup shortening
1 cup sugar
1 egg, beaten
2 cups flour
2 tsp baking powder

½ tsp baking soda
1 tsp cinnamon
½ tsp nutmeg
½ tsp salt
1 cup raisins
1 cup chopped nuts (black
    walnuts if you can get
    them)

Add water to apples. Cream shortening and sugar, add the apples, egg, and flour sifted with baking powder, baking soda, cinnamon, nutmeg and salt. Add raisins and nuts.

Bake in a greased 9″ × 9″ pan in a moderate oven (350°) for about 45 minutes. Test with a straw for just when the cake is ready to come out. You can pour orange juice over it, if you like, after it is done; this keeps it moist for a longer time. You may top with Apple Snow frosting – using your own favorite 7-minute frosting and adding ½ cup grated raw apple.

HOT MILK CAKE

1 cup sugar
2 eggs
1 cup flour, sifted
1 tsp baking powder
1 tsp flavoring (vanilla, lemon, almond, or what-
    ever your taste prefers)
1 cup hot milk
2½ tsp butter (melted in hot milk)

Beat sugar and eggs well together. Add flour and baking powder sifted together. Add flavoring. Last add hot milk with butter melted in it. Pour into layer pans and bake in 375° oven.

Barbara says when you just have nothing in the house but a few scraps and someone phones they are coming – hot milk cake will save your life. You may frost it with your favorite frosting.

HELEN PETERSON'S CHERRY SPICE CAKE

1 cup sugar	2 cups flour
½ cup butter or margarine	½ tsp cinnamon
3 eggs, beaten	½ tsp cloves
4 tbsp sour milk	½ tsp nutmeg
½ tsp baking soda	1 cup sour cherries, drained

Cream together sugar and butter. Stir in beaten eggs and sour milk to which baking soda has been added. Sift together flour, cinnamon, cloves and nutmeg, and mix with the other ingredients. Stir in drained sour cherries.

You can use any canned cherries for this—but the tart ones are really the best. It can be frosted, but I think that spoils it.

SOUR-CREAM CAKE

1 cup sugar	¼ tsp baking soda
1 cup sour cream	1 tsp baking powder
2 eggs, well beaten	Pinch of salt
1½ cups flour	

Add sugar and sour cream to well-beaten eggs; sift together flour, baking soda, baking powder and salt; resift and add them to the first mixture. Stir until smooth. Pour into two layer cake tins, or into one loaf tin which has been greased and dusted with flour. Bake in a moderate oven (350°) about 40 minutes. The cake is done when a straw plunged in the center comes out clean.

CREAM FILLING

½ cup sugar	1 cup milk
1 tbsp cornstarch	2 egg yolks, beaten
Pinch of salt	

Mix sugar, cornstarch and salt and put in a heavy pan. Add the milk and cook over low heat, stirring constantly until the mixture thickens. Add egg yolks and cook 3 minutes longer. Let cool and flavor as desired. (I use lemon extract or instant coffee.)

Frost with butter frosting.

BUTTER FROSTING

¼ cup butter
½ cup confectioner's sugar, sifted
2 egg whites
1 cup confectioner's sugar, sifted

Cream the butter well. Add the ½ cup of sugar. Beat egg whites until stiff; then beat in the cup of confectioner's sugar. Combine the two mixtures and if necessary add a little more sugar. Flavor as desired.

JERRY'S CHEESE CAKE

1¼ cups graham crackers (crushed)
¼ cup powdered sugar
1 tsp allspice
⅓ cup melted butter
2 8-oz pkgs cream cheese (at room temperature)
2 eggs, beaten lightly
⅔ cup sugar
2 tsp vanilla
1½ cups sour cream
4 tsp sugar
2 tsp vanilla

Combine crumbs, powdered sugar, allspice, melted butter. Spread in bottom of a 9-in. spring form pan, pressing some up the sides to form a rim about ½ to ¾ inch high. Stir cheese until soft and creamy. Add eggs, ⅔ cup sugar, 2 teaspoons vanilla. Beat until thoroughly creamed and smooth. Pour into crust and bake in moderate (350°) oven for about 25 minutes. Meanwhile, combine sour cream, 4 teaspoons sugar and 2 teaspoons vanilla. Spread over top of cheese cake, return to oven. Increase temperature to 450°. Bake 7 minutes. Cool, then chill.

SERVES 6

If you do not have a spring form pan, you may use a deep round cake pan or angel food pan. Then you will have to work the cake out with a pie server or spatula. Still tastes extra special.

TOMATO-SOUP CAKE

1 pkg spice-cake mix
1 can (10½ oz) tomato soup
¼ cup water
1 cup chopped pecans

Mix cake as directed on the package (using the soup and water for the liquid called for). Add nuts. Bake in a greased and floured 9-in. tube cake pan. Bake as directed on the package, or until cake draws away from sides of the pan.

Frost with lemon icing.

This is an old-fashioned cake made the easy modern way. For the icing you may use sifted confectioner's sugar blended with lemon juice. A little grated peel helps.

ALICE ADAMS' TEA CAKE

¾ cup sugar
½ cup butter or margarine
1½ cups flour
1½ tsp baking powder
½ tsp salt
2 tsp cinnamon
½ cup milk
1 beaten egg

Mix together the sugar, butter or margarine, flour sifted with salt, and baking powder and cinnamon. Reserve ⅓ cup for topping.

Add the milk to the egg, then add the first mixture and beat until smooth. Pour into a greased 8-in. cake pan and sprinkle the reserved topping over.

Bake 20 minutes in a moderate oven (350°) or until a straw comes out clean when inserted in the center. Serve hot.

SERVES 6 — but 3 can eat it all

This is a quick and wonderful addition to tea when guests drop in, better than cake or cookies, in my opinion.

PINEAPPLE UPSIDE-DOWN CAKE

½ cup butter or margarine   ½ cup water
1½ cups soft brown sugar   1 tsp vanilla
7 slices canned pineapple   1½ cups flour
½ cup shelled pecan halves   1½ tsp baking powder
3 eggs   7 maraschino or candied
1⅓ cups white sugar   cherries

Melt the butter or margarine and brown sugar in a heavy large frying pan (iron if possible). Lay the pineapple slices in gently. Fill the spaces with the pecans. Remove from stove and let cool.

Beat the eggs well, add the white sugar and beat 5 minutes. Then add the water and beat 5 minutes. Add vanilla. Sift the flour and baking powder and fold into the egg mixture. Pour the batter lightly on top of the pineapple. Bake in a moderate oven (325°) about 30 minutes (or until the sponge begins to draw away from the sides of the frying pan and the top is light brown).

Carefully invert the pan on a round platter or chop plate. Fill the holes in the pineapple slices with the cherries. You may top with whipped cream.

An electric beater makes this very easy, but when I first made it, nobody had ever heard of an electric beater. I used a single, shaky hand beater. This is the best upside-down cake I ever found.

SOUR-CREAM GINGERBREAD

1 egg, beaten   1 tsp baking-soda, and
1 cup maple syrup   1½ tsp powdered ginger
1 cup sour cream   4 tbsp butter or margarine,
2⅓ cups flour, sifted with   melted

Blend the egg, maple syrup and cream. Add to the dry ingredients, beating until smooth. Then add the butter or margarine and beat again. Pour the batter into a square or rectangular 8″ × 10½″ baking pan lined with aluminum foil or waxed paper.

Bake in a moderate oven (350°) for about 30 minutes, or until it begins to draw away from the pan.

Serve plain or frosted or with cream.

SERVES 6

WELLESLEY FUDGE CAKE

2   cups brown sugar
½ cup butter or shortening
2   eggs, beaten
½ cup cold water
½ cup sour milk
1   tsp baking soda
2   cups pastry flour
1   tsp baking powder
½ tsp vanilla
1   square Baker's chocolate, melted

Cream sugar with butter and stir in beaten eggs, cold water, and sour milk in which baking soda has been dissolved. Finally stir in flour, measured after sifting, and resifted with baking powder, vanilla and chocolate. Bake in 2 square layers.

FROSTING

2½ cups brown sugar
    Butter (size of a walnut)
2   squares of Baker's chocolate
½ cup rich milk or cream
1   tsp vanilla
    Chopped walnuts, about ⅓ cup

Cook together sugar, butter, chocolate, and milk or cream for 10 minutes; then add vanilla. Set in cold water until the frosting is thick at the bottom; then beat to proper consistency and spread on first layer. Cover with chopped walnuts and spread again with frosting. Frost top of cake and sprinkle with chopped walnuts.

GRANDMA'S CHOCOLATE CAKE

1½ cups brown sugar	2 cups cake flour
1 cup milk	½ tsp salt
3 oz grated unsweetened chocolate	1 tsp baking soda
	1 tsp baking powder
½ cup shortening	1 tsp vanilla
2 eggs, beaten	

Heat ½ cup of brown sugar, half the milk and the chocolate in a double boiler until the chocolate melts. Whip with a wire whisk or a rotary beater to blend in the chocolate thoroughly. Cool. Cream shortening and rest of the brown sugar. Add beaten eggs and stir until smooth. Sift together flour, salt, baking soda and baking powder. Add the dry ingredients alternately with the rest of the milk. Then add chocolate mixture and vanilla.

Bake in two 8-in. layer pans in a moderate oven (350°) for 25 to 30 minutes. Remove to racks and let stand for 5 minutes. Then turn out of pans. Spread cream filling (page 280) between the layers and frost with butter frosting (page 281).

Grandma used to wear soft grey silk dresses with white lace at the throat and wrists. She was small and elegant, but when she got into the kitchen, marvels happened. One I liked best was her cake.

DATE TORTE

3 eggs, beaten	1 tsp baking powder
1 cup sugar	1 cup each of chopped dates
1 cup flour	and nuts

Beat eggs and add sugar. Sift flour and baking powder and stir dates and nuts into the flour. Combine with the eggs and sugar. Beat until smooth. Bake about 20 minutes in a moderate oven (350°) in a shallow loaf cake pan which has been greased. Turn out immediately on a board and cut in squares. Nice when dusted with powdered sugar before serving or with whipped cream on top.

This is a fine send-away present. I ate my way through college sustained by frequent boxes of it from home, and later sent it to my own child and to various boys in the services.

ADELAIDE'S BROT TORTE

5 eggs, separated
1 cup sugar
1 cup fine white bread crumbs
1 cup finely chopped or grated almonds, not blanched
½ tsp cinnamon
 Grated rind of 1 lemon
1 tsp baking powder

Beat whites and yolks of eggs separately. Add sugar to the yolks and stir well; then stir in bread crumbs and almonds, cinnamon, lemon rind, and baking powder. Fold in egg whites. Bake in two 8″ layers. Bake in a moderate oven (350°) for about 25 minutes.

CUSTARD FILLING

1 cup milk   1 tbsp cornstarch
2 tbsp sugar   1 egg, beaten

Heat milk in double boiler. Add sugar and cornstarch and, when dissolved, add beaten egg slowly. Cook until custard has thickened.

Before putting custard between the layers, make 1 large cup of hot sweet lemonade from one lemon. Spread ½ cup over each layer. Cake should stand for a time before serving to give lemonade a chance to permeate each layer. Put together with custard filling and serve sprinkled with powdered sugar.

CHRISTMAS RIBBON CAKE

3 eggs   1 tsp vanilla
¼ lb butter   3 tbsp molasses
1 cup sugar   ½ tsp clove
1 cup milk   1 cup seedless raisins
2½ cups flour, sifted   ½ cup citron, chopped
3 tsp baking powder

Beat well together eggs, butter and sugar. Add milk and vanilla alternately with flour and baking powder sifted together. Divide mixture in three parts. Leave two parts as is; to third part add molasses, clove, raisins and citron, well floured.

Bake in 3 rectangular pans of equal size in 375° oven.

With fruit layer in middle, spread with apple jelly, and frost with plain butter frosting flavored with a bit of orange juice. Decorate with holly and red barley candy reindeer.

I hope you can get the barley reindeer — they are delightful. But this is a festive cake, reindeer or no, and a fine change from those endless Christmas cookies.

LEMON SPONGE CUPS

2	tbsp butter	5	tbsp lemon juice
1	cup sugar		Rind of lemon
4	tbsp flour	3	eggs, separated
1/8	tsp salt	1½	cups milk

Cream butter, add sugar, flour, salt, lemon juice, and rind. Stir in beaten egg yolks mixed with milk. Fold in stiffly beaten egg whites. Pour into 7 custard cups. Set the cups in a pan of water and bake for 45 minutes at 350°. When done, each cup will contain a custard at the bottom and sponge cake on top.

This recipe was a prize winner at a Connecticut contest. Rose Canny, who lives in the charming village of Brooklyn, invited me for tea and the lemon sponge cakes. They should win a prize any day!

MRS. BEWLAY'S RHUBARB CRUSTY

- 4 cups rhubarb, cut into 1-in. pieces
- 1/4 to 1/2 cup sugar (depending on how sweet you like it)
- 5 tbsp flour
- 2 tbsp butter
- 4 tbsp brown sugar

Mix rhubarb and sugar. Place in a buttered baking dish. Rub together with your fingers the flour, butter and brown sugar and sprinkle over the rhubarb. Bake in a moderate oven (350°) for 35 minutes, or until done.

SERVES 4

If you have a garden and grow rhubarb you know the feeling of being just swamped with rhubarb. It can, and does, get tiresome. This is a nice variation from stewed rhubarb, rhubarb pie, baked rhubarb, etc.

ORANGE CAKE

1½ cups flour	½ cup butter
2 tsp baking powder	1 cup sugar
¼ tsp salt	2 eggs
1 tsp grated orange rind	½ cup orange juice

Sift flour once, measure, add baking powder and salt and sift three times. Add orange rind to butter and cream. Add sugar gradually. Add eggs one at a time, beating thoroughly. Add flour alternately with orange juice. Pour in loaf pan and bake in 375° oven between 20 and 25 minutes.

ORANGE-BUTTER ICING

1 tbsp grated orange rind	1 egg yolk, unbeaten
½ tsp grated lemon rind	⅛ tsp salt
3 tbsp butter	2½ cups confectioner's sugar

Add orange and lemon rind to fruit juices and let stand ten minutes. Cream butter. Add egg yolk and salt and mix well. Add part of sugar gradually, blending fruit juices after each addition of sugar. Do this with sugar and juices alternately. Enough frosting for two layers and sides of cake.

CHOCOLATE MOUSSE

1 pkg semisweet chocolate bits
1 large square bitter chocolate
7 eggs
　Salt
1 tsp vanilla

Melt chocolate over hot water. Separate eggs. Beat yolks till light, add salt and vanilla. Cook melted chocolate a couple of minutes. Pour into yolks. Blend well. Beat whites very stiff, fold into yolks. Pour into big dish. Stand in refrigerator overnight.

SERVES 10

This does take a lot of eggs, but you have a wonderful dessert for a party! And all done the day before, too.

CHOCOLATE SOUFFLÉ

3 tbsp butter	2 squares baking chocolate
2 tbsp flour	3-in. piece of vanilla bean
¼ tsp salt	4 beaten egg yolks
½ cup sugar	5 egg whites, stiffly beaten

Melt butter in a saucepan and slowly blend in the flour. Gradually add milk and salt. Then, stirring constantly, add chocolate and vanilla. When chocolate is melted and sauce is smooth, remove vanilla. Cool. Add the egg yolks and beat well; then fold in egg whites.

Butter a soufflé dish or deep casserole, sprinkle lightly with sugar and then pour the batter in. Set dish in a pan of hot water and bake in a hot oven (400°) for 15 minutes. Reduce heat to moderate (375°) and cook 20 minutes longer. Serve hot with cream.

SERVES 6

The soufflé is done when puffed up and firm in center.

LEMON BREAD PUDDING

2 cups milk	2 eggs
½ cup sugar	Grated rind 1 lemon
2 cups inch-size bread cubes	

Soak bread cubes in milk 5 minutes. Add sugar to the milk; then add the beaten egg yolks and lemon rind. Put in buttered baking dish and bake in slow oven (300°) until firm like custard. Bake ½ hour. Beat egg whites until stiff, add 2 tablespoons sugar and spread over top. Brown in moderate oven and serve with lemon sauce.

LEMON SAUCE

½ cup sugar	1½ tbsp lemon juice
1 cup hot water	Dash of nutmeg
1 tbsp cornstarch	Pinch of salt
2 tsp butter	

Mix and cook in double boiler until smooth.

SERVES 4 to 6

NEW ENGLAND RICE PUDDING

3   eggs, slightly beaten
½ cup sugar
    Pinch of salt
½ tsp vanilla
3   cups milk, scalded
¾ cup rice, cooked
    Cinnamon

Mix the first 4 ingredients until well blended, then add the milk. Pour into a greased baking dish, then add rice. Sprinkle cinnamon over. Set baking dish in a pan of hot water and bake in a moderate oven (350°) until the pudding has set and begins to turn golden on top. It will take about 30 minutes.

SERVES 6

This may be served either warm or cold, but in our family it comes to the table warm. A spoonful of thick cream adds a nice touch to each dish.

FLOATING ISLAND PUDDING

1   qt milk   Dash of salt
3   egg yolks, well beaten   1   tsp vanilla
2   tbsp cornstarch   3   egg whites
2   tbsp milk   ¼ cup sugar
1   cup sugar

Scald the milk in the top of a double boiler. Stir in the egg yolks and add the cornstarch dissolved in the 2 tablespoons of milk. Then add the sugar and salt. Cook in the double boiler, stirring constantly until it thickens; add vanilla, and pour into a bowl.

Beat the egg whites until stiff but not dry and then gradually add the ¼ cup sugar, folding it in. Add vanilla and turn the meringue into a mold greased and dusted with sugar. Place the mold in a deep pan in 2 inches of hot water, cover, and bake in a very slow oven (250°) for 20 minutes, or until it is firm.

Cool, unmold in the center of a serving dish, and surround it with the custard. Or leave the custard in the bowl and top with the island.

SERVES 4–6

CHOCOLATE CREAM

½ cup semisweet chocolate bits
8 marshmallows, cut in pieces (or use the new tiny
   ones)
½ cup heavy cream, whipped
¼ cup water
⅔ cup heavy cream

Cook the first four ingredients over low heat in a saucepan until chocolate and marshmallows melt. Remove from heat and chill. When thoroughly chilled, whip remaining cream and fold in. Freeze in ice tray in refrigerator.

MAKES 1 quart

You may use evaporated milk instead of the cream. To whip evaporated milk, chill in ice tray in freezing compartment until the edges begin to stiffen. Put milk in a cold bowl and beat with a rotary beater which you have chilled in the refrigerator.

Whipped evaporated milk may be substituted for cream in most recipes and makes a smooth, satisfactory and inexpensive substitute.

LEMON SOUFFLÉ

4 eggs, separated	2 tbsp lemon juice
½ cup honey	Dash of salt
½ tbsp grated lemon rind	¼ tsp cream of tartar

Beat egg yolks until thick and then add honey, lemon rind and juice, and continue to beat until mixture about doubles in bulk.

In a separate bowl, beat the egg whites with the cream of tartar, then fold into the yolk mixture.

Turn into a greased 2-quart casserole. Set the casserole in a pan of hot water and bake in a moderate oven (350°) about 45 minutes. When it is done, the center is firm to the touch of a finger.

Serve plain or with boiled custard.

SERVES 4–5

This is not hard to make. Just be sure to do the folding gently so the whites will not lose the air. And be sure the oven is not hot.

LEMON BISQUE

        3   tbsp lemon juice
            Grated rind of 1 lemon
        1   can evaporated milk
        1   pkg lemon gelatin
        1¼ cups boiling water
        ⅓ cup honey
        ⅛ tsp salt
        2   cups rolled vanilla-wafer crumbs

Put gelatin, honey, lemon juice, rind, and salt into the boiling water. Let stand until slightly congealed. Then beat evaporated milk and add gelatin mixture. Put half the crumbs in the bottom of a pan (14″ × 8″), add the gelatin mix, top with the rest of the crumbs.

Set in refrigerator to chill well.

Cut in squares for serving.

SERVES 4–6

Evaporated milk must be thoroughly chilled in order to beat well.

This is a delicious dessert, or may be served at teatime. Because of its delicate flavor, it is perfect after a heavy dinner. Fewer calories than cake, and so easy to make.

RASPBERRY PARFAIT

        1   qt raspberries
        1   cup sugar
        ¾ cup water
        3   egg whites, whipped until stiff
        ¼ tsp salt

Crush berries. Meanwhile, boil sugar and water until it threads when dropped from a spoon. Whip egg whites with salt added. Pour the syrup slowly over the whites, beating constantly. When cool, fold in the berries and freeze.

SERVES 4

You may use strawberries if you prefer, but somehow, to me, raspberries are the best.

KING'S ARMS GREEN-GAGE PLUM ICE CREAM

1 pint preserved green-gage plums
Juice of 2 lemons
2 cups sugar
1½ qts milk
1 qt of cream
Dash of salt

Skin and seed and mash the plums, add the lemon juice, sugar, milk, cream and salt, and mix well.

Freeze. If you have a home ice-cream freezer, freeze the ice cream in it. If not, turn your refrigerator to fast freeze. Put the ice cream in the ice trays and freeze. When partially frozen, remove, and stir well to break up the crystals. Or use a French whip. Put back in the freezing unit and freeze until firm.

SERVES 6

This is the best I ever ate. I begged the recipe from John Egan at the King's Arms in Williamsburg after a dinner that made dessert seem impossible. What with the chicken, the rosy Virginia ham, the cornsticks, the creamed celery with pecans, I had no wish for ice cream. I ate a whole huge serving!

ZABAIONE (SHERRY CREAM)

3 eggs, beaten slightly
¾ cup sugar
¼ cup sherry or Marsala
Juice and grated rind of one lemon

Beat eggs in top of a double boiler. Add sugar, sherry or Marsala, juice and grated rind of lemon. Cook over hot water, beating with a rotary beater until the mixture is the consistency of whipped cream. Serve in small glasses, hot or cold, garnished with whipped cream and a cherry.

SERVES 4

Actually the number it serves depends on the size of the glasses. This is a very old recipe and belongs with Queen Anne dining rooms and somebody playing a spinet.

COMPANY SHERBET

2 cups cranberry juice, fresh or bottled
1 envelope unflavored gelatin
1½ cups apple juice
3 tbsp lemon or lime juice
1 cup sugar

Put one cup cranberry juice in a saucepan and sprinkle the gelatin over. Heat gently, stirring constantly, until gelatin dissolves. Remove from heat and add remaining cranberry juice, apple juice, lemon juice. Let cool; then pour into 2 ice trays. Place in freezing compartment until mixture is nearly frozen. This takes about 2 hours. Now pour it into a chilled bowl and beat with a rotary beater until it is smooth. Return the mixture to the ice trays and cover them with foil. Freeze until firm. This takes about 3 hours.

SERVES 6–8

This makes a colorful, refreshing summer dessert, but my daughter Connie makes it all year round. The only trick, as she found out, you must watch it to be sure it doesn't freeze too solid before you beat it.

MAPLE FLOATING ISLAND

4 egg yolks, beaten
⅔ cup rich maple syrup
Speck of salt
4 cups milk
A little vanilla
4 egg whites, beaten stiffly
½ cup sugar

Beat egg yolks and maple syrup and salt. Add milk and cook in a double boiler until the custard coats the spoon. Remove from heat, pour into bowl and cool. Add vanilla.

Beat egg whites and fold in sugar. Put into buttered mold, cover and cook over steam for 20 minutes. Remove mold, but not the cover, and allow to cool. When cold, remove cover and turn onto custard. Chill and serve.

SERVES 4–6

LEMON CHEESE SHERBET

2   3-oz pkgs cream cheese
2   cups milk
½ cup light corn syrup
⅓ cup lemon juice
1   tsp grated lemon rind
2   well-beaten eggs
     Few drops yellow vegetable coloring

Soften the cheese with the back of a spoon. Blend in the milk, syrup, lemon juice, grated rind and eggs. Add tint.

Pour into freezing tray of your refrigerator, and set indicator to coldest position. When almost frozen, scrape into a chilled bowl. Beat quickly with a rotary beater.

Return to refrigerator tray and freeze until firm.

MAKES about 1 quart

CHOCOLATE CARAMEL ICE-CREAM SAUCE

2   1¾-oz milk chocolate bars
¼ cup milk
14 caramels
2   tsp vanilla
     Pinch of salt

Melt the chocolate in the milk in the top of a double boiler over boiling water, stirring until smooth.

Remove wrappers from the caramels and add. Stir again until sauce is smooth. Remove from heat and add the vanilla and salt. Cool.

Serve with ice cream.

Could scarcely have more calories but keep the rest of the meal low in them.

MERINGUES

3 egg whites
Pinch of salt
1/8 tsp cream of tartar
3/4 cup sugar

Put a layer of aluminum foil on your cooky sheets (you need 2) and grease it, then dust with flour. Beat the egg whites until frothy, add the salt and cream of tartar and beat until the mixture is stiff enough to form a peak.

Add the sugar gradually, beating as you add. When the meringue is stiff and begins to look shiny, spoon onto the foil with a tablespoon.

Meanwhile have the oven pre-heating to 225° , or very slow. Slide the meringues gently into the oven and bake 35 minutes, but don't peek. You may then open the oven door and if they are firm and turning beige-colored, they are done. If not, leave them a few minutes more.

Cool them, after removing from foil.

Serve with fresh crushed strawberries, raspberries, or ice-cream in the centers.

MAKES about 16 meringues

An electric beater is a great help, but even without it, once you make meringues, you will use them often. You may make them ahead of time, and store them in an air-tight container.

JOYCE'S PECAN PUFFS

1 cup pecan meats   1 tsp vanilla
1/2 cup butter   1 cup sifted flour
2 tbsp sugar   Confectioner's sugar

Measure 1 cup pecan meats and grind very fine. Cream butter and sugar, add vanilla; add sifted flour. Roll into balls and bake at 300° for 45 minutes. Roll in confectioner's sugar when hot and again when cold.

MAKES about 20, or more

When you make the Christmas confections, don't miss this! It is rich but delicate in texture.

CREAM PUFFS WITH COFFEE FILLING
AND CARAMEL SAUCE

1/4 cup butter or margarine
1/2 cup water
1/2 cup flour with a pinch of salt added
2   unbeaten eggs

Put the butter or margarine in a pan, add the water, and bring to a boil. Then add flour. Keep heat medium high. Now take a spoon – a large one, preferably wooden – and beat the mixture as hard as you can until it comes away from the sides of the pan and makes a ball. Take saucepan from heat. Add 1 egg and beat mixture until smooth. Add the second egg and beat hard again.

Now drop the dough from a tablespoon onto a greased baking sheet, leaving several inches between each puff. Bake in a hot oven (400°) for 20 minutes. Reduce heat to medium (350°) and bake 25 minutes more. Cool.

Slit one side or cut off the top of each puff and fill with coffee cream. Serve with caramel sauce.

MAKES 8 puffs

COFFEE CREAM

1   cup heavy cream, whipped stiff
1 1/2 tsp instant coffee
2   tbsp sugar
1/4 tsp vanilla

Sprinkle coffee on cream, add remaining ingredients, and beat until stiff.

CARAMEL SAUCE

28 caramels
1/2 cup water

Place caramels and water in the top of a double boiler and cook over boiling water until caramels are smooth. Stir occasionally. Cool.

HERMAN SMITH'S GINGER MOLD

2 egg yolks	¼ cup preserved ginger, cut fine
1 cup milk	3 tbsp ginger syrup
½ cup sugar	1 tsp grated orange rind
1 tbsp gelatin dissolved in	1 tsp vanilla
¼ cup cold water	½ pint cream, whipped stiff

Beat egg yolks slightly, add to sugar and milk with a pinch of salt. Put in a double boiler and cook over boiling water, stirring constantly. When it is thick as a custard mixture, add dissolved gelatin. Cool. Then add vanilla, ginger, syrup, orange rind. Fold in whipped cream. Chill in a mold.

Unmold and serve with sprigs of fresh mint and slices of crystallized ginger.

SERVES 4–6

Once, when Herman Smith and I were trading recipes, I admitted desserts were my downfall. This is one of my favorites, and the only difficult thing is to get preserved ginger. The crystallized is sold in most drugstores.

PINEAPPLE CREAM CHEESE DELIGHT

Graham cracker crust	1 8-oz pkg cream cheese
1 cup hot water	1 medium can well-drained
1 pkg lemon jello	crushed pineapple
1 cup sugar	1 can (14½-oz) *chilled*
1 tsp vanilla	Carnation milk

Prepare graham cracker crust according to directions on package. Bring crust up along sides of dish or pan, approximately 12″ × 8″. Prepare jello with 1 cup hot water. Cool to lukewarm.

Cream sugar and cream cheese together. Do not beat. Add crushed pineapple to cream cheese mixture. Add jello to pineapple-cream cheese mixture slowly. Whip chilled milk until peaks form. Fold in 1 tablespoon vanilla. Fold cream cheese mixture in whipped milk. Pour into pan or baking dish and chill until firm. Top with a few crumbs.

SERVES 4–6

This is a rich and elegant finale to a main course of thin sliced cold ham, tossed green salad and bite-sized biscuits.

GRANDMOTHER RAYBOLD'S ENGLISH PLUM PUDDING

1 lb English currants
1 lb raisins, chopped
¼ lb citron, cut small
1 cup beef suet, chopped fine
2 cups sugar
1 qt sweet milk, scalding hot

4 eggs, well beaten
2 cups crackers rolled fine
1 tsp salt
2 tsp (heaped) ground cinnamon
1 tsp ground cloves
1 grated nutmeg

Mix ingredients well. Use a 4-quart tin pail, rub well with butter, set in kettle and fill kettle with water to within 2 inches from top of pail. Make one day before serving. Cover kettle tightly to keep in steam. Put something on bottom of kettle so pudding will not burn on bottom. Cook 8 hours. Serve with hard sauce.

HARD SAUCE

⅓ cup soft butter
1 cup sifted confectioner's sugar
½ tsp vanilla

Cream butter and sugar thoroughly. Then slowly beat in the vanilla. If the sauce separates, add a few drops of boiling water.

SERVES 6–8

You may add a few drops of rum or brandy, if desired.

MRS. TRUMAN'S RASPBERRY DELIGHT

1 pkg raspberry jello
1¼ cups boiling water
1 cup frozen raspberries
   Dash of salt
1 cup heavy cream, whipped
8-oz angel food cake (or less)

Add boiling water to jello; add frozen raspberries and salt. Whip till fluffy. Fold in whipped heavy cream. Pour this over bits of angel food cake. This can be done in layers, too. Chill.

SERVES 6

COTTAGE PUDDING

1/4 cup shortening
1　cup sugar
1　egg, beaten
1/2 tsp lemon or vanilla extract
1¾ cups flour
1　tsp salt
2½ tsp baking powder
2/3 cup milk
1/2 cup chopped nuts
1/2 cup chopped raisins or
1/4 cup thinly sliced maraschino or candied cherries

Cream together shortening and sugar; then add beaten egg and lemon or vanilla extract. Sift together flour, salt, and baking powder. Add these dry ingredients alternately with a total of 2/3 cup milk to the first mixture, and stir in chopped nuts and chopped raisins or thinly sliced maraschino or candied cherries. Pour into a greased cake pan and bake at 350° for about 40 minutes, or until the cake has pulled away from the sides of the pan. Serve with melted jelly or cinnamon or hot chocolate sauce, or with leftover fruit and its juice. The pudding should be served while still warm.

SERVES 6

INDIAN PUDDING I

4　cups milk
1/3 cup cornmeal
1　cup dark molasses
1/4 cup butter or margarine
1　tsp each of salt, cinnamon and ginger
1/2 cup seedless raisins.

Boil milk in top of a double broiler. Smoothly stir in cornmeal and cook 15 minutes; then add molasses and remove from the heat. Add butter, salt, cinnamon, ginger, and seedless raisins. Place this batter in a greased baking dish and pour one cup milk over it. Bake in a slow oven for 1½ to 2 hours. Serve with hard sauce or cream or vanilla ice cream.

INDIAN PUDDING II

3 cups milk	1 whole beaten egg
3 tbsp yellow cornmeal	Butter (size of a walnut)
1/3 cup molasses	1/2 tsp powdered ginger
2 tsp salt	1/2 tsp cinnamon
1/2 cup sugar	

Scald milk and stir the cornmeal in slowly. Add molasses and salt and stir until thickened. Remove from the heat and add sugar, egg, butter, ginger, and cinnamon. Pour into a buttered baking dish and place in a 300° oven. After 30 minutes pour 1 cup of milk over pudding and bake for 2½ hours. Serve with rich cream or vanilla ice cream.

This is an old-fashioned dessert which does not resemble what passes for Indian Pudding in some restaurants. It is moist and light and calls for second helpings.

OZARK PUDDING

¾ cup sugar
1 egg
2 tbsp flour
1½ tsp baking powder
⅛ tsp salt
1 tsp vanilla
½ cup chopped tart apples
½ cup chopped nuts

Beat egg, add sugar and beat 5 minutes with rotary beater or in a mixer.

Sift dry ingredients and add to the egg mixture. Then add vanilla, apples and nuts.

Turn into a greased pie plate and bake in a moderate oven (350°) for about 35 minutes.

Serve with whipped, sweetened cream.

SERVES 4

HILDA'S CHOCOLATE UPSIDE-DOWN PUDDING

1   square unsweetened chocolate
2   tbsp butter or margarine
¾ cup white sugar
1¼ cups cake flour, sifted
2   tsp baking powder
¼ tsp salt
½ cup milk
1   tsp vanilla
½ cup nutmeats, chopped

Melt the butter and chocolate together; mix with milk and vanilla. Sift dry ingredients together. Stir the chocolate mixture into the dry ingredients, add nuts and stir. Pour into a well-greased casserole.

TOPPING

½ cup white sugar
½ cup brown sugar
2   tbsp cocoa
1   cup boiling water

Mix dry ingredients together, and cover the pudding. Pour the boiling water over all. Bake in a moderate oven (350°) until a straw inserted comes out clean. This will take about an hour.

Serve topped with whipped cream.

SERVES 4–6

APPLE PIE ROYALE

1 pkg cream cheese
½ cup butter
1 cup flour
   Pinch of salt

Let cheese and butter soften, then mix together, and blend in the flour, mixing lightly with fingertips. Form in a ball and chill 30 minutes in the refrigerator. Then roll out and set aside.

FILLING

6 tart apples sliced thin
1 cup sugar
½ tsp cinnamon
¼ cup white raisins
   Butter the size of a walnut
   Juice of ½ lemon
1 jigger brandy

Mix apples, sugar, cinnamon, raisins and butter. Pour the lemon juice and brandy over. Let stand 15 minutes. Then place in an 8-inch pie pan, fit the pastry over, prick with a fork, and bake in a medium hot oven (375°) until the pastry is brown and the apples tender (you may test with a fork).

SERVES 4–5

This is the most elegant of apple pies, well worth the time it takes.

CHOCOLATE FONDUE

2   squares unsweetened cooking chocolate
1   cup soft bread crumbs
1   cup milk
1   tbsp butter or margarine
½   cup sugar
    Salt
3   eggs, separated

In a double boiler, over hot water, melt the chocolate. Add the milk and heat, stirring until blended. Then add butter, sugar, a little salt.

Beat the egg yolks lightly and stir in 2 tablespoons of the hot milk, then add them to the rest of the milk mixture. Then add bread crumbs. Let it cool until lukewarm. Meanwhile beat the egg whites until they form in peaks when you hold the beater up. Fold into the cooked mixture.

Turn into a greased baking dish (1½ quart size) or into greased individual custard cups. Bake in a moderate oven (350°) until the soufflé begins to draw away from the sides of the dish, and is delicately puffed on top. This takes from 30 to 40 minutes.

Serve hot with whipped cream.

SERVES 4

The already-prepared crumbs are not soft enough for this dessert. Cut the crusts from freshly sliced bread, and break the centers up with your fingers, crumbling until fine. Pack firmly into the cup to measure.

LEBKUCHEN

    4 eggs, well beaten
    2 cups light brown sugar
    2 cups flour, sifted
    1 tsp cinnamon
    ¼ tsp allspice
    ½ cup mixed candied fruits and peels (or ¼ cup
            each citron, cut fine, orange peel, cut fine)
    1 cup coarsely chopped pecans (unsalted)

Add sugar to eggs, beating until smooth. Resift the flour with the cinnamon and allspice. Add mixed fruits and nuts to the flour, then combine with the liquid mixture. Spread the dough in a greased oblong pan (8″ × 11½″ approximately) so that it is ½ inch deep. Bake at 375° or a moderate oven for 20 to 25 minutes, or until it begins to pull away from the sides of the pan and is golden on top (test with a straw if necessary).

ICING

Sift two cups confectioner's sugar and gradually stir in 3 to 4 tablespoons boiling water or hot cream. Flavor with 1 teaspoon rum, vanilla, or lemon juice, fresh, frozen or canned, until right for spreading easily. This should be thin and runny, it will harden. Decorate with candied cherries, citron peel, and blanched, slivered almonds, or chopped pecans.

This keeps—unless you have children standing around, and in that case, you make three or four, and then find two empty pans. It is hard to stem the tide, especially when the icing is still warm. We serve it for Christmas breakfast and hope a few pieces will be left for afternoon coffee. This also can be made ahead and frozen, provided nobody knows in what part of the freezer you have stashed it.

BROWNIES

2   squares chocolate, melted   ½ cup sifted cake flour
⅓ cup butter or margarine   1   cup chopped walnuts
2   eggs, beaten until light   or pecans
1   cup sugar   1   tsp vanilla
¼ tsp salt

Melt together chocolate and butter or margarine. Beat eggs and add sugar and salt. Continue beating while adding the melted chocolate and butter. Add sifted cake flour and, finally, stir in chopped nuts and vanilla.

Place in a buttered 9-in. pan. The mixture should be only about ¾ inch deep. The whole trick with brownies lies in the heat at which they are baked. Set oven to preheat at 425°. When the brownies are put in the oven, lower the temperature immediately to 350° and bake 18 to 20 minutes, or until the dough draws away from the sides of the pan and a straw comes out clean. Cut into squares while still hot. When cool, store in a crock or tightly closed metal box so they will remain moist. We usually double this recipe.

MAKES 12

SPICE COOKIES
(Sour Cream)

⅔ cup butter   1   tsp cloves
1½ cups sugar   2   tsp cinnamon
2   eggs, beaten slightly   ¼ tsp salt
1   cup raisins   ½ pint sour cream
1   cup nuts   2½ cups flour
1½ tsp mace   1   tsp soda

Cream butter and sugar. Add slightly beaten eggs, raisins, nuts, mace, cloves, cinnamon and salt; then alternately add sour cream and flour with soda, dissolved in a little water, to the first mixture. Beat until smooth. Drop on a greased cooky tin. Bake at 375° until the tops of the cookies look firm and dry. Test with a straw.

MAKES 16–20

MRS. YOUNG'S COOKY CROCK SPECIAL

1 cup shortening	1 tsp nutmeg
1 cup brown sugar	1 tsp cinnamon
2 eggs	1 cup hot water
1 cup molasses	2 tsp baking soda
4 cups flour	

Cream shortening and sugar well; add eggs and molasses. Add flour, nutmeg and cinnamon stirred together. Add hot water with baking soda dissolved in it.

Add water and flour alternately. Drop by teaspoons on greased cooky sheet and plop a fat raisin in middle of each. Bake until a golden brown.

MAKES 40 or more

Mrs. Young keeps these on hand for the children and grandchildren. and grown-ups too! They are easier to make than cookies you cut out with a cooky cutter, when you always have bits and pieces of leftover dough to reroll.

CHOCOLATE MOLASSES CANDY

2   cups sugar (white)
1   cup molasses
2   sticks butter or margarine
4   squares unsweetened chocolate
1   cup milk
1   tsp vinegar
½   tsp salt

Put all the ingredients in a saucepan and boil until it becomes brittle in cold water.

Grease a pan, a flat one and let the candy harden in it. Crack the candy in medium-sized pieces.

The best thing about candy is everyone in the kitchen singing favorite songs and smelling the sweet sugary richness. This candy is fun to make during the holidays.

BROWN SUGAR CHEWS

1   egg
1   cup (packed) brown sugar
1   tsp vanilla
½ cup flour
¼ tsp salt
¼ tsp soda
1   cup coarsely chopped walnuts

Stir together egg, brown sugar, vanilla. Add sifted flour, salt, soda. Add walnuts. Bake for 18 to 20 minutes in greased 8-in. square pan at 350°. Cool in pan, cut in squares and enjoy!

MAKES 12

These are just right for midmorning coffee when friends drop in.

Pickles and Preserves

THE DAYS ARE GONE WHEN A HOMEMAKER HAD TO MAKE ALL her own jelly, pickles and preserves. Almost everything conceivable can now be bought at the nearest grocery, from mint jelly to beet relish. The food processors, bless them, have lifted a burden from us and I am grateful.

There is, however, a kind of joy in "putting up" one or two special treats, and even apartment dwellers can find room for a few jars of their own personal favorites. It's fun, too, to make Christmas gifts into which you have put loving care. Homemade is still a magic word.

I am sharing my top favorites with you. If your kitchen is small, cut the recipes in half and just spend a short time puttering. If you have a big family and plenty of space, these will help the budget and provide for extra treats.

KENNEBUNK PICKLE

3 lbs green tomatoes	1½ bunches of celery
3 lbs red tomatoes	9 tbsp salt
1 medium-sized head of cabbage	1½ qts vinegar
	4½ cups brown sugar
3 sweet red peppers	4½-in. stick cinnamon
3 green peppers	1½ tsp cloves
1 qt onions	1½ tsp dry mustard

Chop the vegetables very fine. Add the salt and let stand overnight. Drain; then add the vinegar and brown sugar. Place the cinnamon, cloves, and mustard in a cheesecloth bag, and boil all ingredients together for 30 minutes. Remove the bag of spices. Pour into sterilized jars and seal at once.

YIELD is 12 half pints

This is presumably a Maine recipe, since Kennebunkport is in Maine. But it fits in any place and is one of the best.

OLIVE OIL PICKLES

4 qts sliced (not too large) cucumbers
12 small sliced onions
   Vinegar
2 tsp cinnamon
½ cup sugar
½ tsp each, cloves, allspice, celery seed
½ cup each, white mustard seed and good olive oil

Cover cucumbers with dizzily boiling water. Let stand until cold. Drain and cover with weak brine. Let stand overnight. Drain again and mix with onion rings.

   Use enough vinegar to make a smooth paste of rest of ingredients. Add enough cold vinegar to cover thoroughly. Use glass to pack in.

This is an old-fashioned pickle that should be in every house.

BREAD 'N' BUTTER PICKLES

12 dill-sized cucumbers or	1 tsp celery seed
6 large, sliced not too thin	1 tsp white mustard seed
6 onions, sliced not too thin	1 tsp ginger
3 cups cider vinegar	1 tsp turmeric
1½ cups granulated sugar	1 tsp pepper

Sprinkle sparingly with salt and let all ingredients stand an hour or two. Boil all together 10 minutes. Pour into sterilized pint jars and seal.

YIELDS about 6 pints

When my first beau walked me home from school (4 miles), we were hungry. We always went directly to the kitchen and had slices of fresh crusty bread on which we put as many layers of bread and butter pickles as would stay on. Kept our strength up so we could walk another mile and play tennis!

WILMA'S SPECIAL BEETS

1	gal. small beets	1 tbsp allspice
2	cups sugar	3½ cups vinegar
1	long stick cinnamon	1½ cups water

Cook and skin the beets. Slice in medium-thin slices. Add sugar and spices to vinegar and water and simmer 15 minutes. Add the beets and boil 5 minutes. Pack the beets into hot pint or quart mason jars and cover with the boiling syrup. If there is not enough syrup to cover, add more vinegar. Process 5 minutes in hot water bath.

MAKES 8 pints or 4 quarts

This is by all odds the best recipe for beets I know of. They may be served hot as a vegetable or cold on a hors d'oeuvre plate. If you live in an apartment, you can cut the recipe in half and if you can't manage the processing, store the jars in the refrigerator. They will keep a week. If you can get the tiny rosebud beets, do not slice them but use whole.

HARVEST SPECIAL
(Garden Special)

4 qts ripe tomatoes	7 sweet peppers, diced
(quartered)	3 tbsp salt
6 cups chopped celery	2 tbsp sugar
8 cups diced onions	4 bay leaves
1 qt water	1 tbsp Worcestershire

Cook together 20 minutes. When it boils, place in hot mason jars and process in hot water bath for 30 minutes for quarts, 25 minutes for pints.

Seal jars and set on a rack in the canning kettle in boiling water that comes 1 inch above the lids of the jars. Cover the kettle and keep the water boiling.

MAKES 7–8 pints

This was one of my first attempts at canning, and the recipe came from a county bulletin many years ago. It was before the days of pressure cookers and deep freezers. But it was worth the struggle. This is a versatile product, which you can use as Creole sauce or Spanish sauce. It is excellent to bake fish in and fine as a casserole with cubed beef and potatoes.

PEPPER RELISH

12 red peppers	2 cups vinegar
12 green peppers	2 cups sugar
12 onions	3 tbsp salt

Chop red and green peppers and onions together. Cover with boiling water and let stand 5 minutes; then drain. Add vinegar, sugar, salt and boil mixture for 5 minutes. Pour into clean hot jars and seal at once.

YIELD 4–6 pints

I almost missed a train once because I was determined to finish a batch of pepper relish. When I jumped on that train, I did not smell of Chanel No. 5, but a strong aroma of vinegar and onions and peppers was with me!

SARAH PARENT'S MUSTARD PICKLES

2 qts tomatoes	1 qt string beans
2 qts small cucumbers	1 large head cauliflower
2 qts small white onions	1 bunch celery
4 qts water	1 pint salt

Prepare vegetables, keeping pieces bite-sized. Break the cauliflower in flowerets. Mix salt and water and add vegetables. Let stand overnight. Drain in the morning and pour boiling water over briefly.

SAUCE

6	qts vinegar	24	tbsp mustard
½	box mixed spices	2	cups sugar
2	heaping cups flour	½	oz turmeric

Tie spices in a cheesecloth bag and add to the vinegar and bring to a boil. Mix dry ingredients well, add enough vinegar to make a smooth paste (let vinegar cool slightly first). Remove spices and add vegetables and sauce to the vinegar.

Then add:

4 small green hot peppers, chopped.

Bring to a boil. Place in sterilized jars and seal.

MAKES 16 pints

Sarah is a true Cape Codder. She says sometimes she puts more of something in and something less. It was a real chore for her to write this down and I did appreciate it.

BAR – LE – DUC

3 qts ripe currants
6 cups sugar
½ cup honey

Stem the currants and put them in a large kettle. Crush gently but do not mash. Add the sugar, bring to a boil, and boil 5 minutes. Drizzle the honey over and boil 3 minutes more. Fill sterilized glasses with the Bar-Le-Duc and cover immediately with paraffin.

YIELD 8 – 10 half pints

This is the best dessert with toasted crackers and cream cheese. Picking currants is an adventure, because wasps are always thick. Connie (my daughter) used to go with me to the currant bushes, but spent a good deal of the time leaping in the air and saying nervously, "Oh, Mama!" Eventually we were told our lovely currant bushes were giving the maple trees some kind of rust and really should be moved a quarter mile away. Well, it was lovely while it lasted. A day of hot sun and dreamy air and glowing currants plopping in tin pails is a wonderful day, wasps or no.

SPICED CRANBERRIES

2½ cups sugar
½ cup water
2 2-in. sticks cinnamon
2 tbsp lemon juice
1 tbsp grated lemon rind
1 tsp whole cloves.
4 cups cranberries

Combine sugar, water, cinnamon, lemon juice and rind, and cloves, and boil the mixture for 5 minutes. Add cranberries, picked over and washed, and cook the mixture very slowly, without stirring, until the cranberries burst open. Pour the cranberries into hot sterilized jars, cover them with the syrup, and seal the jars with paraffin.

MAKES about 2 pints

SPICED CHERRIES

7 lbs tart cherries   1 tbsp ground cinnamon
4 lbs sugar   1 tsp ground cloves
2 cups cider vinegar

Use a heavy large kettle and add all the ingredients at once. Bring to a boil and boil gently until the cherries are fairly soft. Remove the cherries and boil the syrup until it is thickened, then put the cherries back and bring to a boil. Fill hot sterilized jars with the hot mixture and seal with paraffin. Store in a cool dark place.

YIELDS 12 half pints

This is a favorite with cold sliced meat or chicken. When I was growing up, we spent summers in Door County in Wisconsin near Ephraim, a small Moravian village set deep against green cliffs. My mother did not exactly rest during July because Father kept going to the cherry orchards and bringing home bushels of cherries. While he and I went fishing or swimming, Mama was making spiced cherries. On a kerosene stove. Father did carry water from the spring for the kitchen.

SPICED PLUMS

5 parts plums
4 parts sugar
1 part vinegar
1 heaping tsp ground cloves
1½ tbsp ground cinnamon

Take the blue plum that is in market late in October, cut in small pieces, remove stones but not skins; cook everything together. Cook, stirring to keep from sticking, until the consistency suits you.
    Serve with cold meat or duckling.

If you wish to can the plums, use your pressure cooker and follow directions. Ten cups of the cut-up plums, about 6 or 7 pounds, makes 8 pints.

CAPE COD CRANBERRY RELISH

1 lb fresh cranberries
2 oranges
2 apples
2 cups sugar

Put the fruit through a food grinder using medium blade (include rind of oranges and some of the apple skin). Stir in sugar and let stand overnight.

YIELD 4 half pints

This is fine with almost any meat, but elegant with turkey or roast duckling. Takes well to chicken.

Beverages

COFFEE AND TEA ARE THE STANDARD BEVERAGES IN OUR country. At least for adults. The tons of soft drinks that clutter the stores are fine for teen-agers, but I always look with awe at a grown-up who asks for orange pop any time any place. I was never allowed to drink anything but ginger ale when I was growing up, and I will say dry sparkling ginger ale is good for a stomach upset.

I drink coffee morning, noon, and night. At Stillmeadow the coffeepot is always going, and, when the children are home, someone is always asking, "Is there any coffee?" It hasn't ever upset our nerves or kept us awake, but we are a healthy group. In summer, I often have tea for breakfast, but I use only English tea, such as Earl Grey (the brisk tea). I deplore tea bags because I like the true flavor of tea, and for a real diffusion the leaves have to float free. The manufacturers shouldn't be put out by this because tea bags can always go in your suitcase when you are off on a trip when loose tea is impossible, plus teapot, hot-water jug, and the rest of it.

The smoky teas, such as Lapsong, are nice in the afternoon, and the Jasmine tea is delicious on a hot afternoon. I also like Constant Comment, but not for breakfast.

As far as coffee goes, I have tried every brand there is, as far as I know. No two people like the same type, heavy or light. Nobody can agree, either, on the best method of preparing it. I have tried everything and now use an automatic coffeemaker with a fine grind of coffee. I grind my own, but I am not sure this is really necessary. Vacuum-packed coffee does not lose much of the volatile oils. The main thing is, if you grind your own, the smell is delicious while you grind.

During the holiday season, the punch bowl comes out and we serve various eggnogs and such. I keep cranberry juice and tomato cocktail for those who prefer it. If you like wine for company dinners, there are excellent, inexpensive American wines to serve. The general rule is white wine with fish and red wine with meat, but a delicate Rosé is good with anything. Sweet wines are for dessert, and champagne is for weddings. Some people like a glass of sherry before dinner, and I always have some on hand. I use it for cooking, too, on the theory that if you use it, you may as well use the best sherry. The alcohol cooks out, leaving the herb flavor, and I think the more expensive sherry has better herbs.

STILLMEADOW PUNCH

    1 lb sugar, dissolved in boiling water
    ½ lb black tea, steeped (about 4 qts)
       Juice from 7 dozen lemons
    3 cans pineapple (chunks)
       Slice ½ dozen oranges for decoration

MAKES enough for a big, happy crowd

ESTHER'S PARTY ICED TEA

Juice of 3 lemons	½ cup mint leaves
Juice of 1 orange	11 bags Tetley tea
2 cups sugar	7 cups boiling water

Combine juices and sugar. Brew the tea 5 or 6 minutes, then pour the strong tea while it is hot over the sugar and juice. Float mint leaves on top. After 30 minutes remove mint leaves, and allow to cool. Strain into milk bottles and cap tightly. Keep in the refrigerator. When serving, fill glasses with ice, pour tea in, and add fresh sprig of mint. If possible, use apple mint. Keeps about 3 weeks.

MAKES 1½ or 2 quarts tea

Mrs. Bromley's tea is famous, and on hot August days she has it ready when guests drop in. I have already said that I never use tea bags (see comment on beverages), but for this tea I have to go along with the tea bags because it is so easy.

"SALTER SPECIAL" MINT TEA

1 *large* handful fresh brook mint. Place in 2-qt container and bruise lightly.

4 heaping tbsp loose black tea on top of mint. Over these items pour

4½ cups boiling water (best to measure cold and bring to boil). Cover and let steep 5 minutes. Strain.

This makes about 1 quart of "concentrate" which keeps in refrigerator till used.

In a 2½-quart pitcher put 1½ cups of sugar, 1 cup of tea concentrate, juice *and rinds* of 2 lemons and 1 orange (the Californias are best), and fill pitcher with cold water; add a few ice cubes if concentrate was used hot. More or less sugar may be used to suit taste.

Mrs. Salter says her family couldn't get through a hot summer without this. They make so much of it a neighbor asked them if they also used it in their car radiator! It takes a little time to make this, but is wonderful to have on hand.

CHRISTMAS EGGNOG

6 eggs. Beat whites and yolks separately.
Add ½ cup sugar to yolks.
Add ¼ cup sugar to whites when stiff
Mix yolks and whites
Stir in 1 pint cream and 1 pint milk
Add 1 pint rye whiskey and
1 oz Jamaica rum.

Stir.

MAKES 5 pints

It was once the custom for friends to call during the holidays, coming in blowing snow from their mittens. The eggnog in a silver punch bowl was on the trestle table, and the mistletoe hung from a beam a few steps away. Toasting the holidays was traditional.

HOLIDAY EGGNOG

6 egg yolks
¼ cup white sugar
1 cup brandy
2 cups cream
2 cups milk
¼ tsp salt
6 egg whites

Beat egg yolks until very light and then beat in gradually sugar, brandy, cream and milk. Whip the egg whites until very stiff with salt and fold them lightly into the other ingredients. Serve the eggnog into individual punch glasses with a silver ladle and top each glass with cinnamon or nutmeg, as desired.

MAKES 4 pints

This is a traditional Christmas and New Year eggnog which for some reason I associate with Charles Dickens and the stuffed goose and Tiny Tim.

HOT BUTTERED RUM

    1 tsp sugar or 1 lump of sugar
    ¼ cup cider
    ¼ cup rum
    1 tbsp butter

Place sugar in a thick tumbler. Bring the cider to a boil and add to sugar, then add rum and butter. Fill the glass and sprinkle cinnamon on top.

This is the way Rogers's Rangers made it when they struggled through the bitter wilderness. And this is how I learned what a loggerhead is, while reading the history of those early days. A loggerhead was an iron gadget like a poker and they heated it in the fire and plunged it into the jug of rum. So if you are at loggerheads with anyone, it means a lot of heat and steam!

FISH-HOUSE PUNCH

    1½ cups sugar
    2 qts water
    2 qts Bacardi rum
    1 qt Cognac brandy
    1 qt lemon juice (2 dozen lemons) or frozen
           undiluted lemon juice
    1 wineglass peach brandy

Add 1 cup water to sugar. Heat and stir until sugar is dissolved. Cool. Put in large bowl. Add remaining water, add liquids, stirring. Put big chunk of ice in bowl. Let stand untouched for two hours.

MAKES 50 cups

SHELF MAGIC

The first time a carload of unexpected guests arrived at Stillmeadow, I was desperate. I was defrosting the refrigerator and had divided up the remains of the pot roast and the last of the creamed chicken among a bevy of cockers and two Irish setters, who were happy to help out. The half loaf of bread went to the birds, along with some stale doughnuts. I had three eggs and that was about it. I try not to remember that day.

The next time, I was prepared. By then I knew nobody ever arrives at Stillmeadow except in a state of extreme starvation, no matter whether they come at ten in the morning or ten at night. There is always some reason they were not able to have a meal at the usual time. It goes like this: "Oh, I am so glad to get here. I left in such a hurry I didn't have time for breakfast." Or, "Do you have a glass of milk? We didn't get any dinner on account of . . ."

Hence, the emergency shelf. Jill whitewashed the area at the top of the cellar stairs and built four deep shelves. True, you have to be careful not to get a concussion when you try to get down those stairs, but if you turn sidewise and bend sharply you can make it. On the top shelf, we put extra spices, mustards, Worcestershire sauce, pepper, salt, instant coffee, cocoa and powdered milk, and cereals; along with pickles, olives, and snacks (like lobster paste, sardines, smoked turkey pâté).

The second shelf is reserved for mixes, bless them, and spaghetti, noodles, rice, dehydrated soups, gravies, sauces. Packaged rice dishes and dehydrated scalloped potatoes and dried mushrooms go there.

The third shelf holds two cans each of our favorite canned soups, vegetables, canned fruits, canned gravy, baked beans, chili, tamales, canned onions, and potatoes.

The fourth shelf houses two cans each of different kinds of fish, chicken, beef tongue, frankfurters, and the meal-in-one-cans, such as beef stew, corned beef hash, spaghetti and meatballs, canned ham, canned whole chicken, canned chicken cacciatore, and canned creamed salmon and peas, and canned brown bread.

From time to time, I add a new product, such as canned artichoke hearts or canned stuffed peppers, and I keep a list of what has been used so that the next time I shop, I buy replacements.

Even in a small city apartment, emergency supplies can be stored somehow so you never need fear the delicatessen will be closed just when you need to get a meal. For this, it takes figuring. A few of the seldom used utensils can go in a carton in that overcrowded closet. I once gave up a bureau drawer when I lived in a city apartment. The dehydrated soups and gravies and sauces are space-saving; I got ten in a stationery box. Larger packages such as rice Provençal, scalloped potatoes, and so on, have to be stacked up—which is a nuisance, because you always want the one at the bottom, but it can't be helped. Canned fish is a boon because you can stretch a small can of crab or salmon with hard-cooked eggs and cream sauce or with diced celery for salad. If your space is very limited, I think it is better to have two cans of one product (two of crab rather than one tuna and one crab) because this means you can serve four or five in one round. I once used a can of baked beans and had to add a can of kidney beans and it worked all right, but I wished I had stocked two cans of the same kind of beans.

In using mixes and cans, you do need to add a dash of imagination. For instance, canned beef stew takes a dash of burgundy and is topped with parsley dumplings made from biscuit mix. Baked beans go in a casserole with a small onion, cut through into eighths, buried in the center. A sprinkling of dry mustard, a bit of brown sugar and some seasoned salt and pepper, and a couple of partly cooked bacon strips on top and this bakes until bubbly. The possibilities are endless. If you are short of salad makings, chill a jar of canned asparagus and serve it as salad with chopped hard-cooked egg sprinkled over it. For a quick dessert, chill canned pears and serve with crème de menthe drizzled over them.

HERBS, SEASONINGS, SPICES

Cooking with herbs is a fine art. But you do not have to use all the herbs there are when you start the rewarding adventure. Buy small containers, for herbs lose their freshness after long storage. If you grow your own, harvest them as they begin to flower, wash well, and dry in a dark cool room.

Here is my basic list:

Bay Leaves, a must for topping meat loaves, and in soups, stews.

Basil, for tomato dishes, in beef stew, and when cooking shellfish.

Dill, for salads, dressings, sauces. (Tay Hohoff uses canned lentil soup and adds dill and lets it stand a while before reheating; then adds 1 tablespoon sherry per person.)

Marjoram, roast beef, lamb, or veal, and in egg and fish dishes.

Mint, sauce for lamb, with boiled potatoes, with tea.

Oregano, in spaghetti sauce, potato salad, in fish butter for shellfish.

Parsley, salads, dressings, soups, stews.

Rosemary, in chicken, pea, spinach soup, in stuffings, in scrambled eggs.

Saffron, in rich dishes, Arroz con Pollo (chicken), in chicken soup.

Sage, stuffing for poultry or roast pork.

Savory, bean or pea soup, fish chowders, beef, boiled fish, salads.

Tarragon, salad dressings, sauces, aspics.

Thyme, lamb, chicken stuffings.

Herb butter is made by blending herbs and butter (preferably sweet butter). Use 1 level tablespoon of minced fresh green herbs or ½ teaspoon dried herbs to 2 ounces of butter. Add a dash of lemon juice. Use on fish for broiling, with eggs, on asparagus, with broiled meats, or in sandwiches.

Garlic is in a category by itself. It is often called an herb, but it is a root vegetable as is the onion, the way I look at it. Its uses are infinite, from rubbing a cut clove on a steak to mincing it for barbecue sauces. Besides the garlic cloves, garlic powder and garlic salt are essentials.

Here is a list of my basic spices:

Allspice, for soup stock, pea soup, pot roasts, boiling fish or shellfish.

Cinnamon, stick or ground for pies, toast, apple cobblers, baked pears.

Chili, I use this lavishly in egg dishes, soups, stews, chili con carne, barbecue dishes.

Cloves, stick in ham, add to meat stews or soups, with boiled fish, in pickled beets.

Curry, fish dishes, with lamb, sprinkled over boiled rice, in deviled eggs.

Ginger, crystallized or preserved in fruit compotes, Bavarian cream desserts. Snip crystallized ginger fine and use with canned pears or mandarin oranges.

Mace, in oyster stew, fish sauces, in cream sauce for vegetables.

Nutmeg, on eggnogs and custards and in rice puddings.

My favorite single seasoning is seasoned salt, available in most stores. I use it almost always in place of regular salt, except for some desserts that call for flour sifted with dash of salt, etc. I use freshly ground pepper, wearing out a good many pepper mills in the course of a year or so, but it is worth it. I keep an assortment of mustards, the mild Dijon type, the Bahamian, regular, horseradish, dry mustard (English type), and a barbecue mustard.

I use meat tenderizer for most meats.

I use monosodium glutamate in spite of its hideous title. I keep it with my seasoned salt and pepper mill right by the range. I have not written it in many recipes in this book, simply because I hate to keep copying it down. And if I call it MSG it sounds like an automobile. It is not, strictly speaking, a seasoning, but it reinforces the flavor of whatever you are cooking.

I use wine, but that is a matter for the individual cook to settle for herself. I keep 1 bottle of dry white table wine, 1 bottle of dry burgundy, 1 bottle of dry sherry, 1 bottle of sweet sherry, 1 bottle of rum (a half pint for this), and 1 bottle of brandy (for flaming plum puddings and such). Properly used, just a spoonful of wine adds a delicate flavor. There are available several booklets and one or two excellent books dealing with wine cookery, not to mention the huge *Gourmet Cookbooks* (2 volumes), which make a fine addition to the cook book shelf.

But when all's said and done, the priceless seasoning is not to be bought in any store. Better than fillet of beef in aspic with truffles served in an unhappy silence, is the simplest casserole served with love and laughter.

Index